Spirituality in Counselling and Psychotherapy

Spirituality in Counselling and Psychotherapy

Dennis Lines

SAGE Publications
London ● Thousand Oaks ● New Delhi

First published 2006

SAGE Publications Ltd
1 Oliver's Yard
55 City Road
London EC1Y 1SP

SAGE Publications Inc.
2455 Teller Road
Thousand Oaks, California 91320

SAGE Publications India Pvt Ltd
B-42, Panchsheel Enclave
Post Box 4109
New Delhi 110 017

British Library Cataloguing in Publication data

A catalogue record for this book is available
from the British Library

ISBN 978-1-4129-1957-9

Library of Congress Control Number available

Typeset by C&M Digitals (P) Ltd., Chennai, India

Dedicated to all those on a
Spiritual Journey

Contents

Foreword

Spirituality is rapidly acquiring a certain notoriety both in the psychotherapy and theology fields. It is perceived by many as the ultimate slippery concept which enables ill-disciplined therapists and less than respectable theologians to mount mystical hobby-horses and to engage in ill-founded analyses of the existential struggles of twenty-first century men and women. Therapists who pursue this arcane field of enquiry are often perceived as exceeding the legitimate boundaries of psychological study while theologians and religious educators can be castigated as enemies of true religion and traitors to their faith communities.

It is my hope and belief that Dennis Lines' new book will cause the critics to stop in their tracks. It is certainly an unashamedly mystical book in that it focuses on those experiences in therapeutic relationships where there is a powerfully intuitive interaction on a plane of being characterised by a deep bond of love between therapist and client. At the same time, however, it is a robustly empirical book. In the first place the author is at pains to situate his experience within the historical and sociological evolution of western culture since the Enlightenment and into the post-modern period. With the eye of a philosopher and social commentator he tracks the emergence of psychotherapy as a powerful force in the context of a pricipally pragmatic and scientifically centred culture. He is not blind, however, to the fact that despite the decline of formal religion, the predom-inant discourse in a multicultural Britain remains Christian. His analysis is thorough, balanced and even-handed and not for one moment does the reader sense a hidden intent to insinuate a particular point of view.

Secondly – and here lines one of the book's supreme merits – Dennis Lines anchors his findings in his extensive experience as a therapist. As a school counsellor he has privileged access to the minds and hearts of adolescent clients (many of them from working class environments) and the verbatim extracts from many counselling sessions are both riveting and often intensely moving. A second sphere of work in General Practice surgeries provides an altogether different perspective. Clients in the later stages of life are faced with the inevitability of their own mortality and as a result ontological ques-tions thread their way through dialogues where both counsellor and client move between the immanent and the transcendent with apparent ease. As these conversations with young and old alike unfold, the reader is drawn inexorably to the conclusion that issues of meaning, yearning and ultimate purpose lead to a bonding between therapist and client where a quality of reciprocity is established which is transformative for both participants.

Mystical, empirical but also scholarly, Dennis Lines is not encapsulated in his own experience, wide though it is. He is well acquainted with the current literature in this burgeoning and controversial field and readers will find many references to other contemporary writers, both in Britain and beyond. He also provides a comprehensive list of References which in itself constitutes a mini-feast. Despite this breadth of learning, however, the book remains intensely personal. Perhaps at the heart of all spiritual enquiry there resides the mystery of supreme paradox. And so it is that at the end of a book which courageously addresses universal questions of ultimate concern to every reflective human being, I am left with the sense of a unique individual. Dennis Lines has somehow succeeded in conveying his own numinous presence between the lines of his text. We meet in these pages the person who experienced an appalling accident before he had reached middle age, who knew the full intensity of the dark night of the soul and who came through the tunnel into the emerging light. We learn, without having to be told, that vulnerability, powerlessness and weakness can be the source of hope and relationship and not the ground for despair. This gentle, mystical, empirical and scholarly book is truly inspirational and it is for that reason above all others that it deserves the widest possible readership among therapists, religious educators and all those who care about the spiritual destiny of humankind.

Brian Thorne
Norwich, New Year's Day, 2006

Acknowledgements

This book has been 58 years in the making, the period of my life to this point. From an early memory of fearing death, much of my life has involved reflecting on religious and spiritual issues, and the discourses recorded in this book are contributions not only of clients in therapy but of friends and colleagues who have something to say on such matters. I am grateful for what they have taught me and for giving permission to draw from their material. I am also grateful to Alison Poyner, Louise Wise and the team at Sage for instilling the confidence in me to complete this work. I feel honoured by Brian Thorne's comments and thank him for writing the Foreword. I thank also William West for his encouragement and for directing me to further reading. I am grateful to Nathan Marsh and Jean Barley for their artistic sketches, to Nazar Hussain for a photo image, to the British Museum, the Whitworth Gallery and Scala Archives for granting me permission to have published their photo exhibits. Finally I thank Dierdre Barber for proof-reading the manuscript, and Wendy Oldfield-Austin for initiating the book and for many helpful suggestions.

Dennis Lines
February 2006

Introduction

Every so often something happens during a counselling session that affects the way I feel about my client. It occurs with middle-to-late adolescents as much as with clients in their fifties and it can only be described as a *mystical happening*. I feel a powerful bond of love for my client, which I sense is reciprocal, as though we are intuitively relating with each other on a different plane. It is as though we have become extremely fond of one another and that the words expressed are merely the means of communicating a spiritual attachment rather than the means of resolving a particular problem brought to therapy. It is as though there is a need to move from a customary mode of working to satisfy a vastly different requirement, a need that may be as obscure for my client as for myself. This book explores this dimension of therapy with two principal client groups: adolescent and mid-life clients. I will occasionally describe this *relational happening* as a numinous phenomenon or more commonly a spiritual experience.

Some may have reservations about viewing the counselling relationship in terms of love, attachment and bonding, but the love-relating I speak of has no sexual designs, the feeling of growing attachment has no latent parenting plan for a young person, or a hidden agenda to save a person close to my age who is in existential crisis. The feeling of bonding has no wish to transgress the essential ethical boundaries of professional psychotherapy. It is just that the feeling of love of one for another within the counselling relationship is the only emotion that conveys adequately the powerful dynamic of the interrelating of one with another.

Many therapists have reservations about addressing spiritual issues within counselling. This is largely because spiritual and related terms like religious, sacred and transpersonal are not often viewed as value-free terms. I hope all readers will bear with me and enquire further into this therapeutic landscape, not only because human spirituality is universally experienced but also because my treatment aims to be all-inclusive and impartial. Psychotherapists and counsellors have long recognised that their clients have *peak experiences* in life and that a heightened level of relating can emerge from the therapeutic relationship. Some think that the process of therapy itself is a spiritual activity.

Psychotherapy and Spirituality

There has been considerable interest recently in the spiritual dimension in therapy amongst psychotherapists and counsellors. Along with a few stimulating books and articles on spiritual themes and religious issues in therapy, this book hopes to make a contribution by balancing two realities of experiencing which are often held to be in tension: there is a down-to-earth empirical outlook and then there is a mystical one. Various schools of psychotherapy give differing emphases to these realities, sometimes unwittingly. Psychodynamic, Jungian, existential, humanistic and transpersonal therapy, along with many integrative models, including pastoral counselling, have addressed religious, spiritual and humanistic themes, and have created a repertoire of approaches and interventions and applied them effectively in practice. This book will draw on this developing experience, but will present a rationale for working with religious and spiritual issues that recognises sociological accounts of culture together with the numinous or transpersonal dimension. These two realities are reflected in social discourse within a broad context of pluralistic values.

Spirituality and its derivatives will need defining in spite of its imprecise usage in common speak. Spiritually-centred counselling, as I understand it, and in the following pages will demonstrate, is a particular mode of interaction that calls practitioners to step aside from their preferred manner of working to engage in a therapeutic process of being with being, and to respond to their clients in a reciprocal engagement as though both are on a continuing journey of transcending Self (by capitalising self I stress the individual sense of personhood). The customary model of client and therapist, with all its variant poses, is temporally suspended to enter into a spiritually bonding relationship of mutual Self-growth. It is as though both feel the need to *centre* on their own sense of being; both become caught up within a *mystical moment* through relating within a different sphere of experience before resuming their customary focus on the presented problem.

Religion comes in many guises, and counselling has become popular in religious contexts. As the religious traditions have become humanised, however, personhood and what it means to be human have become central. Amongst those counselling within a spiritual context there are a variety of opinions as to whether there are therapeutic resources that are quite specific to the context. Some religious counsellors believe that their main resources can be found in scripture and prayer, whilst holistic therapists value meditation and centring on forces outside of Self. Some pastoral counsellors work within a religious ethos that is more implicit than explicit, whilst others bring religious matters to the forefront of therapy.

One characteristic of religion, which does not apply as much to spirituality, is the embodiment of a range of beliefs and assumptions which collectively become the worldview of the particular community. Such beliefs may remain intact irrespective of the fact that they may be unverifiable and beyond empirical testing. Atheists dispute the basis of religious belief-systems, but most people in postmodern times tend to position themselves at a less extreme stance, as is shown in randomised surveys that reveal a high positive declaration for believing in God, or a higher power, superstition, elements of the paranormal, or omens of good and bad luck.

Psychotherapy has similar features to religion, and has occupied a role and position in modern society that was formerly held by the Christian Church. As the state has increasingly taken over from the Church as the secular counterpart in education and social welfare, so has the therapist replaced the priest as 'father-confessor' but without ceremony and without reference to the sacred. But there is another parallel. Psychotherapy is indeed a broad church of many denominations, and each school has a theoretical basis of belief about persons and their psychological functioning, which in some cases are unverifiable.

The various schools of psychotherapy subscribe to an underlying theory of working which is informed by a belief-system. Many practitioners of all schools of psychotherapy now respect the theoretical assumptions of other approaches in these days of integration and eclecticism, and I suspect, if pressed on the point, might even concede that their own theoretical constructs serve more as a working tool than as a basis of empirical fact. With reference to psychoanalysis, I am thinking of the evidence for the unconscious to consist of id, ego and superego, for the Oedipus complex, and for physical symptoms to be the cause of particular emotional blockages. Regarding Jungian analysis, I am thinking of the evidence for the collective unconscious, for the archetypes, and for dream content to be related to archetypical themes which have influence on emotional difficulties. And in respect to Rogerian therapy, I am thinking of the evidence that human beings have an innate, intrinsic Self that is submerged within environmental expectations but which can re-emerge within the context of a therapeutic relationship. Or that the individual may have become ill through faulty cognitions and may become healthy again through cognitive restructuring as held by cognitive therapy and REBT. We could go on, but the point is that belief-systems that regulate a person's living and functioning are not the sole province of religion, but exist in many professional walks of life, including those of scientists and psychotherapists.

Social Attitudes towards Religion

In addressing issues of spiritually-centred counselling, this book will not be dismissive of religion in spite of the tensions which may result. Various accounts will be offered as to why forms of institutional Christianity are in decline in Britain and other western democracies, whilst, paradoxically, spirituality and spiritual orientations have become popular and appear to be flourishing. For some traditional cultures, religion has become so embedded and monolithic that it would be unthinkable to presume that its relevance for modern times would be questioned. It is certainly not the case in multi-cultural, twenty-first century Britain, Australia, China, parts of Europe and the non-Bible belt region of North America.

Ask people what comes to mind when they think of religion and their responses will fall into two camps of opinion. If they are affiliated to a church, a mosque, a temple, or a fringe sectarian group and you further ask them of the value of being religious, they may well point to the benefits of living in some mystical harmony with a superior power. Those who consider themselves secular, or atheist, or humanist, or even postmodern, may express diffidence and regard the world-wide atrocities that have occurred in the name of religion as indefensible. The Crusading battles between Christianity and Islam, the Spanish Inquisition, the missionary movement, papal opposition to early science, or some of the military campaigns of the modern world, all illustrate the dark side of religion.

The motivations that led radicals to strike the Trade Towers and young martyrs to blow up innocents have as many political interests as religious ones, clearly, but the case for religion to come over as amoral and inhuman is reasonably strong. Religious apologists see evidence of a decadent society – soaring crime figures, sexual promiscuity, spread of AIDS, breakdown of the nuclear family, etc. – stemming from an erosion of traditional religious values, and further reason that without religion the world would not have been graced with such figures as Jesus of Nazareth, Mohammed, the Buddha, Ghandi, Martin Luther King, Mother Teresa or the Dalai Lama. But atheists counter-claim that venerated figures can be identified who are not driven by religious conviction but by humanistic values. The fact that corruption and vice can be found as much in religion as in society freed of its control illustrates the tension between religion and secularisation in modern western society.

What is meant by Spirituality?

Spiritually-centred counselling is meaningless without common agreement on what is meant by spirituality and how it may differ from similar, and possibly related terms, such as religious, existential, humanistic and transpersonal. Spirituality and religion are as old as humanity and are inseparable from early culture, so we are not only dealing with topics which reach back in the mists of antiquity but also as having crucial importance for a good many people and over a considerable period of time. When first planning this book, I thought it would be simple to create watertight definitions of religion and spirituality that were clear and universally acceptable. It seemed a natural enough starting point. After reflecting on what I understood by these terms, however, the task became virtually impossible. How can definitions of spirituality and religion meet the need to be fully inclusive and all-encompassing? I thought that with more reading, and after conducting workshops on the subject, it would make the job easier. But studying spirituality more extensively and after having engaged in dialogue with course delegates, the multiple insights drew a mist over the landscape, which left me feeling that precise definitions were unattainable. Nevertheless, I have attempted to define religion and spirituality, if only tentatively, to serve as a working hypothesis. What philosophers and psychologists understand by Self also requires consideration. I raise in this book the question of whether our consciousness of who and what we are is innate or a constantly evolving construct shaped by our social environment.

If we were to ask folk what comes to mind when they think of spirituality, I suspect their replies would be as varied as their personalities. That is the problem with definitions of terms which have such a history of connotations and associations. What further confuses the issue is the relationship between religion and spirituality. Whilst religion may be related to spirituality, the latter is not dependant on the former, since spirituality has its secular dimensions in that the term has become generic in accounting for aesthetic and artistic creativity in transcending natural limits of personal being.

Religious people tend to view the Spirit as an ontological external agent, whilst humanists recognise the human spirit as an innate ability, shown as resilience in hardship and endeavour in achieving difficult tasks. A question this book poses is the relationship of the two. One underlying presumption for sceptics is that spirituality is somehow superior to religion, as though it antedates and may outgrow it, but this is unfortunate and suggests that the two are easily definable terms. This book draws on the rich narratives of clients' lived experiences, as reflected through therapeutic sharing, to reveal the substance of spiritual phenomena, and, although quantitative research is presented, in the main grounded theory of qualitative analysis underlies this study (Glaser and Strauss, 1967).

What is crystal clear is that what we *choose* to see as reality cannot be separated from what we *the observer* can make sense of. In aiming to cover the vast topic of religion and spirituality within counselling and psychotherapy, it is imperative to declare openly my hand, and to inform you the reader of my formative experiences in youth, the cultural factors that have shaped my thinking and my current presuppositions, since bias will determine the selection of theorists I use in support of my position. In order to further expose my limitations, then, and in common with other authors on spirituality in psychotherapy, I present a brief biography of my spiritual development so that you may view my stance within its formative religious and cultural context.

My Formative Religious and Spiritual Experiences

My parents were not religious, at least in terms of taking me to a place of worship. My mother was a housemaid in a vicarage during her late teens before going into nursing during the Second World War, and I recall her becoming critical of religious hypocrisy after serving the clergy, but the details of what had happened were kept from my brother and me. After serving as a soldier, my father was a factory worker in Birmingham for the rest of his life before passing away three years after retirement. Neither parent consciously led me towards a religious life, but they brought me up with a respect for discipline, good manners and hard work. The only religious influences I remember were occasional comments which served as moral imperatives, such as 'cleanliness is next to Godliness' if I went to bed with dirty knees, and 'God helps those who help themselves' if I was lethargic. My early spiritual inclinations were to be in the natural world, where I had a fascination for bird-spotting and animals generally – I recall spending hours in youth walking in the countryside looking for bird's nests.

My adolescence is largely lost to memory. There were a few brief dates and much time was spent making models, but at 15 I attended a Christadelphian youth club and Sunday School. The Christadelphian brotherhood is a small Christian sect that holds within its central belief-system the propositions that Jesus was not divine, but born a human, that he rose from the dead and would come back again to earth as God's appointed Messiah. Christadelphians believe the Bible is inerrant. After my adult baptism, becoming initiated into this brotherhood gave me a new family and satisfied my ideological spirit. I preached in churches and ran the youth club, taking literally hundreds of young people camping during my twenties.

At 27, still single, I decided to have a career change from engineering to teaching, and I entered Newman College for teacher training. Here in a Catholic environment, I trained as a teacher of religious education and studied modern theological thought and higher critical methods of interpreting the Bible. At this point I found the beliefs of my former Christian brotherhood untenable and after a brief spell trying to modernise the community decided to move on in my spiritual journey. Catholicism gave me a new perspective of the Church and its role and place in history, though I did not become converted.

Approaching mid-life, I had a tragic accident and broke my neck from falling downstairs. The next ten months were spent in a spinal injury hospital for rehabilitation, and during this time I became depressed and once contemplated suicide. Strangely, my disabled condition did not shake my faith in a higher power, but presented new possibilities and an awareness of untapped inner resources. My spinal injury closed the door to teaching but offered an opportunity to become a school counsellor, and to learn to rely on others for life's basic needs.

My spiritual experience of the numinous (defined later) was fourfold. I felt a sense of awe in early youth when walking in the countryside feeling close to nature, and having a sense of the earth as a living being (Gaia). It felt pleasant to be in natural surroundings of birdsong and green pastures and to remain there, to feel the numinous of life in vibrant activity. Experiences of sitting high on the slopes of Snowdonia, musing in contemplation as buzzards soared overhead, also rekindled a spirit of something Other, of a *presence* that seemed more than the sensual attraction of the pass, the tumbling waterfalls and the echoing wind to my face.

But the numinous was also experienced in a sense of belonging to a religious family, first in late adolescence when being 'converted' and enjoined with a community engaged in singing and hearing the scriptures come alive with existential relevance, and then during my thirties becoming enthralled by the symbols, the ritual and the worship in the *beauty of holiness* in a Catholic church or monastery. In such locations and settings the numinous becomes real in emotion if not in reason.

The mind-body-feeling link of holistic being, where tensions are as real as harmonies, was tested in the spinal injury unit where my existence seemed pointless and futile, and where the *dark night of the soul* introduced me to that aspect of the numinous that is revealed in existential nihilism. My sense of being was face to face with non-existence, and the deep *shadow* of non-being seemed more magnetic than the wish to remain alive.

Finally, coming through that tunnel, there was the emerging light of opportunity of a new numinous *presence* through interrelating, in meeting real pressing needs of young people during therapy and by receiving support in my disabled condition. These genuine bonds were rich social interactions that endorse our human interdependence and social connectedness. All these numinous themes will be developed in what humanistic therapy views as *peak experiences* or as religious mystics see as *ineffable moments* of spiritual encounter.

Book Structure

The first three chapters set the context of spirituality and psychotherapy within the western postmodern world. This material is comprehensive, and readers may prefer to return to this heavily theoretical analysis after having first considered the nature of spiritually-centred therapy. I feel that therapists are better able to understand and contribute to their client's stories if they have a grasp of the intellectual framework that has informed the social outlook of their lives. After explaining key terms of secular society, the first chapter outlines postmodern consciousness as traced from the Enlightenment to our present time, where religious pluralism has become an ideal. We consider the rational mind as shaped by philosophy, critical theology and the sociology of religion. The following chapter asks in the light of declining interest in church attendance whether there is evidence of a spiritual revolution taking place in the West. After discussing the nature of inward spirituality, I present definitions of religion and spirituality to help pave the way to a clearer understanding of spiritually-centred counselling in practice.

The beginnings of psychotherapy and counselling can be traced within the altered social conditions of the industrial revolution. During this period the various sciences were formed and psychiatry emerged within a rapidly changing religious and secular world. Treating the mentally ill became institutionalised as the health service delivered professional psychiatry and psychotherapy. The third chapter examines the religious and spiritual insights of Carl Rogers, Sigmund Freud and Carl Jung as representatives of many clients in therapy whose discourses reveal constructs of reality which lie somewhere along an empirical-mystical continuum. When I ask what is an individual, a unique and inviolate separate consciousness, I am asking what is Self. It is clear that there are different images of the person underlying psychotherapeutic theory, and this will be considered in relation to transpersonal approaches which see as their central task the transcendence of Self.

Chapter 4 considers the indications for therapists to move into a spiritual mode of therapy. An indicator for young clients might be a need to share their experiences of the paranormal, and I shall ask whether such mysterious happenings, as related in discourse, are part of a developing integration of opposing poles of consciousness, evidence of an imagination running wild from uncanny sights and sounds, or an intuitive reception of the numinous. At the other end of life-span development, some clients become more confident in discarding superstition and those metaphysical elements of religion that served them in youth. Their certainties are brought into question. For many, cognitive disillusionment coincides with poor health and social change. Retirement forces them to redefine who they are, and to adjust to loss and changing roles as their children grow up and their loved ones die around them. Spiritual therapy is also indicated when a client's sense of being needed alters to being needy and where the time for their own decease becomes a daunting, fast approaching, reality. From client we next move to practitioner.

An attempt to specify the characteristics of a spiritually-oriented counsellor is the topic of Chapter 5, where I draw distinctions between pastoral and religious counselling, transpersonal and humanistic psychotherapy and spiritually-oriented therapy. Analogies of other mentoring guides are considered to help make clear how the therapist might align himself with the client in spiritual work. This chapter urges the need for practitioners to develop an internal dialogue of self-supervision, often in later reflection through listening and re-listening to recorded interviews, not as an alternative but as a complement to formal supervision. Such an exercise clearly shows where the practitioner's values and assumptions lie, and where the course of therapy and the nature of intervention are affected thereby. None of us are value-neutral, but being aware of our prejudices and predispositions undoubtedly enhances our effectiveness and avoids the pitfalls of unhelpful projections commonly associated with counsellor countertransference.

The next two chapters move into the process of therapeutic healing. Chapter 6 asks the basic questions of what might be happening in spiritual work, and what form of healing is likely to take place. If spiritual work involves transcending Self, rather than bolstering an ego, an understanding of Self seems a necessary undertaking. Fragile senses of Self are considered through the discourse of four boys engaged in bereavement group therapy. The emotional turbulence and social instability resulting from the death of a parent can in part be restored through religious belief, and the transcript reveals fascinating insights of evolving cognitive structures that make sense of individual loss. Healing occurs amongst peers through shared social discourse to normalise individual experience. A further case is presented to help illustrate how Self may be transcended. Analysing discourse exposes the therapist's values, however subtly disguised, and through the brief selected transcript an invitation is given to detect my own leanings in order that others may practise such skills in their own work.

Chapter 7 opens another tier of counselling process through looking at the potential for the therapist to use metaphors of the spiritual journey through life. Religion has provided an invaluable library of journeying motifs, which will still have currency for many. In light of a loosening hold of religion for many living in a postmodern world, however, religious examples taken from scripture will have less import even if they carry psychological potential for growth. Enlightenment for the Buddhist and insight through psychotherapy are not dissimilar, but for those who find religion irrelevant to their everyday consciousness, I explore the possibilities of demythologising some traditional journeying motifs.

Chapter 8 deals with religious doubt through obstacles that often occur through misfortune, or through inner-questioning as life events and human experience become out of sync with religious accounts of reality. Such self-doubt takes place commonly, but not exclusively, during two phases of development. In this chapter, I examine doubt for mid-life clients. Two extended cases of an atheist and a devout Muslim are presented to illustrate how spiritually-centred counselling can facilitate both and yet open up for each new possibilities for transcending Self through integrating the opposite poles of thinking. These extracts cannot hope to illustrate the whole process as much as show where therapy can move. The chapter raises issues of faith and evidence by looking at the relationship of faith and mental health. Common obstacles lying at the heart of religion are examined before reviewing the therapeutic potential for clients to preserve a trust in life and in a transpersonal dimension.

Chapter 9 reviews a broader range of techniques and tools as used in religious and transpersonal therapies than have been illustrated in earlier chapters. The rationale for praying in session is discussed along with meditation and mindfulness. My intention in this book is to encourage all to consider integrating a spiritual mode of therapy in practice, and as such the approaches I have illustrated are not too enterprising. For the more advanced practitioners, however, I cover some of the holistic techniques regularly applied in body psychotherapy. A range of exercises of my own is presented to assist your clients in recognising their most dominant mode of spiritual functioning. The chapter closes with a consideration of the mystical elements in counsellor relating.

The final chapter acknowledges the common difficulties in ending sessions, particularly for a style where there is no clear closure. The terminus point for most of the world faiths is salvation, variously conceived, but the different belief-systems were constructed in an age when metaphysical reality had more impact than it has today. As such, schemes of salvation have little hold on any but the religiously devout. I have not played off one belief-system against another, simply because these are held with conviction and are meaningful discourses for many. That said, I have offered in concluding this book five features of hope revisualised that may help to shape a pluralistic outlook that is necessary for the spiritually-centred therapist.

Throughout this book, theoretical principles and the mode of spiritually-orientated counselling are illustrated with case vignette material. Customarily, I present composite characters to protect client confidentiality, but, in giving spiritual therapy an authentic feel, I have asked a few of my mid-life clients for permission to represent their discourse verbatim. Transcript material is presented not only from 'clients in therapy', but also from discourse amongst fellows who have a profound interest in spiritual matters. Ethically, I am less troubled to relate spiritual issues of my client's material than I would be with more intimate details of their social relations. The teenage-to-late adolescent client material is exclusively taken from the secondary school where I serve in full-time employment, and my elderly clients were drawn from GP referrals and from private therapeutic practice. Some were either struggling over religious or spiritual issues, whilst others had profound insights and experiences of rich and relevant material. In all cases, extracts of verbatim narrative were shown to each contributor within context before going to print. Where clients stress their deliberations I have illustrated this in italics.

Regarding use of the terms psychotherapy, counselling and therapy, they are used interchangeably for style with no intention of being hierarchal, but I have tended to reserve the term psychotherapy and its derivatives when discussing founding figures or their theoretical reasoning. The gender of client is varied to reflect the whole male and female experience, but since my own casework is exclusively given the male personal pronoun for therapist is retained for ease of reading, again with no intention of being discriminatory.

Most of my teenage clients are drawn from secularised poor to middle class families, of an area designated as social priority (54 per cent of families on income support and 39.6 per cent of pupils eligible for free school meals) with the majority of pupils living in council accommodation of single-parented families, normally mothers (80 per cent of pupils receiving counselling have had at least one stepfather cohabiting within their life-span). My adult clients, in the main, were reflective educated people, both male and female.

The ethnic mix of the cultural area where I work is designated statistically as being 88 per cent 'white', 11 per cent 'ethnic minority' (5.1 per cent 'mixed race' and 3.2 per cent 'African Caribbean' being the larger groups) and 1 per cent 'not known'. These percentages do not reflect those of the city of Birmingham, since my clients are, arguably, more secular than those of the inner-city, where ethnic minority communities tend to be more religious. Christian, Islamic and Hindu experience is represented, and the voice of an atheist with humanistic values is heard. Though theoretical perspectives of Jewish and other eastern religious experience are covered, there have been no representatives of these persuasions. In the main, spiritually-centred counselling is demonstrated purposely with clients who have little to no formal religious affiliation.

1

The Enlightened Mind

The air above Jerusalem is saturated with prayers and dreams,
Like the air above industrial towns it's hard to breathe.

Richard Holloway

It ain't necessarily so
The things that you're liable to read in the Bible
It ain't necessarily so!

George Gershwin

This chapter addresses the intellectual climate of western society with reference to formal religion, leaving the intuitive legacy of religion and inward spirituality to Chapter 2. The modern outlook has evolved over a period of social and ideological change, principally from influential philosophers of the Enlightenment. The development of science in the West, together with literary criticism that questioned the inerrancy of the Bible, began a process of eroding faith in God, and this has led to a decline in Christian adherence and a drop in numbers regularly going to church. The sociology of religion drove a further nail in the ecclesiastical coffin by presenting a new discourse that robbed religion of its mystical impulse. The critical themes of rational and reductive enquiry, biblical criticism and the sociology of religion take up this chapter, in as much as these new sciences have affected the postmodern perspectives of clients in therapy.

Joy came for counselling over a six-month period because she could not adjust to retirement and felt she had lost life-meaning. She was diagnosed as having chronic fatigue syndrome by her GP, a condition he thought to be more related to psychological than to physical factors. She was divorced from her husband and after eight years had still unresolved issues of unfairness and belittlement. She had been an Occupational Therapist but when retired had become isolated, rarely seeing her ex-colleagues or her extended family. More importantly for her, she no longer felt she could attend church for social and spiritual support.

Joy:	I've tried to go back to church. I'll sit at the back but the service passes over me. Nothing seems the same anymore.
Dennis:	In what way Joy?
Joy:	It's irrelevant. People come over and greet me; they're kind; they invite me to their homes, but I can't be doing with it. Perhaps I'm scared of being drawn in again, I don't know. Perhaps I'm anti-social … People say when you're older you turn to religion, but it's the opposite for me. A lot of my friends are not with us – I always seem to be going to funerals … I never questioned my faith before, but it doesn't seem real now. I want to believe in God. I dearly want to be part of it all again. But I just can't seem to swallow religion anymore, even though I should and need to … Why do you think this is?
Dennis:	I'm interested in why you feel you *should* and *need* to 'swallow religion'.

Joy's experience is not untypical of many clients brought up within a faith community that in post mid-life fails to provide meaning in an age of heightened personal expectations. Western culture has passed through a modern period, where meaning was uniform and religiously determined, to a postmodern stage where all meaning is individually determined. Western culture is understood to be secular, postmodern and pluralistic.

Western Culture

Secularism

Secular is defined in the *Oxford Dictionary* as 'concerned with the affairs of this world, not sacred, not ecclesiastical, not monastic'. For the last one and a half millennia, western culture was defined within a Christian context, then for the last two centuries humanism made inroads. Today, countries like Britain have become multicultural with a social composition of broad opinion and adherence to many faith and non-faith communities of diverse persuasions. Many more people attended church regularly and had quite strong Christian convictions a few generations ago than is the case today. Young people need only to ask their grandparents about the influence of the Church on their lives and upbringing to see how times have changed. Even after the mass immigration of recent British history, the dominant outlook still remained Christian. Laws of parliament and much pageantry in Britain stem from the Christian worldview. Social values and moral conduct were exclusively biblical, as interpreted by the Church.

When campaigners voice disapproval on controversial topics such as gay and lesbian sexuality, abortion, euthanasia and the rights of going to war, it is not necessarily Christian but secular morality that underlies their convictions. Religious injunctions on how *we should live or behave* are no longer binding and use of the Bible for swearing oaths has become largely meaningless. Christian teaching on every conceivable topic – Creation, existence beyond death, gender relations and sexual mores, etc. – has been replaced by humanistic non-religious beliefs and scientific paradigms. Even though scientific paradigms shift with new knowledge and cultural diversity (Kuhn, 1996 [1962]) they are compelling for those who live by them. This is secularism.

This book will reason that two conceptual frameworks – 'spiritual' and 'empirical' – co-exist in light of the paradigm shift from Newtonian physics to quantum physics, from fixed law theory to inherent indeterminism and chaos.

Postmodernism

Dictionary definitions of modernism and postmodernism fail to encapsulate the meaning of these terms as applied to philosophical thinking. The modern world at the turn of the last century was optimistic in the sense that there was a large-scale view that science would solve every conceivable problem. Science and technology were reshaping the modern world and were pushing the frontiers of the unknown forward, and at an unimaginable pace – this was modernism. A 'positivistic desire for absolute certainty' was the governing principle (Swinton, 2001: 13). Knowledge of human origins, physical and mental health, chemistry and materials, technology, manufacturing industry, atomic physics, commerce and communications, were undergoing relentless progress. Mechanical robots would replace human labour and leave everyone wealthy and free to indulge in every conceivable passion.

The disillusionment spread, however, and this heralded the postmodern period. Science had claimed too much (Gergen, 1999) yet religion remained unverifiable (Holloway, 2004). Research in science, religion and philosophy showed that the more that was known the more there was to discover. The underpinning of knowledge was also beginning to be questioned, recognising that the 'knowable' was only a reflection of the presuppositions of the 'knower', that hypotheses only self-reinforce, and that knowledge is relative. Philosophers and sociologists recognised that science could never be truly objective but was socially constructed, just like religion. The European world of the late nineteenth century had become postmodern and, in spite of recent signs of a return to a modernist spirit of dogmatism in some religious quarters, postmodernism is the current reality for the majority.

Pluralism

Pluralism is probably self-explanatory. The *Oxford Dictionary* defines pluralism narrowly as 'holding more than one office (ecclesiastical) at a time'.

I spoke earlier of Christianity being the dominant worldview of the past, but as communications led to the global village and westerners began to brush shoulders with eastern peoples then communities became more cosmopolitan and competing religious and non-religious systems of knowledge have claimed equal validity. Many social communities within British culture are now as much Islamic, Jewish, Hindu, Sikh or New Age as Christian, and the non-religious beliefs of Zen Buddhism attract many thinking intellectuals of the western world. The implications of this social and ideological admixture cannot be understated. As I write, the demographic composition of citizens where I live in Birmingham, Britain's second City, has ethnic minorities as the majority culture, which makes ethnic minority a curious contradiction in terms. Added to which, the majority of my clients are from non-religious backgrounds. Inevitably, internal law (where people do what *they* judge to be right) supersedes religious morality, and the Court of Human Rights has become the determiner of social justice in Europe. Within this flux of religious and non-religious viewpoints, it is broadly recognised that no one belief-system can claim superiority. This social situation of integration combined with polarisation, apathy living beside fanaticism, atheism as co-existent with fundamentalism, and humanism sitting alongside religion constitutes what has become to be understood as pluralism.

When speaking of pluralism, I am not thinking of pluralistic relativism. Wilber's (2000, 2001a) preference for 'universal integration' appears too monolithic and synthesised, for, in what follows, I aim to validate each person's reality within their own cultural worldviews (Gergen, 1999), not to amend their perspectives to fit my preconceived programme. In therapy I invite clients to see things differently, yes, but to override their valuations, no. This book will promote egalitarian principles by valuing similarity and difference through re-viewing the philosophical issues of various truth claims and through looking at the possibilities of enrichment by validating differing discourses of meaning. The point is that each person's reality will be defined within a cultural dialogue of meaning-making (Gergen, 2001), but this is not to deny that there may exist a 'perennial philosophy', or universal quest, to transcend human finitude (Wilber, 2001b: 77–88).

Postmodern Discourses

Postmodernism is characterised by a range of discourses that collectively describe the way the world is viewed, and some are more prominent than others (Howard, 2000). There are discourses on duties and responsibilities, personal happiness, religion and politics. Social discourse has had and continues to have a profound affect on counselling and psychotherapy (McNamee and Gergen, 1992). Traditionally, religious discourse determined the worldview of the community, but since the Enlightenment competing discourses have had a marked affect upon religion and brought about a new understanding of Self.

Enlightenment

The overarching hold of religion for many people in the past, as it is today for Islam and Catholicism and for many fundamentalist sects and denominations, is partly due to its beneficial effects in binding a community together and partly to the absolute claims of its belief-system (Holloway, 2004: 124–7). But the postmodern climate of opinion has little tolerance for such claims, and the requirement for changing beliefs in the light of critical study and pluralistic ideals has had an affect upon counselling and psychotherapy in the transition from purist ideology to integration. Space will only afford a thumbnail sketch of the writings of influential philosophers, theologians and sociologists that have shaped the postmodern consciousness of the developed western world.

The Enlightenment is a classified period of European philosophical thought whereby the human spirit was raised above religious and imperial authority. Religious groups saw this wave of thought as a threat to the revealed truths of scripture. Such antagonism was caricatured as the elevation of man over God. The Enlightenment was evident in the birth and rapid development of modern science after a seventeenth century French philosopher, Rene Descartes (1596–1650), laid the philosophical building blocks upon which science was erected. Descartes reasoned the case for mistrusting the senses and for testing absolutely everything; to take nothing for granted unless it was self-evident or established by logical inferences from self-evident premises. He even advocated that we should begin by doubting our own existence and the existence of God. Happily, he concluded, since we are aware of our doubting then it is evident that we exist: 'I think, therefore I am' was his rhetorical certainty (*Discourse on Method* and *Meditations*). Proving God's existence was a little more tenuous and rested on the ontological argument (God's existence by definition is as real as the fact that a triangle has three sides) and a curious logic which reasoned that God would not allow human beings to be deceived. Commentators on Descartes' work have decried his absolute materialism and have supplemented the mechanical body with the soul, or *the ghost in the machine* (Ryle, 1990).

Liberating the human spirit created 'modernity' and formed the rational-industrial worldview that ushered in beneficial social changes, including the rise of democracy, the banishing of slavery, the emergence of liberal feminism, the widespread rise in empirical science, the systems and ecological sciences, an increase in life-span of almost three decades, the introduction of relativity and perspective in art and morals and science, the move from ethnocentric to universal morality, and the dismantling of social hierarchies (Wilber, 2001a: 63).

Towards Existentialism

Existential philosophers have left their mark on the public psyche. Existentialism is a way of assessing individual existence (Yalom, 1980).

Immanuel Kant (1724–1804) believed that the only satisfactory proof of God's existence was the moral argument – I take this up with John in Chapter 8. This proof remains for many Christians the basis of human conduct, in spite of its anti-pluralistic implications for determining what is right and wrong, and the implausibility of how we can know. Kant reasoned that we can know what is right by critical and rational reflection but Sartre (1973) later disputed this (Lynch, 2002). Kant dismissed the belief in Natural Theology – that God's existence could be verified in the natural world – yet he did a great service to psychology, in formulating experience as being arranged in perceptual schemas, or categories of reality. His point was to illustrate that the human mind is not passive but active, that we unconsciously order reality within pre-developed concepts, and that all awareness of our environment is an interpreted awareness (*Critique of Pure Reason*).

George Hegel (1770–1831) described the tendency in scientific and philosophical thought to follow laws of a particular pattern of thesis, followed by antithesis, followed then by synthesis. The vitality for Hegel, his lifeblood so to speak, was faith, but the emerging situation is where philosophy is tested. So faith stands in tension with scepticism, Christianity with the Enlightenment, mysticism with rationalism, and the synthesis in his philosophy was found in the Spirit. In *Philosophy of Mind* (1807), Hegel wrote about the psyche (*Geist*) which for Paul Tillich (1976) is best translated as Spirit. Hegel saw the point of identity between God and man within the philosopher's mind: God becomes real in the self-consciousness of man, and the essential nature of man belongs within the inner-life of God. Speaking of 'finite-infinite', he claimed that the mind of God becomes actualised via the minds of his creatures. This is an interesting perspective of synthesising the empirical with the mystical within a social merging with the divine, and this has implications for spiritually-centred counselling, as we shall see.

Søren Keirkegaard (1813–1855) and Martin Heidegger (1889–1976) wrote extensively about the givens of human existence, about human hopelessness, giving Hegel's terms of 'alienation' and 'estrangement' a poignant significance in the human search for meaning. Existence is punctuated by human tragedy. The existential philosophers developed a new 'individualist' reality of living within a 'thrown condition'. The human situation is that of being-in-the-world, such as it is, and of having to face conflict with respect to the Self, others and the physical world (McLeod, 1993). Existentialism holds that we have to survive within the givens of birth, freedom, meaninglessness, isolation and death. These were the founding thinkers of Existentialism, from which a school of psychotherapy emerged. Existential therapy subscribes to a range of basic assumptions that help clients to clarify life meanings by confronting everyday existential paradoxes (van Deurzen-Smith, 1984). But one philosopher above all has had a profound influence on postmodern consciousness, and his name is Friedrich Nietzsche (1844–1900).

Nietzsche

'All postmodern roads lead to Nietzsche', said Ken Wilber (2001a: 55). It is to Nietzsche that the existentialist term of *nihilism* is to be applied, and whilst the Scottish philosopher, David Hume (1711–1776), has made a contribution, it is to the thoroughgoing radical frankness of Nietzsche that humanism and atheism find an authority. Nietzsche contracted syphilis in his student days and suffered a mental illness before his death – some fundamentalist Christians view his demise as an act of God. Nietzsche wrote about the need for us to stand upon our own two feet and to face the world in confidence without appealing to higher authorities and beneficiaries to help us get through. Though judged negatively by some, he spoke of his love for mankind and said 'yes to life' through man's *Will to Power* and *The Superman*.

Nietzsche discussed the nature of truth. 'What is truth?' asked Pilate of Jesus. Nietzsche's reply was that no truth is discoverable except the truth which *you yourself are*. There is no sense or meaning in the world except the truth *you yourself give it* (Hollingdale, 1969: 25). The answer to Pilate's question is that truth is the will to overcome the nihilistic devaluation of life; it is the arrival of the Superman of self-authority, and this, in turn, led to the death of God.

In *Thus Spake Zarathustra* (1969 [1883–5]), Nietzsche, ingeniously, turns the biblical teaching of revelation on its head through his prophet Zarathustra (the founder of Zoroastrianism). Moses and Elijah came down the mountain with a revelation from God, just as Jesus delivers his Sermon on the Mount. Zarathustra likewise goes into the mountains for solitude but then descends with a gift because 'he loves mankind'. He meets an old man collecting roots in the forest and speaks to him. He learns that he is a saint who lives in a holy hut and that he continually praises God in song. When they part, Zarathustra reflects in his heart: 'Could it be possible! This old saint has not yet heard in his forest that *God is dead!*' (1969: 41).

A graphic account of the death of God is recorded in his next book, *The Gay Science*, in which a madman goes in search of God in the marketplace at night with a lantern. He shouts incessantly, 'I am looking for God'. But his mocking bystanders suggest that God may have got lost like a child, or gone on a voyage. The madman yells in anguish: 'I shall tell you. *We have killed him* – you and I. We are all his murderers' (Hollingdale, 1969: 14).

I have given more space to Nietzsche because I think his work, whilst unheeded in his own day, has had an enormous impact upon the intellectual perspectives of modern times. One criticism of long drawn-out styles of psychotherapy is the tendency to pamper Self through excessive introspection. Extensive therapy can foster narcissism for individuals who are so absorbed with themselves that they fail to see that healing may require them to seek an engagement with others. At this point, however, it is worth noting that much of the movements of human rights, person- and child-centredness, self-fulfilment and humanistic morality against religious teaching are the natural outworking of Nietzsche's teachings of personal autonomy. One clear strand of the anti-religious authority of postmodern consciousness that serves as the basis of atheism is that God is presumed to be dead, and this creed lies at the basis of Jean-Paul Sartre's (1973) deduction that we have to live our lives in the self-evident fact that God does not exist and 'that there are no ultimate values' (Lynch, 2002: 37).

From the Enlightenment through to modern times science has been heralded as the salvation of mankind, particularly for those who have abandoned religious faith. In spite of two World Wars, the Holocaust, and the enlightened mind of postmodernism (Howard, 2000), reality for western peoples is embedded within a causal scientific paradigm. Descartes is regarded as the father of modern science through creating the intellectual culture from which a methodology of hypothesis, experimentation and measurement could thrive. Isaac Newton established the fixed laws of gravity and the planetary orbits, upon which the reality of certainty beyond perception could be framed. Galileo and Darwin made observations that would challenge orthodox Christian belief of God as the Creator and of Genesis being a historical account of the origin of the universe. Existentialism liberated the closed mind to find expression in great literature, poetry, art and the modern-day novel. The human spirit was free of constraint and through drama and the expressive arts, individuals like Michelangelo and Blake dared to challenge the establishment (Schaeffer, 1972). Michelangelo's frescos represent Catholic traditions through the eyes of the human subject. Through Renaissance influence and humanism, he retains the divine as transcendent but through human concerns and connectivity (see Figure 1.1).

The most significant feature of Existentialism in terms of psychology, however, was the emergence, or re-emergence, of the psychology of individual Self.

Philosophical Perceptions of Self

Self, according to Heraclitus, is an illusion since everything is flux, change, process, continually becoming something else. I am not some solid essence: *I cannot step twice into the same river.* A great intellectual gap exists between Augustine's divine-Self-consciousness and David Hume's scepticism. Augustine's God was in continual dialogue with him and served as his personal counsellor, and so he made a deity of my Self. Hume, when looking inwards, could not catch his Self that would be separate from his perception. John Locke was the last serious philosopher to suggest that Self could be observed directly (Howard, 2000). Rousseau advocated a return to nature as the map for finding Self, whilst Hegel postulated an essentialist doctrine of Self that was integral with absolute Spirit, the unifying Agent of all reality. For Schopenhauer, Self was a

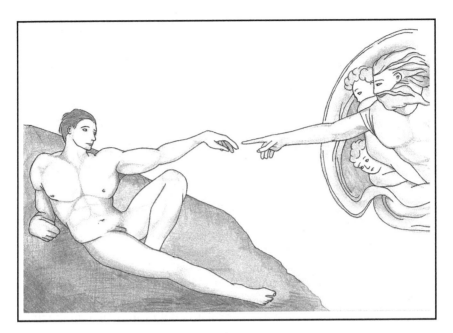

Figure 1.1   Michelangelo's 'God creating Adam', Sistine Chapel, sketched by Nathan Marsh

noumenal subject, not a phenomenal object, and as such could not be observed – *there is no separate Self; we are all an expression of the one subject.* Kierkegaard, along with other existentialists, believed that Self could not be found so much as be created. Self development was a process of continual becoming to reach intrinsic potential, either being grounded with, or released from, the religious Object:

> Kierkegaard's existentialism consisted in finding oneself within and before God. Nietzsche's self was a bridge leading to 'superman'. For Heidegger, self was inextricably interwoven with, and emergent from, its larger context. Hegel's self was part of the absolute idea. For Sartre, self was similar to Descartes' self, but without God. Self, for Sartre, was its own God. (Howard, 2000: 341–2)

Western philosophers have wrestled perpetually with understandings and conceptions of Self, and Alex Howard (2000) has made a valid point when highlighting the importance for counsellors to consider this vast corpus of material when forming their own understandings of Self and therapeutic theories. In summary, he writes: 'From Hume onwards, naive ideas about a simple core self have become increasingly implausible' (Howard, 2000: 357) and feels that the modern tendency to individualise and psychologise Self has been damaging to society. Our examination in what follows will take on board this observation, yet will explore psychological constructions of Self more through analogy and metaphor than through the logic of reductionism.

Higher Criticism of Scripture

In the 1940s, Dietrich Bonhoeffer was arrested and imprisoned by the Gestapo after an attempt to assassinate Hitler had been foiled. It was not that he was personally involved, but more that he was suspected of being part of a conspiracy. Bonhoeffer was a Lutheran theologian, and from his cell he wrote a remarkable series of letters that collectively became an uncanny forecast of modern times. In one letter he wrote: 'We are moving towards a completely religionless time; people as they are now simply cannot be religious anymore' (Bonhoeffer, 1970: 279). This prediction has a ring of truth for religion, but not necessarily for spirituality, as we shall see.

The absolute certainty that kept the old religious order intact was based upon religious authority. For the Catholic Church this was an infallible papacy, tradition and the biblical scriptures, and for Anglicans, from the Reformation onwards, it was the Bible and the Christian believer's relationship with God. The religious authority for Muslims is the Qur'an and the Hadith (sayings and deeds of the prophet) whilst for Judaism it is the Torah, the Prophets and the Mishnah. The authority for Hindus is the Vedas, for Buddhists it is the Pali Canon, and for Sikhs it is the Guru Granth Sahib.

Many of these sacred scriptures are based on revelations during altered states of consciousness, which are described by Grof (Bray, 2004) as holotropic experiences (oriented towards wholeness), and which are claimed to be repeatable (Grof, 1996). The Bible, particularly, has been the first sacred text to have been subjected to higher criticism to expose human elements behind divine inspiration (Lines, 1995b). The Talmud has had a long tradition of interpreting the Law and the Prophets, but the Qur'an has received little public scrutiny (Manji, 2004). In the interests of brevity, I trace a few milestones of Christian scholarship through New Testament literary criticism.

Ruddolf Bultmann (1952, 1953) began a controversial debate in 1948 on Christian mythology by demythologising the New Testament (the resurrection and ascension of Jesus) and by reinterpreting the Christian message in existential terms, following the philosophy of Martin Heidegger. A group of British theologians in 1997 confronted orthodoxy by disputing biblical inerrancy and by questioning the historicity of the incarnation (Hick, 1977). These theologians followed a reputable line of German and European scholars who dismantled Christian authority right at its core, the infallible nature of holy writ. Don Cupitt (2001) has attempted to reformulate Christianity, but on the whole the absolute authority of sacred scripture interpreted literally is now judged to be untenable by biblical exegetes.

Postmodern biblical scholars discount any claims that the Bible is inerrant (Lines, 1995b) if by such terms is meant that scripture presents absolute truths of history (i.e. what is written *actually* happened) and science. Although the trend has occurred a little less in Judaism and hardly at all in Islam, it is feasible that higher criticism will be applied to almost every religious text in the not-too-distant future. The corollary is that no one sacred text can be claimed to have the whole truth – an obstacle many clients wrestle with in therapy.

The postmodernist ideology abandons the notion of a single absolute truth that can be found with objective certainty, in favour of relative, conditional truths, even to the acceptance of paradox (McNamee and Gergen, 1992: 8–15). The old 'Cartesian-Newtonian paradigm' we must now abandon, argues Edwards (1992).

Apart from the challenge of religious authority through higher literary criticism, there are three assumptions that the new spiritual paradigm of postmodernism cannot tolerate (Lines, 2002):

- From the sociological perspective, the religious organisation is prone to exploit the individual's spiritual needs without satisfying them, and to create a hierarchical system that pursues power and control (Lines, 1995a). Religion has often lost touch with its spiritual sources and become a secular institution, a 'benign social custom' or, at worst, a 'pathological reflection of infantile ego development' (Boorstein, 1996: 182).
- Secondly, the 'chosen people' concept of divine election (Judaism, Christianity and Islam) is reprehensible in the modern world. Some religious writings were once thought to be the authorisation rather than the product of the 'holy community', having no bias or propagandist motives. Primitive, homogeneous societies reinforced their sacred truths through group cultic acts and through communal ceremony, which collectively became their reality. Thus, individual identity was synonymous with cultural identity and was ratified by membership of the 'religious community'. Such exclusivity must now give way to universalism and pluralism (Hick, 2001).
- Finally, the Enlightenment gave birth to the individual (Tillich, 1976), and Freud identified the various drives that underpin the Self (Freud, 1933). But this division of community and of Self has become outdated and is becoming superseded by a new reality that stresses the relationship of parts to wholes.

Sociology of Religion

One major discourse of postmodernism is the sociological account of religion. Nearly every political, religious and ethical discussion of the modern period will contain a strand of opinion which is influenced by this outlook. Whether the debate centres on Islamic–Christian relations, homosexual clergy, voluntary euthanasia, etc., communications are at cross purposes when one party reasons from a 'revealed insight' perspective and another from one that views religion as a product of social influences.

Karl Marx (1818–83) was the most influential social scientist in history, yet Emile Durkheim (1858–1917) and Max Weber (1881–1961) have had a considerable influence on the religious outlook. They were classical theorists writing in agrarian societies; both were reacting to the initial stages of the industrial and democratic revolutions, and both visualised many of our modern structures and problems.

Durkheim (1933) coined the term 'anomie' to describe the dissolving of regulation and the breakdown of norms within society which religion had established over the centuries. The advance in capitalism during industrialisation required individually led citizens to detach themselves mentally from tradition, but, for Durkheim, this would lead to a society where 'individualism' would lead to a breakdown of mutual dependence and an increase in deviant behaviour. Durkheim forecast what today we call a 'dog eat dog', 'every man for himself', mentality, but he was not predisposed towards religion. Durkheim robbed religion of its numinous content and reasoned that religion was not supernaturally inspired but the product of society, 'something eminently social' (Thompson, 1982: 125). He studied the cultural history of the *sacred* and the *profane,* and reasoned that both serve a complementary social function. Regarding religious experience, Durkheim acknowledged that 'it does exist' but 'it does not follow that the reality which is its foundation conforms objectively to the idea which believers have of it' (Bellah, 1973: 190).

In *The Protestant Ethic and the Spirit of Capitalism,* Weber (2003 [1905]) explained the shift from traditional to rational action in the religious and economic systems of many civilisations. He came to believe that the rationalisation of action can only be realised when traditional ways of life are abandoned, as occurred in the Industrial Revolution. After careful study, Weber came to the hypothesis that the Protestant ethic broke the hold of tradition and encouraged men [sic] to apply themselves rationally to their work. Calvinism had developed a set of beliefs around the concept of predestination. It was believed by followers of Calvin that a place in heaven could not be earned by good works or acts of faith, since people were either among the 'elect', or they were 'damned'. However, wealth for a person was taken as a public sign that they were elected by God; thereby the acquisition of money as a Christian virtue was promoted. The Protestant ethic therefore sanctioned a spirit of rigorous discipline, and encouraged all to strive to become prosperous.

Weber asked why capitalism did not occur in other non-western and preindustrial societies when some of them had the technological infrastructure and other necessary preconditions for economic expansion. One significant reason was the absence of something akin to the Protestant ethic. He did not believe that the Protestant ethic was the *only cause* of the rise of capitalism, but thought it was a powerful force in fostering its emergence.

This analysis of the cause and continuance of religion being attributable to natural factors within society is widespread for many today, and has appeal for those who believe in the power of society to mould the minds of its citizens. Essentially, the sociology of religion states that 'the gods whom people worship are imaginary beings unconsciously fabricated by society as instruments whereby society exercises control over the thoughts and behaviour of the individual' (Hick, 1990: 30). Religious feelings evoked by the numinous are delusions since no supernatural Being exists; it is society's environing reality. And the supposed demands made upon worshipping subjects is society's moral imperative of its subjects, since we are social beings through and through.

Not withstanding, John Hick (1990) remains unconvinced that the sociological account of religion is proven, for the following reasons. If the call of God has to be translated as 'only society imposing upon its members forms of conduct that are in the interests of that society', then how are we to account for those charismatic individuals who are led by a developed conscience to speak out against the confined interests of the social group? Where does the creative vision to innovate change from the moral norm come from? What inspired the insights of the great religious reformers – such as the biblical prophets like Amos and Hosea – to denounce the ways of their own people? If it is society, then there is a contradiction (Hick, 1990). Kenneth Gergen (1999) proposes a socially constructed reality, but Wilber (2000) questions absolute constructionist accounts of reality: if there are no worldviews that are not socially constructed, how can the 'socially constructed worldview' be the true reality? It must be socially constructed – it is to argue in a circle (Wilber, 2001a: 56).

Towards Religious Pluralism

A central question that concerned me during the religious idealism of my early twenties was the tension between a parochial belief-system and universal salvation; whether only those of my religious denomination might be saved on the last day or whether God's grace would extend to all mankind. I could not see how a simplistic notion of 'salvation only in Christ' could mean anything for the many millions in India who are brought up as Hindus, or for the tribes in remote parts of the world who had never even heard of Christ, let alone have become Christian. Such questions seem irrelevant for me today, but in that early period of staunch religious conviction, where the decisions for right and wrong living had eternal consequences, it was crucial. One philosopher of religion who has addressed the implications of religious pluralism is John Hick (1990, 2001). Hick (1976) argues for universal salvation with an intriguing theory of post-death consciousness developed from the Tibetan *Bardo Thodol*, or *The Book of the Dead*. Hick's major interest, however, is in finding a common language for different religious concepts.

Redemption in Judaism comes through the covenant relationship of Yahweh with the Jews as the chosen people, as revealed in the Torah. Muslims believe that salvation depends entirely upon the graciousness and merciful nature of Allah, as self-revealed in the Qur'an. Christians believe their salvation rests in Christ alone, as revealed in the atonement through the cross, and through the conferring of eternal life for the believer, as declared in the New Testament. The Buddhist sees salvation quite differently, as surrendering and releasing the ego, as reaching Nirvana by being absorbed within the unity of Brahmin. These salvation claims of different religions compete with one another, as though one is superior to the rest; one holds pre-eminent truth and the others are by definition secondary, or even erroneous. Hick maintains that if we move away from a model of conflicting truth-claims towards a model of seeing different religions as different concrete manifestations to humanity of the ultimate divine reality within varied cultural settings, then we begin to embrace a more rational philosophy of universalism where there is no conflict. Reality is known to the Christian through the love and forgiving nature of Jesus who is worshipped as Lord, and whose salvation is celebrated through the Eucharist in bread and wine. But Reality for the Muslim might equally be evident in the holy Qur'an, as a strictly unitary Being, who responds to the supplicant in the pattern of prayer, fasting, alms-giving and pilgrimage as required in the Qur'an. As Hick reasons:

> We have here something analogous to different maps of the religious world ... But that one map is correct does not mean that another, drawn in a different projection, is incorrect... For when we try to map the infinite divine reality in our finite earthly human terms we inevitably distort it, some of us within one theological projection and some in another. (Hick, 2001: 200)

If we are to address God as *the Real*, then, reasons Hick, we must recognise that *the Real* in itself lies beyond the range of our entire network of concepts, other than purely formal ones. We can only conceptualise it within our human terms, following Kant. The religious traditions thus stand between us and *the Real*, constituting different lenses through which we are aware of it (2001: 191).

Hick prefers the title for God as *the Real* rather than such equally suitable alternatives as Ultimate Reality, the Transcendent, the Divine, mainly because the English term *the Real* is not only acceptable within Christianity but also because it corresponds sufficiently with Sanskrit and Arabic terms for God. The basis on which we know *the Real* will be differently formed within the different traditions. But we can never be conscious of the deity or of the absolute in general, for it has to be personal, as concretely experienced (in Kant's language, schematised) in historical time and within a culture. Take, for example, Jewish history and the Torah. God is intimately part of their history but the Bible knows nothing of the peoples of China or India or the Americas, just as the God of over one thousand names in the Vishnu is restricted to India, with no apparent awareness of the Jews, and so on.

Finally, Hick draws the necessary distinction between the numinous experience of *the Real* and the everyday experience of the senses in the world. One is a transcendental phenomenon and the other is a natural phenomenon. Experiencing the wind in my face, as I view the mountain and drink the cool water from a mountain stream, is a phenomenon available to me in my senses in the natural world. But if I stand in the presence of God and feel the closeness of his being, then this experience is not available to me through the senses, and it is likely that this awareness has occurred not intuitively but because I have been introduced to God through teaching or through the medium of religious worship – the knowledge of the mountain experience is not compatible with the knowledge of God (Hick, 1990).

Conclusion

This chapter has examined the social and ideological effects of the philosophical liberation brought in by the Enlightenment, by biblical scholarship and by the sociology of religion. Although Britain is a multi-cultural society, the dominant though diminishing discourse is still Christian in spite of numbers meeting to worship every Sunday morning being in decline. The postmodern worldview in the main is pragmatic and scientifically centred and sociological accounts of religion are persuasive to many clients entering therapy.

The implications of religious pluralism for spiritually-centred counselling cannot be underestimated. In closing this chapter we have seen that rival religious truth-claims are merely different theological projections of the ultimate divine reality. Already, metaphors have been used without qualification, such as maps and lenses, but as we begin to focus more on the language of spirituality in counselling and psychotherapy, *differing discourses* will employ personalised metaphors. Although this book will embrace Hick's pluralistic values, when referring to the divine I shall not adopt his preference of *the Real* but will speak of 'the numinous', so as not to exclude my colleagues and clients who have difficulty in accepting the existence of a divine Being, but who nevertheless wish to engage in spiritually-centred counselling.

2

The Spiritual Revolution

There was once a time when all human beings were gods, but they so abused their divinity that Brahma, the chief god, decided to take it away from them, and hide it where it could never be found. Where to hide their divinity was the question. So Brahma called a council of the gods to help him decide. 'Let's bury it deep in the earth,' said the gods. But Brahma answered, 'No, that will not do because humans will dig into the earth and find it.' Then the gods said, 'Let's sink it in the deepest ocean.' But Brahma said, 'No, not there, for they will learn to dive into the ocean and will find it.' Then the gods said, 'Let's take it to the top of the highest mountain and hide it there.' But once again Brahma replied, 'No, that will not do either, because they will eventually climb every mountain and once again take up their divinity.'

Then the gods gave up and said, 'We do not know where to hide it, because it seems there is no place on earth or in the sea that human beings will not eventually reach.' Brahma thought for a long time and then said, 'Here is what we will do. We will hide their divinity deep within the centre of their own being, for humans will never think to look for it there.' All the gods agreed that this was the perfect hiding place, and the deed was done. And since that time humans have been going up and down the earth, digging, diving, climbing and exploring – searching for something that is already within themselves.

(Elkins, 1998: 37–8)

The Enlightenment raised the European social consciousness to become aware of the effects and consequences of reason applied to religious belief. This chapter will consider the mystical element of human makeup in order to argue the case for plural discourses of religion and spirituality. As human beings are advanced social animals through their cognitive faculties, so are they distinctively spiritual. Christianity offered salvation to those of the first century, a belief-system which continued steadily through the Middle Ages in Europe, but there has been declining interest in formal religion with noticeable consequences in modern times. New expressions of spirituality, and not only New Age movements, have led many social commentators to wonder whether we are living at the dawn of a spiritual revolution. This chapter considers this hypothesis, and then makes an attempt to define the indefinable nature of religious and spiritual experience, in order to lay the foundations of the model of spiritually-centred counselling which follows.

Christianity in Decline

A few scholars who take an active interest in such matters have attempted to compile statistics on measurable factors of religion and spirituality, and below I summarise the findings recorded by William West (2000, 2004). West draws principally upon the studies of David Hay (Hay and Hunt, 2000) to illustrate that the secular society of Britain in modern times is post-Christian, that, whilst the constitution, civil institutions and public ceremonies and holidays in Britain still reflect the Christian narrative, it has to be recognised that 'Christianity itself is in decline and the largest spiritual grouping would have to be New Age or unaligned' (West, 2004: 16). West predicts: 'I do not honestly believe we can get back to a massive adherence to Christianity despite the hopes of many evangelical Christians. Indeed I do not think a resurgence of Christianity in that form would be a spiritual step forward' (2004: 16), a point inferred by Sam:

> *Sam:*   Around here I read the Church Newsletter and they're all old folk, and it'll be like the National Trust. People of a minimum age will be fifty. Some churches may attract the broader family, but many are elderly single women.
>
> *Dennis:*   Do you think that was the heyday of the Church during our youth?
>
> *Sam:*   There are still people involved in Church groups, who believe in it hugely, but my kids now spend most of their day at school, in travelling, and by the time they get back they have little time to themselves before going to bed. The school is a long day. During holiday time it's just time to chill.

Summarising the statistical research on the status of the Christian Church in postmodern Britain, it has been estimated that 27 per cent of the adult population attended church regularly on Sunday morning in 1850, 54 per cent attended Anglican morning services according to the 1851 census, but in 1990 this figure dropped to 14 per cent. In 1989 regular church attendance in Britain fell from 4.74 million to 3.71 million in 1998, a drop of more than 20 per cent in a decade. Today, on an average Sunday morning, there will be less than 8 per cent of the population going to church, and of these congregations, especially in the Church of England and the Methodists, the majority are increasingly elderly. The only Christian communities that appear to hold steady numbers, or are growing, are the evangelical churches, the black churches, and some of the fundamentalist denominations (Brierley, 2000; Bruce, 1995; West, 2004: 18).

The common outgrowth of religion for adolescence is illustrated in the case of Anthony, a 13-year-old client. He was born in Jamaica and he reflected on some of the differences of life in the UK.

Anthony: My nan still goes to Church in Jamaica. She helps out in the neighbourhood. My granddad just likes his garden- ing [*Anthony laughs, and I laugh along*]. My mum went to Church, and I used to go to Church when I was really, really young. I used to go to this Sunday School where I used to live. I was probably about four, or three.

Dennis: At three or four would you have some memories of what it was like?

Anthony: Yeah, I used to not want to go because it was boring; except I liked the sweets [*Anthony laughs*].

Dennis: So you'd go for sweets?

Anthony: Mm.

Dennis: Did you stop when you moved to England?

Anthony: I just grew out of it; I had different interests.

In spite of declining numbers attending Christian churches there is an increasing number of mosques and temples of Sikh, Hindu and Buddhist communities in the UK. Non-Christian religions are similarly increasing, and the Pagan Federation, according to West, claims to be the fastest grow- ing religion in Britain with over 100,000 followers. House fellowships and new religious movements led by charismatic leaders appear to attract large followings amongst the young. New Age spirituality has become a very popular form of religious expression that overlaps with some forms of humanistic and transpersonal therapies. Finally, there are now many people actively involved in meditation, yoga and other spiritual practices without being aligned to one religion or another (West, 2004).

In spite of this decline in nominal church attendance, many people in Britain today still view themselves as Christian, will declare that they believe in God and will often attest to unusual experiences occurring in life which they understand as being spiritual. West draws out the impli- cations of this in terms of how we might measure the spiritual base of people living in Great Britain today. Hay discovered that one-third of sub- jects in a poll survey affirmed that they had been influenced by 'a pres- ence or power, whether referred to as God or not, which was different from your everyday self' (Hay, 1979, 1982; Hay and Morisy, 1978). A recent study broadened the scope of the question to include ecstatic and paranormal experiences in nature, a pattern of events, answers to prayer, an awareness of the presence of the dead and of evil, and 76 per cent of respondents recorded positive results (Hay and Hunt, 2000).

From analysing the work of Elkins et al. (1988) and Greeley (1975) on public opinion surveys in the USA, West deduces that one-third of respondents report having had religious or spiritual experiences, but Americans are three times more likely to attend church or be members than is the case in Britain (West, 2000: 11). Hay is convinced that religious experience is universal and that 'its continual survival as a phenomenon irrespective of church attendance points to its value to us as a species' (West, 2000: 12).

The Spiritual Revolution

David Tacey (2004) believes that a Spiritual Revolution is occurring in Melbourne amongst students from the evidence of over-subscribed courses on the subject. Trained in literature, theology, sociology and history of religions, and with a leaning towards Jungian depth psychology, he was curious about an undeveloped interest in spirituality amongst young adults. Against the advice of his colleagues, he decided to offer a course on spirituality and was overwhelmed by the high take-up. It was as though there was a dormant interest waiting to be stirred. Near his home town in Alice Springs, the River Todd can be seen to appear from the ground after heavy rainfall, and this, he says, is like the spiritual revolution. The underground stream of spirituality beneath our ordinary world is rarely noticed, as with the Tao (2004: 51). His task is 'to educate the spirit in the person, by enabling students to see and recognise the spirit in culture, literature, art and their experience of life' (2004: 76).

Tacey thinks that the youth of today are indicating that their spirituality is *engaged* spirituality, since they are concerned with the welfare of the world and the sacredness of endangered nature; it is pragmatic and worldly and is seen as a cure for racism and as a new ecological awareness. Spirituality for youth is not a quest for perfection through piety and devotion, but a search for guiding visions and values within this world, 'for the deep currents of spiritual impulse and reality that give life meaning and direction' (2004: 65).

Tacey is not anti-religious even though he recognises that religion has little relevance for much of Australian youth. He acknowledges that there is a lack of confidence in the clergy and religious leaders as guides or holy men, and sees the whole process as little more than social conditioning and functional engineering rather than as a genuine contact with the sacredness of life. Feminists regard Christianity as patriarchal, and pagan students regard religion as partly responsible for the desecration of the earth and the destruction of the environment. Esoteric and occult students claim that Christianity had lost its spirituality many centuries ago, and evangelicals insist on receiving Jesus into our hearts as the answer (2004: 99). Through literature, art and personal experiencing, Tacey works alongside students' personal reflections to help them develop a relationship with the sacred: 'Man today hungers and thirsts for a *safe* relationship to the psychic forces within himself' (2004: 28).

The question that remains is whether this personal vision of Australian youth is universally experienced; whether there is evidence of a spiritual revolution taking place elsewhere under the principle of what Jung refers to as *synchronicity*, or meaningful coincidence? The question has been the topic of a sociological study carried out by Paul Heelas and Linda Woodhead (2005) from 2000 to 2002 at Kendal in the north-west of England. The authors recognise the 'subject turn' in modern culture encapsulated by a comment made in 1966 by Madeleine Bunting:

> People are turning inside themselves for answers rather than look-ing to external religions which people have to fit into rather than finding something which fits them. People are taking more control over all aspects of their life, spiritual and health, rather than letting other people tell them what to do or believe. (cited in Heelas and Woodhead, 2005: 125)

The researchers studied the religious and spiritual activity of this isolated region to examine trends from earlier statistics and then compared the data with that covering other parts of Britain and the USA. They described the religious activity of Kendal as the *congregational domain* – or 'religion-as' experience – and the *holistic milieu* – or 'subjective-life' experience. The holis-tic milieu includes Zen meditation, New Age movements, and alternative or holistic (body-mind-spirit) spiritualities like spiritual yoga, reiki, meditation, tai chi, aromatherapy, paganism, rebirthing, reflexology and wicca.

The overall difference was clearly evident, as Heelas and Woodhead (2005: 13) observe: 'As we pushed open the doors of churches, chapels and meeting houses on consecutive Sunday mornings, we became aware of a similarity that overrode all other differences. To step into a service is to find one's atten-tion being directed away from oneself towards something higher'.

There were differences, however, and they are categorised under four headings:

- Congregations of difference
- Congregations of humanity
- Congregations of experiential difference, and
- Congregations of experiential humanity.

Congregations of difference are those which stress the distance between God and humanity, creator and creation and the necessary subordination of the latter to the former – *We are called by God to give our lives to him, since salvation – as defined in the Bible – is granted by following his commandments and having a relationship with the Lord Jesus.* Such congregations include Independent Evangelicals, Mormons, Jehovah's Witnesses, Christadelphians and Anglo-Catholics.

Congregations of humanity limit this distance by singling out 'humanity' as something that God and human beings have in common; they tend to emphasise the importance of worshipping God by serving humanity – *God comes first, love of neighbour comes second, and self comes last.* The Church of England, Roman Catholic, Methodist and the United Reformed Church were of this category.

When both these groups emphasise the authority of subjective experience in religious life they take on more of an experiential form. Congregations of experiential difference continue to stress the gap between the divine and the human but believe that God can enter directly into subjective experience as the Holy Spirit – *At the point of conversion you surrender individual life and your uniqueness and autonomy to God.* This group includes congregations of the Salvation Army, Church of England and the Community Church (Independent).

Congregations of experiential humanity, whilst diminishing the gap between the divine and the human, close it still further by teaching that the divine is more likely to be found in inner experience than in the externals of religion like scripture and the sacraments – *It is not necessary to merely* **become** *better, one should* **feel** *better.* These congregations were of the Spiritualist Church, the Society of Friends (Quakers), Unitarian Chapel and the First Church of Christ (Scientist).

Given that modern life has become secularised, and that the sacred landscape has become more subjective-life than life-as experience, the survey through headcounts and other means of assessment attempted to measure the relative health of these activities, and to see their relationship. Overall the study concluded that there was no evidence of a spiritual revolution, if by spiritual revolution we mean that the holistic milieu had taken over from the congregational domain. There was evidence of declining numbers in the congregational domain and rising figures in attending subjective-life forms of spiritualities, but the contrasting trends were not significant in numbers to portray this as a spiritual revolution – the evidence points to the co-existence of two forms of data.

The authors offered bold speculations with interesting qualifications. The evidence in Kendal (matched by national figures in Britain) suggests that headcounts at religious congregations are continuing to decline – early polls from 1950 onwards record 12 per cent of the population, which reduced to 7.9 per cent in 2000. In 1957, 73 per cent of Britons claimed they had attended Sunday School regularly, but this figure fell to 4 per cent of the population in 2000 (Heelas and Woodhead, 2005: 72). The reasoning offered is that association with congregations of 'life-as spirituality' is not supportive in a culture where education (child-centred), health (patient-centred) and politics (human rights) have taken a subjective turn.

It is feasible, however, to speculate that other factors may lead to a bottoming-out. The authors predict an overall congregational decline to continue for the next 25 to 30 years as attendance at congregations of humanity shrinks to around 1 per cent of the population, and since they expect attendance at congregations of experiential difference to remain fairly steady, this would lead to a levelling out of the congregational domain at around 3 per cent of the population by 2030 (Heelas and Woodhead, 2005: 148). If groups within the congregational domain who follow life-as religion are able to steer their faith toward subjective-life spirituality, then there may be hope of survival.

The evidence from this study showed that whilst there has been a large scale interest from the 1960s and 1970s in subjective-life spirituality, and that interest has grown steadily and consistently till modern times, the growth has not been sufficiently substantial to warrant describing the trend as a spiritual revolution. This is not to say that the modern fascination for subjective-life spirituality may not increase in popularity but neither is it to say that the numbers may not remain steady, or even decrease. The authors point out that since this growing interest may have stemmed from the 1960s, it is possible, considering the particular age groups who are primarily caught up in subjective-life spirituality and who would have been at university or delving into alternative experiences at the time, that this number may not also bottom-out. Conversely, if young people are brought up to see value in holistic spirituality, it can be argued that the numbers might increase considerably, and thereby bring about the spiritual revolution. As the authors concede, 'predicting the future has its limits'. They are not confident that Christianity will stage a revival, as in the past, since Christian capital is no longer high as it was in the eighteenth century when revival last occurred with the rise of Methodism: 'Religion which tells you what to believe and how to behave is out of tune with a culture which believes that it is up to us to seek out appropriate answers for ourselves' (Heelas and Woodhead, 2005: 126).

Whilst this study appears comprehensive and well reasoned, it does not take into account the multi-faith constitution that makes up British society more generally. The authors acknowledge this and also recognise that not all the activities listed by them as belonging to the holistic milieu might be described as being spiritual. Questionnaire data informing respondents involving themselves in subjective-life activities are largely women (80 per cent), of middle age (48 per cent were between 45 and 54, 23 per cent were older) who described themselves as believing in spirituality (90 per cent) even though some did not regard their holistic activity as being spiritual. It strikes me that there are other sociological factors (feminism, disposable income) to account for these trends. Of this group, 58 per cent reported that they had been 'brought up with a religious faith' at home, and with so many church people attending yoga and alternatives, these groups may not be wholly distinctive for comparison (30 per cent practised more than one activity).

Nevertheless, their data reinforces the general trend of life becoming more subjective, and it remains to be seen whether the Australian experience will be replicated elsewhere and whether either the congregational domain or the holistic milieu will alter significantly to bring about a spiritual revolution. It is another question to ask what meaning we might give these cultural trends. What is clear is that 'spiritual traditions are enormously important within the culture, but have been generally eliminated from the psychologist's vocabulary' (Gergen, 2001: 34).

West and Tacey, along with other counselling practitioners who engage in spirituality (Thorne, 2002), are open to what might be termed a mystical experience, and as such quantifying spirituality in Britain is more encompassing than counting heads that turn up to church every Sunday morning. The next chapter will discuss the variant understandings of individuality and the notion of Self, as enshrined in different worldviews in today's postmodern western world.

Defining Spirituality with Reference to Religion

Within the history of religion, the Spirit, in its various terms, is almost universally understood as a supernatural agency operating in the universe or in peoples' lives, where it is often termed 'transpersonal'. As will become apparent later, when speaking of spiritually-centred counselling and transpersonal therapy the substance of what is understood is so similar that the two may be regarded as the same. The Spirit stands as a powerful metaphor in communicating human-divine relations. Spirituality, whether understood as an element within the person needing to be identified and cultivated, or as something externally 'given' from a metaphysical source (Cupitt, 1980), makes little sense without its predicate, the Spirit – from the Latin, *spiritus*, meaning 'breath' (i.e. 'breath of God': Genesis 2: 7).

Classically, within many traditions, the Spirit is the medium by which a transcendent Being has communion with a human being. In eastern thought, and non-rational Christianity, spirituality is inextricably tied to the idea of transcendence, the idea that there is 'something out there' that is bigger than we mortals 'down here', and upon which we are contingent (Elkins et al., 1988). The medium of contact is understood to be through the Spirit. The Spirit is the inexplicable bridge between the human and the divine, then, but must remain as a metaphor, since delving into its essence is conjecture that takes us into metaphysics, which finds no place in postmodern thinking.

Wilber (2001a) traces two paths of spirituality – the Ascending path towards a higher transcendence and the Descending path towards this world – in the evolutionary record: 'Evolution is best thought of as *Spirit-in-action*, God-in-the-making, where Spirit unfolds itself at every stage of development' (Wilber, 2000: 9). But I think it is possible to categorise three overall transpersonal elements in religion and spirituality:

- The traditional picture of an omnipotent 'God out there';
- An immanent divine element within; and
- The relational character between a person and a higher being or a person with a person.

Figure 2.1   Images of a transcendent and immanent God by William Blake – 'The Ancient of Days' and 'The Union of the Soul with God' – sketched by Nathan Marsh

Transcendent and immanent emphases of the divine occur frequently in the history of religion and often appear in classical works of art (see Figure 2.1).

The mystical-human poetry of Taoism places this wisdom teaching as an esoteric form of this-worldly immanence, whilst the Indian traditions of reincarnation would link Hinduism with the monotheistic faiths of Judaism, Christianity and Islam as being other-worldly transcendent.

In *Beyond Religion*, Elkins (1998) promotes mystical spirituality 'outside the walls of traditional religion'. His father once said that 'Sitting in a church house will no more make you a Christian than sitting in a chicken house will make you a chicken' (1998: 25). The work of Elkins (1998) presupposes that many find formal religion inadequate in spite of reports to the contrary (Richards and Bergin, 1997). Elkins prescribes a humanistic, non-religious spirituality, which has appeal for secularists in the postmodern world. Spirituality can be traced through:

- the feminine side of the personality
- the arts
- the body
- psychology
- mythology
- nature
- relationships, and
- the dark nights of the soul

The distinction between spirituality and religion – whatever definition we give these terms – was not clear until recent times, to such an extent that early spirituality was indistinguishable from religious experience. Theorists have defined spirituality in very different terms:

> Bucke (1923) refers to spirituality as 'cosmic consciousness'; Maslow (1970) called it 'being cognition'; Ouspensky (1934) called it 'the perception of the miraculous'; Fromm (1986) refers to spirituality as 'to be' rather than 'to have'; Assagioli (1975) claims that all activity which drives the human being forward towards some form of development – physical, emotional, mental, intuitional, social – if it is in advance of his or her present state, is essentially spiritual in nature. (Kirkland, 1996: 261)

Measuring 'spirituality' is almost a contradiction in terms for some (Mott-Thornton, 1996; Thorne, 1998), whilst others think it possible (Elkins et al., 1988; Tart, 1975). Spirituality has been described and defined in humanistic-phenomenological terms (Elkins et al., 1988). A team of researchers led by David Elkins (Elkins et al., 1988: 10) arrived at the following definition of spirituality, which for West (2000) is difficult to improve upon:

> Spirituality, which comes from the Latin *spiritus*, meaning 'breath of life', is a way of being and experiencing that comes through awareness of a transcendent dimension and that is characterised by certain identifiable values in regard to self, others, nature, life, and whatever one considers to be the Ultimate.

Their Spiritual Orientation Inventory consists of nine categories and is broadly referenced by therapists working in religious and spiritual areas (West, 2004):

1 A transcendental dimension
2 Meaning and purpose in life
3 Mission in life
4 Sacredness of life
5 Challenging material values
6 Altruism
7 Idealism
8 Awareness of the tragic
9 Fruits of spirituality

The Numinous

I have used the term numinous to portray the ineffable, indescribable element of religious and spiritual experience, and since transpersonal and humanistic psychologists, following Carl Jung, use this term I shall need to amplify its use and meaning. Ruddolf Otto (1958) brought a new synthesis to the opposing extremes of objective reasoning and subjective experiencing. He coins a term to describe the ineffable part of spiritual experience, the 'numinous' – from the Latin *numen* meaning deity. He encourages reflective people to consider *moments* of deeply felt spiritual experience, such as being rapt in worship, and to use this word to describe the 'pure' feeling-state:

> The feeling of it may at times come sweeping like a gentle tide, pervading the mind with a tranquil mood of deepest worship. It may pass over into a more set and lasting attitude of the soul, continuing, as it were, thrillingly vibrant and resonant, until at last it dies away and the soul resumes its 'profane', non-religious mood of everyday experience. (Otto, 1958: 12)

There is also the identification of personal Self with transcendent Reality through *moments* of religious experience, to quote William James:

> The perfect stillness of the night was thrilled by a more solemn silence. The darkness held a presence that was all the more felt because it was not seen. I could not anymore have doubted that He was there than I was. Indeed, I felt myself to be, if possible, the less real of the two. (James, 1961: 66)

The numinous leaves the recipient with a sense of awe and wonder, or alternatively in dread of a *presence* that is indefinable but powerfully felt, like that of Jacob at Bethel when in fear of his life. After dreaming about a ladder bridging heaven and earth he was forced to exclaim: 'How awesome is this place' (Genesis 28: 27). Numinous experience is related in letters by Paul to Christians in Corinth where he speaks of being 'caught up to the third heaven' and God revealing 'through the Spirit' what 'no eye has seen . . .' (2 Cor. 12: 2–3; 1 Cor. 2: 9–10). Theologians have attempted to quantify the numinous experience of encountering the divine through visions and callings (Rahner, 1963 – summarised in Lines, 1995b). Mystics present it in poetic verse (St John of the Cross) and some transpersonal scientists have even tried to measure it or compare it to paranormal phenomena (Tart, 1975). Lewis (1940) thinks that it is illogical to conceive that the numinous could have emanated from human imagination without a divine substance having produced it.

Spirit Within

Don Cupitt (1980) asks whether religious experience is an 'extra sense' that some people have which others lack. Does the mystic gain knowledge in a way which is inaccessible for most others? Has he or she some special sense or faculty that is generally dormant in most of us? Cupitt is sceptical about establishing authentic criteria for separating the subjective from the objective in mystical experience. Mystics, he says, do not produce consistent descriptions of the supernatural; such descriptions reveal metaphysical beliefs, such as 'reality being one', 'time being unreal', and so on, which is incompatible with modern experience.

With 'introvert mysticism' we *abstract away* from the senses and discursive thinking, and our thought becomes very still, absorbed and undifferentiated, but with the opposite kind of mysticism, known as 'extravert' or 'nature mysticism', we gain a heightened awareness of the external world *through* our ordinary senses. In both cases 'a good deal of intellectual interpretation is interwoven with the experience', concludes Cupitt (1980: 31). Curiously, the English philosopher, Bertrand Russell, felt that mystics had attained a universal experiential knowledge, by placing greater store on *knowledge through intuition*, by seeing a *plurality of meaning* behind the universe, by viewing *time as being unreal*, and by maintaining *no ambiguity between good and evil* (Russell, 1986 [1917]).

In pressing for the need for inward spirituality, Elkins (1998) endorses the view that spirituality is universal. The common core of spirituality is found in the inner phenomenological Self and has to do with our capacity to respond to the numinous (following Otto). Principally, he viewed spirituality as a mysterious energy associated with the soul. As a Jungian, Elkins viewed archetypes as being connected to the soul, as inherited patterns in the human psyche that predispose us to react to life events in a somewhat similar manner, like 'river-beds in the desert that predict the river flow when the rains come'. Human reality suggests that we have lost our soul, he said: 'Our problem is not that the sacred has ceased to exist, but rather that we have lost our connection to it' (1998: 63). His personal programme of spirituality makes no appeal to the 'otherness' of conventional religious encounter, yet other theorists wish to retain the sacred in their own work (Thorne, 1998; West, 2004).

Personal Definitions of Religion and Spirituality

To understand spirituality we shall have to surrender our positivistic need for absolute certainty in order to capture that aspect of human experience that transcends final categorisation and which through the limitations of language we try to express the inexpressible (Swinton, 2001). In the interests of preserving a comprehensive understanding, whilst not thereby losing what is distinctive to the term *spirituality*, Crawford and Rossiter (1996) suggest that all definitions should avoid the following:

- defining spirituality exclusively in formal religious terms
- defining spirituality with the exclusion of any reference to religion
- defining spirituality so broadly that all aspects of life are regarded as spiritual

Elkins' construction above, though reasoned and imaginative, seems to fall foul of the second and third suggested categories to be avoided, as listed by Crawford and Rossiter (1996).

I use the term *religious* to denote adherence to group or individual ritualistic acts through perceived instructions from a divine source, whereas *spiritual* is that part of our inner being that relates to a divine source but which is independent of performing particular actions. Although I recognise linguistic limitations in such language, I am drawn to view the *spiritual Self* as an intuitive, inner-sense of being, which relates to the numinous, and which results in feelings of contentment, or of awe and wonder for the sacred in life – however that is imagined.

In what follows, an attempt is made to meet these three perspectives of spirituality with the proposition that in spiritually-centred counselling the numinous may be experienced through focused human interaction. Any discussion of religious experience, talk of the soul, the transpersonal dimension, and spirituality – in its many facets and broad manifestations – cannot avoid looking at the role of mythology in individual and collective discourse, in accounting for extraordinary phenomena and for giving meaning to ritual. The purpose and role of mythology will be taken up in Chapter 8.

Conclusion

In this chapter the decline of nominal Christian influence in the West has been considered in light of falling rates of attendance and adherence. The Christian Church has many diverse expressions and it is predicted by sociologists that those which have become more humanised, rather than remaining religious and distant, will probably continue into the foreseeable future. Whilst New Age spirituality his become popular amongst the well-to-do secular folk of modern times, we have seen that this trend could hardly be described as a 'spiritual revolution'.

I have attempted to define religion and spirituality to serve as a working hypothesis for what follows in subsequent chapters. Theorists have viewed spirituality within three basic perspectives of transcendence, immanence or as something which relates to the numinous – as an ontological Being, or as within people. Spiritually-inclined counsellors view spirituality as being either anchored in *otherworldly* transcendence or *this-worldly* immanence, where the latter is expressed as an experience in natural phenomenon.

As a shorthand description of the indefinable element of religious, spiritual and secular experience, I shall use the term numinous to include all. Throughout this book, I will avoid questions of truth and falsity, because, as clients' narratives make plain, personal experience is valid and must be viewed as an authentic discourse not only for the individual concerned, but also for the community from which it is a projection.

3

Psychotherapy and Spirituality

Religious experience is absolute; it cannot be disputed. You can only say that you have never had such an experience, whereupon your opponent will reply: 'Sorry, I have.' And there your discussion will come to an end.

C. J. Jung

Having examined the intellectual and religious world that fashioned postmodernism, this chapter will outline the particular social context within which psychotherapy emerged. Within a radical period of social change, psychotherapy responded to a need for healing that was formerly the remit of the local priest. Throughout this book, I will be juggling two balls of empiricism and mysticism, and will endeavour to show how leading figures in psychotherapy have tended to catch one of these balls and let the other drop to the floor. From the empirical outlook of Chapter 1, the emphasis switches to the opposite pole, that of mystical experience, as understood within the theoretical framework of transpersonal therapy. In the interests of promoting therapeutic pluralism, a sense of balance is imperative. If the therapist has too obvious a bias, and one not matching the client's experience, there will be a failure to address the person holistically.

After outlining the beginnings of psychotherapy and pointing out the role of religion in that process, the discussion moves on to consider the different realities as coined by Sigmund Freud, Carl Jung and Carl Rogers. I reason that these three prominent founders caricature the different discourses of people in the postmodern world.

Traditional therapies subscribe to an underlying theoretical position that implies a particular image of the person, and these vary and have significant therapeutic implications. By comparing and contrasting transpersonal psychology with those of popular approaches, key features will emerge to serve as foundations of spiritually-centred counselling. Our interest is to explore the larger question of whether such models have the capacity to take on specific religious and not-so-specific spiritual themes in their work, or whether there are barriers that arise from theoretical tensions and customary ways of working. The chapter closes with a case vignette to illustrate how a person's theoretical leanings will affect practice when engaging in spiritually-centred counselling.

The Emergence of Psychotherapy

The emergence and early development of psychotherapy has been well documented (McLeod, 2003), particularly with reference to the changing role of religion in society (West, 2000). In what follows, I summarise McLeod's account and illustrate how the supportive function of the Church in society has given way to professional services for mental health over the last 200 hundred years (Halmos, 1965). The displacement of a religious frame of understanding for a scientific one led to the emergence of psychotherapy, and there are implications for clients in therapy today who find practitioners reluctant to engage in religious and spiritual matters (Swinton, 2001; West, 2000), as a result of a preoccupation with outcome research (Mearns and Cooper, 2005; Thorne, 2002).

The transition from rural to largely industrialised communities had a marked effect upon traditional social patterns during the Industrial Revolution. Town populations expanded to service the needs of capitalism at the expense of village communities. The intellectual atmosphere of the Enlightenment throughout Europe created a form of reasoning amongst the intelligentsia that would filter down within the social fabric of the populace. It is improbable that the general public would ever have even heard of Nietzsche let alone have read him, and though the intellectual wing of the Church would have assessed the philosophical climate with due care and reserve, in a time where social control was considered God-given and legitimate, educated clerics teaching the masses was not considered necessary or pragmatic. Every person knew their place! It is social change that affects people most, not always intellectual reasoning.

As in earlier 'magical' cultures, where indigenous diviners and witch-doctors cured the emotional, psychological and behavioural difficulties of one estranged member of the tribe, so in the agrarian communities throughout Europe up to the eighteenth century such people were treated by the parish priest. The means of healing were through the Catholic confessional, but, as McNeil (1951) points out, healing was a communal affair targeted to the *cure of souls* by means of public admonishment, prayer and excommunication. The seriously disturbed and insane were regarded as 'lunatics' but were tolerated by the community. At this point, there was no provision for mental health, no psychiatry and no science of cause or cure for mental illness – there was merely Christian ritual.

Catholic confession was not an individual private affair, as it is today, but a much more public exposure. In addition, the clergy in the sixteenth and seventeenth centuries regularly acted in a counselling role with their parishioners (McNeil, 1951). All this changed when capitalistic values of the Industrial Revolution became prominent. The movement of the masses into the factories had a profound effect upon economic and political life. The social structure was rapidly changing as the ethics of science replaced those of religion.

Capitalism required a high level of rationality and repression of pleasure-seeking. The work ethic required control of personal impulse, autonomy, independence and the repression of sexuality. The fundamental shift was from a tradition-centred society – where communities were close-knit and where everyone knew everyone else, and where behaviour was controlled and monitored by the community – towards a form of society where satisfaction from working hard was the ideal and where individuals were expected to show initiative and inner direction. In the migration from land to factory, life was becoming increasingly mechanised and profit-centred and the economic predicament of those who were socially disadvantaged or handicapped was of having no social welfare to support them. Formerly, the less advantaged were accommodated and had a small part to play in the village economy, but now the discipline of the machine, long hours and fragmentation within the social group, meant that there was no one left to care for the old, the infirm or the insane.

The workhouse system grew as a state provision to accommodate the non-productive members of society. Conditions at workhouses were strictly run on discipline and were labour intensive. Some lunatics were extremely difficult to manage, until the Asylum Act of 1845 compelled local justices to set up separate apartments – known as asylums – to remove the most demanding from those on courses of rehabilitation. Although some asylums were run on religious lines, such as Tuke in York run by Quakers, most were not (West, 2000). The state asylums were the forerunners of mental hospitals, but in those days conditions were appalling and inmates were treated like animals, even to the extent where they could become a spectacle of entertainment for a penny a day. William Hogarth depicts such patients in Bedlam, the asylum of London: one believes he is an astronomer, another the Pope and another the King, whilst the upper classes stare and whisper in mockery and derision (see Figure 3.1).

The beginnings of psychiatry can be traced to the time when the medical profession took interest in the asylums because there were profits to be made from 'the trade in lunacy', not only by running the institutions, but also in receiving fees from the mentally disturbed patients of the upper classes. Subsequent Acts of Parliament in Britain granted the medical profession control over the asylums. During this period of social containment of the insane, medical science was applying itself to understanding and treating madness more systematically, and earlier religious views, such as demonology and witchcraft were largely dismissed. Explanations for insanity were crude and generally centred around phrenology, sexual indulgence and masturbation. The early treatment was by chemical regimes, and much later on by electroconvulsive therapy. Male oppression occurred with the majority of inmates being women. Psychiatry was developing as a specialist profession in its own right, alongside other areas of medicine and a more precise classification of psychiatric disorders was being undertaken.

Figure 3.1   Hogarth's 'A Rake's Progress — scene from Bedlam'
(1735–63) © The Whitworth Art Gallery, The University of Manchester

Not everyone felt happy about locking up lunatics within institutions alongside other lesser disturbed people, however. There was controversy and considerable debate over the wisdom of whether such people were not better served by care in the community. This has a familiar ring for us today. The treatment of the insane in silos echoes biblical times where lepers were left in colonies beyond the village, and it seemed that where rationality was prized society had little toleration for dealing with those classified as irrational lunatics, other than by confinement. By the nineteenth century psychiatry had established itself as the means of dealing with patients who were increasingly being referred to in less pejorative terms of mental illness. McLeod (1993: 11) records that the first psychotherapists as specialists in treating people were in Amsterdam in 1887.

As West (2000) points out, the evolution from Church and priest to science and psychotherapist has not been a one-way process, since various Christian groups in the twentieth century have initiated therapeutic support for a range of emotional and social difficulties (Relate, Westminster Pastoral Foundation, Alcoholics Anonymous, Samaritans and Cruse). Counselling has become a popular ministry in the Church in recent times.

In summary, the history of psychotherapy is the transition from religious means of understanding and curing mental disorders to medical treatment of the very same conditions. The changed social and economical conditions arising from the Industrial Revolution removed the traditional supportive mechanisms of close communities for those who couldn't cope, and the more severe the maladjustment the more it was felt necessary to take them away. The parish priest was replaced by the professionally trained practitioner, first the psychiatrist and finally the psychotherapist. Medical diagnoses of science took over accounts delivered for centuries by religion. With the prizing of rationality, and the capitalistic requirement for autonomy and independence amongst the populace, the treatment programmes for those having less serious mental illnesses were through the *talking cure* of mind with mind in the location of a consulting room between doctor and patient. The psychotherapist had replaced the priest, and ritualistic means of curing the soul became sublimated by therapeutic techniques of healing. By the turn of the century, the provision of mental health was organised by the state, diagnosis had become more refined, theories of 'the unconscious mind' were becoming common in European thought and Freud (1899) had published his seminal work, *The Interpretation of Dreams.*

Religious Influence on Founding Psychotherapists

It is not without significance that many founders of schools of psychotherapy have had formative religious experiences. Freud was a non-practising Jew, but his therapeutic persona, according to West (2004), resembled that of a Jewish Rabbi, as expert and interpreter, and his interest in death and sexuality may stem from Genesis mythology. Jung came from a family of ministers of the Reformed Church, and in his local village was known as 'parson's Carl', a nickname he disliked. Abraham Maslow, a founder of humanistic psychology, was born of an orthodox Jewish family, as were Melanie Klein (Object Relations), Eric Berne (Transactional Analysis) and Martin Buber. Carl Rogers, the founder of client-centred or person-centred therapy, grew up in a strictly religious Protestant family which disapproved of gambling and the theatre and who, in his own words, was raised in an 'uncompromising religious and ethical atmosphere.' In spite of planning to be a minister, he altered course and elected to become a psychologist after broadening his religious perspectives: first by visiting the World Student Christian Federation Conference in China, and secondly by studying liberal theology at the Union Theological Seminary. Donald Winnicott (Child Analyst) was a Methodist, Rollo May (Existential), was a former minister, as was David Elkins (Humanistic).

When first examining the lives of pioneering psychotherapists, I was surprised to find how many were from Jewish and Christian backgrounds, but on reflection I suppose it is not coincidental. Some may view their innovative academic pursuits to be the natural outworking of religious conviction, particularly if their religious imperative was social engagement. Three components of spirituality, according to Elkins et al. (1988), are 'meaning and purpose in life', 'mission in life' and 'altruism', and the relationship between religious conviction and social responsibility is emphasised in Judaism, Christianity and Islam, particularly if the faith is mature and intrinsic (Allport and Ross, 1967). I shall pick up this theme later. As mentioned above, some therapeutic services have been formed on Christian principles, and the Church in latter times has jumped on the 'therapy-speak' bandwagon when struggling to find a role in the secular age.

West (2004: 24–41) thinks that some founding psychotherapists display features of being shamans who characteristically 'become healers after passing through a deep-seated initiatory or creative illness' (2004: 27). Rogers became ill after leaving China, and enters a 'dark period' of 'great personal distress' for two years after counselling a troubled woman. Jung became ill and mentally disintegrated after his break with Freud. The creative genius, as evident in *The Interpretation of Dreams*, and in psychoanalysis, is the culmination of a considerable period of neurosis for Freud when working with Fleiss.

Not disputing West's thesis, it is equally plausible to suggest that not following parental religious expectations results in sublimating guilt for ambition. Freud's strong anti-religious attitudes have led some scholars to assume that his views were the product of reaction formation, and McLeod (1993) infers the same in his brief account of Carl Rogers' redirection. Whatever the case, Freud, Jung and Rogers warrant a fuller discussion, because, as I shall argue, the views of each represent a discourse of modern times.

Sigmund Freud: The Empirical Discourse

What characterises Freud and Jung as prominent commentators on religion and spirituality is that their opinions represent two contradictory discourses, or human constructs, or worldviews, which remain with us today. These conflicting perspectives exist in different people's attitudes to spirituality and may also exist as unresolved ambivalence in the mind of the same person.

It is well documented that Freud was scathingly critical of religion and, whilst it is wondered what form of Judaism and Christianity in Vienna he found so objectionable, it seems futile to deny that his scepticism has been highly influential in shaping attitudes of atheism today. To reason that his position was an overreaction to wishing to be considered as a scientist does not carry weight, since Jung equally saw himself as a scientist yet felt his spiritual scheme was compatible with empirical testing.

Freud's position on religion and spirituality is compatible with theories of the sociology of religion. 'It has occurred to me,' he once said, 'that the ultimate basis for man's need for religion is infantile helplessness' (Letter to Jung in 1910: Palmer, 1997). This kind of statement is insidious because it uncovers an underlying tendency of human beings to be deluded in order to overcome personal insecurity. He dealt a vicious blow to religion, then, not by castigating faith with empirical reasoning, but (echoing Nietzsche) by identifying human vulnerability and a requirement of psychological props to carry us through life. In a sense, he felt that our *psychological need* for religion suggested that many of us have never really grown up. He saw God as an idealisation of our fathers, and wrote:

> Psychoanalysis has made us familiar with the intimate connection between the father-complex and belief in God; it has shown us that a personal God is, psychologically speaking, nothing other than an exalted father, and it brings us evidence every day of how young people lose their religious beliefs as soon as their father's authority breaks down (Freud, 1899/1990: 216).

In analysing patients suffering from 'obsessional neurosis' in Vienna, Freud noticed that many of the ritualised behaviours, such as 'obsessive washing' for no practical purposes, or 'regular repetitive actions' prompted by superstition, were strikingly similar to the practices of many religious people in worship. This repeated observation led him to conclude that religion was a pathological counterpart to 'obsessional neuroses'. For Freud the purpose of life is simply the programme of the pleasure principle (Freud, 1920). Religion at its best was considered to be a 'crooked cure' (West, 2004), 'an expression of the instincts it has suppressed' (Palmer, 1997: 13).

In the closing pages of *The Future of an Illusion* (1927), Freud, in the same condescending manner as Durkheim, concedes that religion has served a purpose for human civilisation in taming asocial instincts and in keeping people happy, and that he for one would not dream of replacing it (1927: 216–27). It would be simple to write Freud off as being wholly negative about religion and pessimistic that it could offer people anything at all in the modern world, but he recognised a spiritual force in life that I shall have course to examine more fully later on, and he refers to this primordial life force as *libido*.

Carl Jung: The Mystical Discourse

It was over the topic of religion and sexuality that the two giants, Freud and Jung, fell out and ultimately parted – Jung founded analytical psychology (the rift has been well documented, and will not take up space here – see Palmer, 1997). While Freud might be direct and outspoken, a ruthless critic who pulls no punches, Jung's affirmative stance on religion is not an easy read. He introduces the reader to obscure concepts which he claims have empirical support. Jung's exhaustive studies of ancient religion led him in the opposite direction to that of Freud. Unlike his former tutor, his research validated religion and led him to conclude that *it is not the presence of religion that is a symptom of neurosis, but its absence*. He speculated that we all have a common human experience, and that it cannot be mere coincidence that many ancient and modern religions have similar motifs, belief-systems and orientations. He suggested that these common themes all emerge from what he termed the 'collective unconscious'; they occur to people spontaneously not because they invent them uniquely but because they are archetypal, and so are received psychically through experiential phenomena, such as when dreaming:

> The typical Jungian archetype is a basic, inherited image or form in the psyche. These basic or primordial images represent very common, very typical experiences that humans everywhere are exposed to: the experience of birth, of the mother, the father, the shadow, the wise old man, the trickster, the ego, the animus and anima (masculine and feminine), and so on... Millions upon millions of past encounters with those *typical situations* have, so to speak, ingrained these basic images into the collective psyche of the human race. You find these basic and primordial images worldwide, and you find an especially rich fund of them in the world's great myths. (Wilber, 2001a: 193)

Jung's theoretical scheme is not without criticism (West, 2000), and some theorists do not equate the collective unconscious – which is common across cultures and through time – with spirituality *per se*, since few individuals achieve higher transpersonal states of consciousness (Wilber, 2001a). Wilber thinks that the collective unconscious is natural not transpersonal (2001b: 179–82).

Freud and Jung were fascinated with dream content and the dreaming process, but they interpreted the dreaming phenomena quite differently. Freud saw dreams as the royal road to unconsciousness, whereas Jung reasoned that dream images were symbolic representations of the collective unconscious. Jungian analytical psychology consists primarily of interpreting the dream material of (largely post middle-aged) clients within the rich repository of religious mythology of the past, in order to trace their archetypal, and therefore, eternal truths and relevance.

Again, opposing Freud's father replacement theory, Jung reasoned that God's reality is that of the archetypal father of the collective unconscious. If asked how he could be so sure of his theory, he frequently responded with the evidence of experience. In fact so sure was he about the certainty of the reality of God that when Jung was asked in a BBC interview in 1959 whether he believed in God, he replied: 'Difficult to answer. I know. I don't need to believe. I know.' What he was saying was that when he knew something then he did not need to believe it, or if he believed in a thing it was because he was not sure that he knew it. I am well satisfied with the fact that I know experiences which I cannot avoid calling numinous or divine. When pressed on the question on what precisely he meant, Jung confirmed the existence of God for each individual by saying that God is a *psychic phenomenon* (echoing Hegel) that is immediate, direct and a self-evident fact of psychic experience encountered by us within the depths of our own beings; that he is a *psychic reality* attested to and known by each individual's response to the archetypal images of God:

> We remember that God as archetypal-form is not individually acquired but is, *a priori,* an inborn mode of apprehension which belongs to the collective unconscious as 'unknowable' and 'eternal' but which is yet manifested in the symbols of religion. (Palmer, 1997: 127)

Jung's style of expression remains ambiguous and unclear, since his use of language is 'more like a lyrical flight than a description of empirical fact' (Hostie, 1957 – cited by Palmer, 1997). Jung acknowledges this when asked to describe specifically the nature of the *libido* psychic energy, and replies that it cannot be conceived concretely anymore than energy can in the world of physics (Jung, 1913). What we can conclude from Jung's structure of the psyche, the collective unconscious and the archetypes is that his understanding of transcendence was of the 'God within', and as such we may regard his psychology as mystical:

> Thus, through the symbolic images of religion, the individual receives and expresses a revelation of the immanent-transcendent, of the suprapersonal centre of his own existence, the numen, 'God within us'. (Palmer, 1997: 141)

Carl Rogers: The Relational Discourse

West (2004) discerns that the therapeutic stance of Carl Rogers following his six-month stay in China resembled that of a Taoist or a Zen Buddhist, that in soaking up Chinese influence he was unconsciously forming the style of an Eastern philosopher and relating like a Buddhist monk. Secondly, along with other theorists (Mearns and Cooper, 2005; Thorne, 2002), West has drawn attention to later developments in Rogers' thinking towards the end of his life. Rogers speaks of his *presence* being 'full of healing' when his 'inner spirit has reached and touched the inner spirit of the other'. It is a therapeutic experience when he is closer to his 'inner, intuitive self,' when he is in touch with something 'unknown' in himself, 'in a slightly altered state of consciousness in the relationship' (Kirschenbaum and Henderson, 1990). Thorne (2002) goes further from the lead of such sentiments to suggest that therapists need to adopt a spiritual discipline to work with transcendence and spiritual energy.

In what I develop in this book, Rogers stands mid-point within a broad spectrum of spirituality where Freud stands at one extreme and Jung at the other. Rogers combines the sociological view of religion with the mystical one, and fundamentally puts great trust in his own personal experience, which Wilber (2001b: 97) understands as a 'phenomenological imperative'. In departing from his Protestant roots, Rogers remained true to its underlying principle. Protestantism rejected papal authority for the direct relationship with God, unconditionally, without mediation, and person-centred theory demythologises the religious forms to become a secular equivalent where the direct experience of relating person to person becomes the source of healing:

> In my earlier professional years, I was asking the question: 'How can I treat, or cure, or change this person?' Now I would phrase the question in this way: 'How can I provide a relationship which this person may use for his own personal growth?' (Rogers, 1967: 32–33)

> Neither the Bible nor the prophets – neither Freud nor research – neither the revelations of God nor man – can take precedence over my own direct experience. (Rogers, 1967: 24)

In summary, Freud stands at the opposite end of the religious spectrum to Jung. Freud is positioned alongside sociologists of religion, such as Durkheim, philosophers, such as Hume, Nietzsche and Russell, whereas Jung is aligned with mystics, such as St John of the Cross, Eckhart and Otto, philosophers such as Hegel and Schleiermacher, and palaeontologists like Teilhard de Chardin. Rogers might be aligned with a Jewish mystic by the name of Martin Buber who spoke more poignantly about quality relating than any other I have read, and his insights will take up later discussion. Psychotherapy has evolved its equivalent expressions of transpersonal, immanent and relational religion, which is graphically illustrated (albeit simplified) in the following diagram (Figure 3.2).

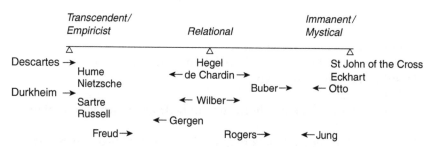

Empirical–Mystical Continuum

Figure 3.2 *The realm of religious social discourse of postmodern consciousness*

Two Clients in Therapy

Imaginary Friend

Children enjoy fairytales of princes, princesses, witches and dragons so much that it is wondered whether they have a greater predisposition for experiencing mystery and awe during childhood than at any other period of development. But cognitive development during adolescence (Lines, 2006) requires an adjustment of reality testing. A considerable number of prepubescent and early adolescent clients coming forward for therapy reveal in their discourses, almost incidentally, their emotional dependence on 'an imaginary friend'. Below I present brief extracts of narrative where 'friends' have names and an undoubted reality. It is common, in my experience, that it is largely boys that have such mystical mentors (Bray, 2004), and in virtually every case young clients share information with me they have never disclosed to any other person, not even to their closest parent or sibling. I select the example of Nathan (aged 13), and invite you to consider which of the above theorists this extract supports.

Nathan came for counselling over worries about his mother's severe drinking problem. In many ways he was a survivor, but when he spoke of his early childhood there was evidence of a restlessness and experiences of a paranormal nature. He told me about moving into a new house where he had nightmares in his bedroom, which his mother then had when they swapped rooms. When I asked him about what support he had had through all this he began to tell me about his imaginary friend.

> *Nathan:*   One dream was weird. This doll changed into a zombie and kept coming and I was running down this road for about an hour but he kept on coming. It never caught me; I just woke up.
>
> *Dennis:*   I used to have a regular nightmare about falling down a well; of spinning around and around and falling down lower and lower, but then never hitting the bottom [*I wanted to normalise his experience*]. Did you ever talk to anyone about what happens in your nightmares?
>
> *Nathan:*   I used to talk to my friend, Johnny [*Nathan grins*].
>
> *Dennis:*   How old were you then?
>
> *Nathan:*   About five. He would talk to me, fight with me.
>
> *Dennis:*   He would fight you?
>
> *Nathan:*   Yea.
>
> *Dennis:*   Did you talk to Johnny in your bedroom when you went to bed?
>
> *Nathan:*   I'd never really talk to him when I went to bed, it was during the day. I would talk to him about what was going on in my house.
>
> *Dennis:*   When else did you talk to Johnny?
>
> *Nathan:*   When I was bored. I wouldn't talk to him with words. I'd be just thinking.
>
> *Dennis:*   It seems a bit like praying. Did you ask him to get you out of trouble?
>
> *Nathan:*   Yea [*Nathan nods*]. We'd only talk for a bit.
>
> *Dennis:*   Do you talk to him now, Nathan?
>
> *Nathan:*   No [*Nathan looks at me adopting a masculine posture*], no, not at all now. No, I don't think so.

Dennis: I wonder why?

Nathan: 'cause I used to think he was real when I was younger, but now I know he's not, obviously!

Dennis: But what's changed?

Nathan: Got wiser.

Dennis: If someone were talking to your mum, would she know about Johnny?

Nathan: No way!

Clearly, different theorists would not interpret this material in common. A Jungian analyst would trawl through archetypal material to interpret Nathan's (and my) dream material. Nathan speaks of a trusting relationship of direct experience, even though of an imaginative nature. The discourse *may* support Freud's theory of a neurotic need for a protective, benevolent figure to carry a troubled psyche through the vicissitudes of life, but I have problems with this, in that the theory was shaped with the traditional, nuclear family composition in mind. Nathan, like so many I counsel, had no experiences at all of living with a father, or stepfather. There were no obvious persons within memory to represent a psychological lawgiver, or an installer of conscience, against whom to rebel.

Further, Nathan's manner of dialogue with Johnny resembled praying, or *spiritual emergence* (Grof and Grof, 1989), and yet there was no evidence of him receiving any formal religious instruction, or being introduced to prayer as an emotional or psychological means of support. (There have been two young clients from a non-religious family I have counselled who have prayed regularly but have had not the slightest idea why they do or who may have introduced them to this means of seeking help, almost suggesting that praying may be innate.) I leave the interpretation of this not uncommon parapsychological phenomenon for you to interpret in your own way.

Mysterious Happening

Ibn is a devout Muslim of middle age whose current faith was shaped by childhood experiences. Consider for a moment this narrative, and again ask yourself which of the above theories Ibn's experience confirms.

Ibn: I'll tell you a short story about how my faith developed. I was about ten or eleven and my mother took me to a shop in a village [in Kashmir]. The shop was just outside the village, just one building, and there were some sweets there and I said to my mother, 'I want those sweets.' And the price of the sweets was two paisa, which is like two pennies, and mother did not have the money. She said, 'Son, I can't buy the sweets because I don't have the money.' But I was insistent; I wanted those sweets: 'Whatever you can do, get me those sweets.' And she said, 'Can't do it.' So she walked out of the shop; I walked out with her, and between the shop and the village there were two or three farms and we had to walk between the farms. Among these farms there was a pathway. About thirty or forty yards outside I noticed on the floor a coin, exactly two paisa, a two pence coin. It was fairly new, you could see it shining. It hadn't been there very long and I picked it up and because I was following my mother, I said to her, 'Mother, here's the money, now get me the sweets!' So she went back and got me the sweets and to this day I simply can't understand where that came from. How did that *exact* money come, the money to buy the sweets?

Dennis: What sense do you make of that – that God provided it?

Ibn: I think God provided it, and that is only one story.

Do such phenomena illustrate wishful thinking, autosuggestion, selective memory of a fickle nature, or does it provide evidence of the numinous, divine providence, faith in action, or God working through natural events? Whatever your views are will clearly affect your practice and will indicate where you sit on the empirical–mystical continuum.

Psychotherapy and Spirituality

Image of the Person

When writing a counselling text for secondary school pupils, I attempted to examine the manner in which each of the major schools of psychotherapy subscribed to an implicit image of the person (Dryden, 1984; McLeod, 2003) within their theoretical underpinnings (Lines, 2000). Below I represent these perspectives with some additions:

- The image of the person for psychodynamic counselling is of a being functioning on different levels of consciousness, and under the impulses of largely unknown forces, some of which reveal themselves in inexplicable symptoms – defences have been unconsciously erected from early life to protect and safeguard the Self from hurt.
- The image of the person in Jungian analysis is of a being moving through the process of individuation, as on a spiritual journey of Self-hood and as living under psychic influences of the collective unconscious.
- The image of the person in person-centred counselling is of an individual as the expert of her own life and experience, as Self in a state of becoming, and as directed by an organismic valuing process which is in tension with the Self-concept formed to survive in a social context.
- The image of the person in gestalt therapy is of a Self engaged in a relentless drive to meet personal needs as they arise in the environment. Self is viewed holistically in body and mind in a wholly interrelated series of activities of thinking, feeling, breathing and behaving.
- The image of the person for behaviour psychologists is of a Self who is principally directed and motivated by environmental factors, as being steered in behaviour by dominant rewarding or punishing stimulants.

- The image of the person for cognitive behavioural counsellors is of a Self principally directed, or potentially directed, by reasoning and cognitive faculties.
- The image of the person in family therapy is of a Self as a member of a unit rather than as an isolated being, as one link of an interrelated and intercommunicating system.
- The image of the person in existential therapy is as a finite individual Self attempting to live out a life productively within the givens of human existence.

These are very general and vague, and I suspect many theorists would word the image of the person underlying their theoretical position quite differently. It goes without saying that the psychodynamic therapist will work with their client's current social difficulties, physical symptoms or psychological problems through their unconscious-unresolved resistances and formulated defence-mechanisms, whether or not the practitioner judges her work to be spiritual. The Kleinian will work on the dynamics of object relations in respect to mother and child, and the Eriksonian will engage with parent or adolescent from the theoretical perspective of role confusion as occurs in individuation; again, it is a question of personal interpretation and classification as to whether any or all of their respective work has spiritual dimensions. The same can be said of other major approaches referred to above. Kenneth Gergen (1999, 2001) reminds us of the pitfalls of diagnosing 'problem' and 'cure' within purist schools of theorising based upon 'observations' and the preoccupation with the *individual mind* at the expense of the *social Self*. He reasons that:

> Social constructionist theories of human action are not built up or derived from observation, but rather grow from a community of engaged interlocutors. It is the conventions of intelligibility shared within one's professional enclave that will determine how we interpret the observational world. (Gergen, 2001: 98)

All therapy is conducted in the light of theoretical frameworks, but what might the spiritual framework look like? Let us broaden the question by examining established approaches of religious and spiritual models.

Religious Counselling

The first significant psychiatrist to introduce spirituality within his writing was Scott Peck (1978). Peck was not brought up in a religious household, and claimed after being drawn to eastern mystical writing that he was a mystic first and a Christian second after entering the church through the back door. Richards and Bergin (1997) prescribe a spiritual strategy for counselling which is theistic – 'God exists', humans are created by God, and are influenced by spiritual forces etc. The authors correlate religious devoutness with healthy functioning (1997: 78–112), but point to the lack of emphasis given to spiritual concerns in psychology. They argue that this results from the founders of psychotherapy carrying with them in their work certain presuppositions and assumptions of scientific method that have recently become discredited (1997: 24–48). In spiritually-centred counselling, their strategy endorses traditional transcendent interventions (prayer, blessing, meditation for guidance and enlightenment) and non-transcendent techniques (debate over religious values and behaviour or the scriptures, influences of religious background, practice of forgiveness, or keeping a journal) (Richards and Bergin, 1997: 239). Whilst this might be appropriate for clients in North America where the authors recognise that 95 per cent of the populace still maintain traditional belief in God, and 70 per cent retain membership at a church or synagogue (1997: 7–8), this would ostracise many within the UK where religion has far less influence upon daily living, and where a broader, more ecumenical and interdisciplinary understanding of spirituality is required.

In spite of the apparent restricted focus, Richards and Bergin recognise the need for pluralistic openness:

> The resurgence of humanistic-existential thought, the emergence of the cognitive revolution, and the postmodern movements in support of hermeneutics, narratives, qualitative research, and social constructivism have created a logical space for a spiritual strategy. (1997: 76)

Practitioners looking for more conventional interventions in practising spiritually-centred counselling will find all they require in this comprehensive text. The authors draw attention to the effectiveness of spiritual therapy for drug-related difficulties (Diamond, 2000; Richards and Bergin, 1997: 244–5), and to the importance of reflecting on therapist values (1997: 131–2), a topic I take up later.

Pastoral Counselling

David Lyall (1995) presents an overview of counselling in the pastoral and spiritual context and emphasises its roots and developments within Christian faith. Counselling becomes pastoral, he says, when it is offered by an ordained minister within a community of faith. The therapeutic scope is limited to a frame of reference where God is central and where Jesus and the Bible become the general topics of conversation. He draws a distinction between pastoral counselling and Christian counselling, however, reasoning that a Christian psychotherapist is going to be committed to the faith which conceptualises the counselling process in terms of Christian terms and values, such as the stress on sin, guilt and Christian responsibility. Secular psychology will be drawn upon, so long as the science of human behaviour does not contradict scriptural teaching.

Although pastoral counselling will have a broader remit than Christian counselling, in practice there is found to be considerable variation in the degree to which psychotherapeutic theory underlies therapy. Some work through the resources of scripture and prayer, whilst others value holistic therapies of meditation and centring on forces outside of Self. Some pastoral counselling centres function exclusively within a Christian ethos that is more implicit than explicit, whilst others operate in settings where spiritual ideas are important, but which are not explicitly evident in their work with clients (Lyall, 1995: 80).

Pastoral counsellors may be less rigid in planning contracts than other practitioners, and therapeutic boundaries may be more flexible (clients may be members of the same congregation). They take an active interest in spiritual direction, and are quite content to pray in session and to merge living the gospel with personal therapy. Leech's (1977) view is to locate spiritual direction within the sacramental and liturgical life of the Church whose role is to transform lives rather than aid the laity in adapting to social conditions, and others reason that those who enter spiritual direction will have psychological concerns that are part of their spirituality, and that it all may result in the difference between content and intent. Lyall (1995) speaks of the Christian metaphors the pastoral counsellor may employ in therapy, which include the evangelical message of *accepting that one is accepted* and a broader calling which entails turning towards the world as opposed to retreating to solitude. In summary, pastoral counselling, though beneficial within the household of faith, will fall out of step with the requirements of pluralistic spirituality. West's early work (2000) has been criticised for being too dismissive of religious and pastoral counselling.

A more pluralistic treatment of pastoral care is provided by Lynch (2002) where the values of the practitioner are given greater emphasis. Lynch sees therapy as aimed towards 'the good life', though Patterson in the preface claims that 'human flourishing' is more meaningful. Lynch (2002) reasons that the aim in pastoral care is to recognise a transpersonal element through an ethical relationship to the *Other*. We are responsible for and obligated to the *Other*, he says, it transcends Self and gives life meaning, exhausts understanding and in concrete terms is experienced by engaging with others: 'I can therefore live out my responsibility to respect and care for that which is beyond me, the "Other"' (2002: 41).

Transpersonal Psychotherapy

A comprehensive collection of transpersonal psychotherapies has been undertaken by Seymour Boorstein (1996), building on the foundations of William James' *states of higher consciousness*, Carl Jung's concept of *individuation*, Roberto Assagioli's work of *spiritual practices*, and Abraham Maslow's notion of *peak experiences*. Scientific research carried out by Charles Tart on *transpersonal states and the paranormal* and by Stanislav Grof on *non-ordinary states of consciousness*, completes an impressive gallery of expertise that may satisfy the reader that research on transpersonal spirituality is not new but has constantly developed (Boorstein, 1996: 2).

Walsh and Vaughan (1996) have assessed those transpersonal elements that extend beyond the personal Self to encompass wider aspects of humankind, life, the psyche and the cosmos, and have drawn distinctions

Table 3.1 Contrasting western and eastern psychology

Western Psychological Methodology	Eastern Psychological Methodology
Aim	Aim

— to discover cause of inner conflict
— to provide awareness, or change
  by direct environmental modification,
  by differential reinforcement, or by
  thought substitution
— to strengthen the ego
	— to help clients not to identify with
	  negative thoughts and emotions
	— to train awareness through meditation
	— to identify illusions and dreamlike states
	— to discover identity through
	  conscious awakening

between transpersonal and conventional forms of therapy. One significant difference lies in examining *consciousness* as opposed to the 'contents of consciousness', and another centres on the Buddhist emphasis of non-attachment and the cessation of desire, in sharp contrast with western approaches which tend to indulge in Self. Ostensibly, the same goals of symptom relief, alleviation of stress, behaviour and thought change are addressed in transpersonal as in other therapies, but transpersonal psychotherapy includes a conceptual framework for handling more expansive experiences by using all life-experience as part of learning, and by exploring existence through altered states of meditation, behavioural modelling (Bandura, 1977) and karma yoga, or the yoga of service.

As we shall see in Chapter 5, the therapist as expert who can provide information is downplayed in favour of *mutuality*. The therapist provides a model of learning-to-cope and in collaboration aims for client *competency*: 'Such modelling provides a high degree of mutuality between therapist and client, because both share the same growth-oriented intention for the therapy, are less hierarchically distanced, and each can learn from the other' (Walsh and Vaughan, 1996: 24). A contrast between traditional approaches and the transpersonal approach is presented in Tables 3.1 and 3.2.

As Walsh and Vaughan (1996) conclude, the greatest limitation of transpersonal psychology is its inadequate experimental foundation; it is not an approach which is easily accessible to investigative arenas of most researchers; the approach therefore is experimentally untested. Whilst this is clearly a shortcoming, the applicability of traditional scientific paradigms to investigate transpersonal phenomena is questionable. A second limiting factor in transpersonal psychology is that it places stringent demands on its practitioners, since the phenomena are largely more subtle and deeper. To date, with a few rare exceptions, the transpersonal has not been integrated with other western psychologies. Hopefully, this may change in the near future.

Towards Integration

The point I am attempting to make is that, as they stand, the major approaches and schools of psychotherapy have nothing about them which is intrinsically religious or spiritual – that is apart from, possibly, Jungian

Table 3.2 Contrasting traditional approaches with transpersonal psychotherapy

Traditional approaches	Transpersonal psychotherapy
Classical psychoanalysis — human beings are inherently locked in mental conflict, which can be reduced but never fully resolved — health comes from having a strong ego to mediate between an irrational id and a controlling superego	— a strong healthy ego is an asset in meeting life demands, but this is not the summit of mental health — health is to transcend ego conflict
Analytical psychotherapy — in-depth exploration of psyche to deal with archetypes and the collective unconscious — myths and images of dreams and active imagination are powerful therapeutic agents — numinous is investigated within mental contents of the psyche in order to release potential for self-healing and self-realisation	— a move from examining the contents of consciousness to explore consciousness itself, as the context of all experience — valuing the direct, imageless awareness attained in the practice of meditative discipline
Behavioural psychotherapy — measurement of observable behaviour prior to changing behaviour through empirically based techniques — subjective experience and consciousness are largely ignored — treat pathologies that are clearly defined, overt and relatively simple to observe	— meditation enhances feelings of love, which inhibit negative emotions, such as anger — replacing anxiety with relaxation is a form of reciprocal inhibition — behaviour modelling for more subtle experiences and behaviours than mere observable ones
Humanistic psychotherapy — growth-centred model concerned as much with health as pathology — holistic in that health is a balanced integration of physical, emotional and mental dimensions — development of personality and the achievement of ego goals	— health includes the extra dimension of spirituality — aim is to transcend beyond self-actualisation — first-hand experience of transpersonal states are imperative for growth and guidance
Existential psychotherapy — search for meaning and purpose — confrontation of death and aloneness — necessity for choice and responsibility to achieve authenticity — a belief that we shape our own reality	— to further grow we have to penetrate the mask of our separate and alienated individuality to reveal the transpersonal Self — to experience the interconnectedness of all life — hope to transcend the ego-defined identity and inescapable perspective of existentialism — personal transcendence must emerge from the existential question of freedom and all its paradoxes to be-in-the-world — the Buddha, in the three remaining Noble Truths, pointed the way to freedom through the transpersonal realm beyond the ego and existential nihilism

analysis. Cognitive therapies have tended to become hedonistic in orientation (ill-fitting numbers 5 and 6 of the Spiritual Orientation Inventory, Elkins et al., 1988) and psychoanalysis in long-term contracts has tended to encourage self-indulgence and a degree of narcissism (Gergen, 2001). This is to make a general point, rather than to suggest that a deeply religious practitioner, or an intuitive spiritually-minded therapist, might not engage in brief focal psychodynamic counselling, or cognitive therapy and REBT, with success.

Therapists of the psychodynamic orientation have indeed addressed spiritual issues in their work (Jacobs, 1993), and so have person-centred counsellors (Thorne, 1998; 2002), and even those belonging to the cognitive-behavioural school (Richards and Bergin, 1997; Scott Peck, 1978). Whilst some humanistic therapists may address spiritual issues within a secular framework (Elkins, 1998), the approach generally will attract many who have unresolved religious issues but who feel nevertheless a need to move towards a non-religious expression of spirituality. There can be little doubt that Jungian analysis and transpersonal psychology will attract both clients and candidates for training who have an intuitive sensitivity for a higher reality and who are not dissuaded by the nihilistic doom of Freudian psychology as applied to religion.

Though I remain optimistic that traditional schools of psychotherapy will continue to travel from dogmatic stances along the stream of the integrative movement, and that books, such those of West (2000; 2004), Swinton (2001), Thorne (2002), Elkins (1998) and Wilber (2000; 2001a), will finally break through the reticence (or refusal) to take on religious and spiritual issues when clients wish them to do so, there may remain something intrinsic about features of some approaches that render them unable to practise spiritually-centred counselling. Those practitioners who find themselves unable to adopt a 'one down' position – with no fixed agendas, no hypotheses in mind, and no subtle agenda, or religious predilection towards which the client should be encouraged to conform – will find the mode of spiritually-centred counselling virtually impossible to practise.

Summarising key features arising from this chapter, which will build a foundation for future spiritually-centred counselling, I would commend the following as being centrally important:

- A need to recognise the empirical and the mystical dimension in life.
- A need to avoid a constricted view of the image of the person.
- A need to value the religious 'other than' persuasion, as well as transpersonal dialogues of altered-states, and material–causal facets of human experience, both in their own rights and as future possibilities for growth.
- A need to enquire into the nature and character of consciousness itself rather than viewing it as the centre of thought-control and receptacle of memory.
- A need to cultivate a therapeutic style of mutuality, aiming for client competency in respect that for the client to grow and heal spiritually the therapist must model the same inclination.
- Therapy should aim at transcending the ego in place of shoring it up to face life's trials.
- Therapists might explore the implications for therapy of the interconnected nature of all life.

A Case to Consider

The context of the following extract is a general frustration voiced by Sam of not feeling she fitted in with various churches during her life. There was ambivalence coherently expressed in balancing integrity with a draw towards the numinous.

Sam: A friend of mine got very involved in the charismatic movement and she described a situation where everybody was throwing themselves onto the floor under the influence of the Holy Spirit. She said, 'I didn't feel anything but I just threw myself onto the floor anyway.' And then I said, 'Well what did you do when you were there prostrating yourself?' And she said, 'Well, I just prayed to God for all the things I need doing.' She regards God as Tesco's: so she goes, 'I need this and I need that.' And, for example, she prays to God because she wants her house to sell, and it won't sell because of a falling market because they're building an airport in Solihull, but she doesn't think that that's inappropriate; it's all about what I can get, not what I can give ...

Dennis: I'm trying to understand what the draw is for you: is it the people, do you think, or the trappings that go along with the church?

Sam: You need someone to animate the process. If someone was there and it was just me, I'd be all right, yeah. That wouldn't matter. In fact, the people are just a bit of a nuisance sometimes.

Dennis: So, you wouldn't say that sitting on your own in a church was beneficial?

Sam: I've done that, yeah.

Dennis: And has that been meaningful?

Sam: Yeah, though the last time I did that was about six months ago when I dropped in at Worcester and I'd stopped at three churches on the way home and in each one I formally prayed in them, just sat in them. I'd gone into a church that was local to us and had asked for something. In a way a bit like standing at the cenotaph to make it a real declaration. And then, over a period of time, this will just sound silly, I really felt that it was impertinent to ask. So, on that day, when I went to the three churches, I basically said, 'Take it back. I don't want the request to be in; it's cheeky'.

Dennis: As though the letter was in the post and you had to go to the sorting office to get it back? It almost sounds superstitious.

Sam: I don't think it was superstition. One thing I learnt from the Baptist church was that phrase, 'Give and it will be given unto you, pressed down and shaken together; it will be laid down in your lap'. That has been constantly true in my life.

Dennis:	And you believe that actually comes true?
Sam:	I actually believe that, yeah. And I have evidence of that happening to me over and over again. I mean, in terms of how people give things to me, even silly things like furniture. I got a job in the Museum and Art Gallery, and if I'd have applied for it I would never have got in. I got a job in a sixth form college teaching A level, and if I'd have applied for it I wouldn't have got in. I got a job in another school because I just turned up one day.
Dennis:	It's almost as though there's a magical text that …
Sam:	I read about Mother Teresa where it said that she said, 'I believe where it says in the Bible, "In as much as you do it unto one of these you do it to me [Christ]."' So, she said, 'And I believe that; I really believe that.' So when she's cleaning the shit off some beggar, she believes she's doing that to Christ. And as long as she believes that, you can't touch her, can you?

Before closing this chapter, pause for a moment and reflect on how you might respond in your next intervention if Sam were your client? Ask yourself what predispositions and feelings might influence your response, whether you might feel threatened by entering and/or sharing in a mystical dialogue, and what encouraging the talk on spirituality might mean for you.

Conclusion

This chapter has illustrated how the emergence of psychotherapy was an evolutionary provision that replaced the local priest in a particular social setting. We looked at the religious influences of various leading figures who became founders of particular schools of psychotherapy. Paradoxically, within the current secular setting of today's therapeutic consulting room, there is a reluctance to engage positively in religious and spiritual issues even though clients may lead their therapists into such territories. Recent movements in religious and transpersonal therapy have become more than a voice crying in the wilderness. The chapter closed with a transcript of a client's religious and spiritual ambivalence, with an invitation to reflect on personal practice with such a case.

In the pages that follow, I hope to present a different lens through which to view spirituality, a lens which pays respect to sociological interpretations of phenomena but which allows both therapist and client to view and explore a mystical dimension of experience. One requirement of this mode of spiritual therapy, which some approaches will not easily accommodate, is to take on a genuine neutral stance that is characteristic of transpersonal and systemic styles of psychotherapy. Throughout this book we will be exploring different understandings of Self and of the human spirit, from religious constructs to spiritual and humanistic ones.

4

Indications for Spiritually-centred Counselling

And before they went to bed that night he said:
  'We must never fear robbers or murderers. They are dangers
from outside, small dangers. It is ourselves we have to fear. Prejudice is the real robber, and vice the real murderer. Why should we
be troubled by a threat to our person or our pocket? What we have
to beware of is the threat to our souls.'

Victor Hugo, *Les Miserables* (1980: 42)

Death in the company of the beloved is no death. The painful thing
is not to leave life, but to leave whatever gives it meaning.

Raymond Radiguet, *The Devil in the Flesh* (2005: 52)

This chapter looks at the criteria for counsellors to engage in spiritually-
centred therapy. I encourage you to detect leading sentiments and expressions raised in sessions by clients that may indicate a need for a change of
approach. As practitioners, you may judge from your own school of thought
and practice where you feel spiritual enquiry will have a place and may
consider broadening your perspective by thinking about the potential of
integrating spiritual work within your customary manner of working.

I raise the common paranormal experience of pre-pubescent and early
adolescents and invite you to consider this as an early manifestation of
the numinous. We consider bereavement and retirement as events which
prompt searching questions as well as leaving clients disorientated and
overwhelmed. Much counselling is centred on fragile relationships and
this chapter explores where the spiritual outlook may have a part to play.
Spiritual therapy will have a significant role for those clients for whom
life has lost meaning.

What Type of Counsellor?

Clients who are religious purposely seek their master, shaman, guru,
priest or minister, specifically for spiritual or religious issues that trouble

them in life. Occasionally, religious people may look for a therapist who is sensitive to spirituality and who may not be religious in order to explore elements of their faith within a value-neutral therapeutic setting. But there are many more who are in therapy and who have no formal religious allegiance and yet wish to explore spiritual aspects of their person. There will be secular-minded individuals who may be indirectly struggling with aspects of their inner-being, or sense of spirituality, that signals a requirement for spiritually-oriented work. For many people, spirituality is an intuitive inner-sense, however vague that may be for the empirical researcher, and some may need to engage with one who can become in tune with what they are sensing. I believe that a significant number of clients in therapy are recognising the spiritual emptiness of a life solely engaged in material acquisition, particularly in later life. In Hugo's popular novel, the police give chase to Jean Valjean, and in spite of being given a room for the night he steals the bishop's candlestick the next morning. A fine gesture to repay our hospitality says the bishop's sister, but to neutralise her disgust, the bishop replies with the charitable sentiments that opened the chapter.

Person-centred and cognitive styles of therapy are in theoretical opposition, in that the former is dependent on the client's intuitive lead and the latter on the therapist structuring the session. This general caricature is not entirely accurate – it is improbable that a client leads in an absolute sense without responding to the counsellor's interventions, and unconscious resistance only allows structuring where a client is willing for this to happen. The position I take is a midpoint one of following my clients' lead to a point when indications suggest that they may benefit from exploring more deeply their inner-Self through a semi-structured range of questioning. Counsellor interventions are fashioned to unearth spiritual possibilities for growth and enlightenment.

Indications for Spiritually-centred counselling

Two principal types of client are predisposed for spiritual awakening and spiritual reflection, and these are adolescents and post middle-aged clients. I am persuaded by theories of individuation (Erikson, 1963; Jung, 1933) which see adolescence as a turbulent psycho-sexual phase of social adjustment that shows signs of *spiritual emergence* (Grof and Grof, 1989), and by Jung's observations that amongst 'patients in the second half of life – that is over 35 years of age – there has not been a single one whose problem has not been in the last resort that of finding a religious outlook on life' (Jung, 1933: 164). I consider Wilber's (2001a: 38) scheme of Kosmic consciousness, whereby the Spirit can be 'awakened to its own true nature', to be a transpersonal potential for all clients.

Spiritual factors may not be the presenting problem brought to counselling, but may underlie the way by which the client sees the world. Spiritual beliefs may predetermine the client's moral options in day-to-day dilemmas (Lukoff et al., 1998). Clinical work, such as bereavement, anonymity and social isolation, alcohol and substance abuse, sexual orientation confusion and suicide ideation have been addressed with conventional counselling – psychodynamic, humanistic-existential, cognitive-behavioural – along with eclectic and integrationist models (Bergin and Garfield, 1994; Diamond, 2000; Lines, 2006), but might just as appropriately be addressed through spiritually-centred counselling (Boorstein, 1996; Richards and Bergin, 1997; Thorne, 2002; West, 2004).

Some clients come specifically for religious-based counselling for issues relating to their personal faith, and the work of Richards and Bergin (1997) addresses the range of approaches and techniques designed around this narrow focus. The authors present a questionnaire, a range of assessment tools and models for 'measuring' religiosity (1997: 184–199), and argue that formal assessment of a client's religious background aids the therapist to understand their worldviews and utilise community and spiritual resources in therapy. Thorne's (1998) earlier work presented a restricted focus, in my judgment, through the healing power in mystical Christianity and biblical narratives, and West's two books (2000; 2004) present research of his own carried out principally with Quaker therapists. The underlying impression here is that clients bring up the topic of religion or spirituality and the therapist responds accordingly. Thorne's (2002) more recent work calls upon therapists within the person-centred tradition to recognise the spiritual dimension inherent in their understanding, following the lead of Rogers' latter writing. West (2000) campaigns for all therapists to explore the spiritual possibilities upon a broader canvas than the Christian worldview, and Elkins (1998) has attempted to engage Jungian and humanistic therapists in a non-religious aspect of spirituality.

I encourage this later perspective for reasons not only of embracing pluralism within humanistic ideals, but also because I believe, and I recognise that this is contentious, that many clients may not be aware that their cognitive, emotional and social difficulties may be an external manifestation of unresolved spiritual dilemmas. This will become evident as we examine casework material.

Elkins' (1998) programme includes creating a sacred place and writing a spiritual journal each day of helpful exercises that have moved his clients deeply. It includes selecting the most poignant medium in which to reflect on momentous events, spending time in a sacred place, and sharing individually suited programmes with a friend with whom the client feels safe. Elkins (1998) offers us a practical, individualistic programme based upon the following presuppositions:

- that we are unique
- that our spiritual needs will change in time
- that we must adopt an open-venturous attitude to redefine spiritual experience based upon our own experience, remembering that soul-work cannot be rushed
- and that we must remain open to the sacred.

It naturally follows, therefore, that in general those clients coming before Elkins may not be healed spiritually if they are not convinced that they are unique, if they cannot adapt during an unsettling period of change, if they have lost courage to welcome growth or to trust their own experience, or if they cannot make sense of what it means to remain open to the sacred.

Transpersonal therapists, as reviewed by Boorstein (1996), engage with problems that are conventionally addressed with psychodynamic, analytic or Gestalt approaches, and this point is broadly acknowledged by contributors who in some cases integrate the transpersonal within traditional styles. The distinguishing features are the central importance given to consciousness rather than 'contents' of consciousness, and the application of mind-altering techniques. Essentially, those clients wishing to explore the nature of their own consciousness may be drawn towards a transpersonal therapist. In order to entice you to consider the benefits of spiritually-centred counselling, I side-step those more ambitious techniques of altered mental states and instead encourage you to consider spirituality within a more secular and commonplace understanding.

Indications for religious and spiritual therapy for the practitioners mentioned above appear conventional in the sense that client and therapist have a mutual prior agreement that their problems are related to common understandings of religion and spirituality, but what about those younger or overtly non-religious clients who come for therapy who are unaware of their spiritual impulses, or who remain unconvinced that their difficulties stem from spiritual roots?

When do Clients Require Spiritual Therapy?

Throughout my practice, I have found seven common areas of concern which may warrant a decision for the therapist to move into a spiritual mode of counselling. These seven areas may be classified generally as follows:

Adolescence
- *paranormal experience in youth* – childhood development and encountering ghosts and spiritual beings
- *bereavement* – shock stimulates emotional insecurity and a testing of belief-systems
- *overcoming obstacles in relationships* – inadequacy when facing difficult relational tasks

Middle-Aged
- *discovering inner-Self* – realising inner resources to meet a challenge
- *growing out of religion* – finding the courage to 'stand alone' without religious security
- *search for meaning* – establishing meaning when identity within roles is no longer sufficient
- *confronting personal extinction or loss of parent* – death closes the doors to opportunity

The first three categories apply principally, but not exclusively, to pre-adolescent to adolescent young people, while the last three are principally, but not exclusively, applicable to adults, particularly those beyond middle age. The fourth category can refer to a person facing a crisis at any stage of development, but, again, will become evident during life-span stages where emotional, social and psychological change is occurring. Below I present extracts of counsellor and client discourse where these spiritual and religious tensions begin to bubble and rise to the surface.

Paranormal Experience in Youth

Wilber (2000: 139–142) thinks that childhood spirituality is possible within certain definitions of spirituality. Clearly, being egocentric, children will not have the capacity to be world-centric or fully empathic of others' concerns, but they may be open to *peak experiences* of psychic dimensions. Early- to mid-adolescents not infrequently have frightening experiences for which they have no language to make sense, apart from borrowed narratives unconsciously lifted from films and television. For some young people, the paranormal features highly – particularly ghosts and spirits (Bray, 2004; Grof and Grof, 1990). During school counselling, a considerable number of young people give accounts of ghosts and spirit visitations with little prompting. In *Brief Counselling in Schools* (Lines, 2006), the case of Des is presented in some detail where spiritual therapy addresses his paranormal experiences in relation to the loss of his father. Paranormal events and spirit visitations occurred for Rory and Jim, 13-year-old lads.

Rory: I used to see little girls looking in my room. I had a vision of a little girl sitting right next to me; not like a human being. It was a soul, it wasn't an image. When I turned my head away and looked back she'd gone. My mum was there sitting on a chair like this one [*Rory points to the seat*] and she saw her but thought nothing of it; and the same happened when she turned her head away she was gone ... When my brother's mate went out of the door he saw the little girl walking in, 'cause it looked exactly the same as our next-door neighbour. So he said, 'Get out?' So she went out but we never heard the door close, but then she appeared in the room ... We used to have this dog called Beethoven, and you know how dogs can see spirits, well, she must have seen her because he was barking all the time at where she was sitting.

Dennis: So, you think there are spirits?

Rory: I believe there's souls, 'cause I think I saw one when I was walking home from my mates. And he lives next to a cemetery. I was walking down this hill and I saw this thing; it was a head and a thing floating towards me. And he said, 'Look behind. What's that thing over there?' So I looked behind me and it came right close to us. It was like an old man with a hat on, all we saw was him floating towards us real fast. Then he stopped at the top of the hill and just vanished. So we ran.

Dennis: So what sense do you make of that?

Rory: Souls, I believe in. I believe that a soul is kind to you.

Dennis: How can you be sure that it's not your imagination playing tricks?

Rory: I don't think so. We all in our family know that the little girl is real. We hear her walking up and down the stairs at night, but nobody is afraid because we know she's friendly. We've been living in our house for over twelve years, and she's got used to us being there. We take no notice, we just go back to sleep.

Dennis: What makes you think that ghosts are real?

Jim: Because I've seen one [*Jim begins to laugh*]. I know I have.

Dennis: Can you tell me about that, Jim?

Jim: When I was staying at my sisters, and my little nephew was crying, 'cause he kept on seeing things, and, then when I went in the room with him. Thingy, err [*he becomes pensive, and looks downward*] … I, I just kept on thinking I could see it …

Dennis: What do you think happens to people when they die?

Jim: If you're burned you burn, and if you're buried, you just, I don't know if you're buried. You just get eaten away, ain it. People say that, just before something happens, you go, and then you die.

Dennis: Has anyone close to you died?

Jim: Yeah, Molly.

Dennis: Do you think of Molly now?

Jim: This is weird [*Jim becomes animated*], 'cause after she'd died, this lady used to go into this shop, and this is where she used to go, and she looked the double of her and we all used to say, 'That's Molly!'

Dennis: Mm.

Jim: And we all couldn't believe ourselves, because she was there, because she'd died.

Dennis: Do you think it was Molly?

Jim: No. I doubt it. She couldn't have been. She'd died.

Reflective questions when engaging in spiritually-centred counselling with young people over paranormal experiences will be more pertinent than in other approaches. If Wilber (2000: 14) is correct when he says that 'peak experiences can occur to individuals at almost any stage of development', and that they are *temporary* yet *direct experiences* of nature mysticism, deity mysticism or formless mysticism, as though an individual catches glimpses of transpersonal states, then the following questions are pertinent:

- Should the counsellor share similar accounts from his own current or past experience, with the intention of 'normalising' the client's experience?
- Should paranormal narratives be downplayed, from a condescending perspective that reasons 'the youngster will soon grow out of magical or mythical reasoning and learn to demythologise the inexplicable'; should they be given no attention, so as to divert the mind to more empirical reasoning; or should paranormal explanations be validated, so as to open the mind further to numinous possibilities?
- Should the spiritual therapist offer 'credible' explanations for what is experienced, so as to induce the juvenile mind to scientific objectivity?

As you answer these questions, search deeper into the underlying beliefs and presuppositions which are steering your reasoning. Where you lie on the empirical–mystical spectrum will largely influence what course you take. In preparing case vignettes, counselling discourses are recorded on video or audio tape and listening and re-listening to the recordings reveals my own values and beliefs (Lynch, 2002; Mearns and Cooper, 2005), which will influence my client's further deliberations (Toolan, 1988). Did you notice my response of 'Mm' when Jim said, 'That's Molly!', and his subsequent rationalisation? Nathan, in Chapter 3, may also have detected a subtle scepticism on my part, even though it was not apparent to me in session.

Paranormal tendencies are not the only indication for a spiritual mode of counselling. Some young people experiencing trauma or bereavement within their family may be forced to enquire into the Big Life Questions, and in some circumstances be required to draw from their deeper resources to cope in altered social circumstances that inevitably arise from loss.

Bereavement

The tragic death of a parent or close relative or friend, or particularly a pet, can leave a youngster devastated. One developmental task during adolescence is the adjustment to the loss of childhood and this itself has been likened to bereavement (Noonan, 1983). The psychodynamic interpretation of adolescent development involves the psychological murder of father [*sic*] as competitor through the Oedipus complex (Jacobs, 1993), but if father suddenly dies there can result irrational guilt, which thwarts development with possible symptoms, unhealed psychological scars, or paranormal experiences. Mario had witnessed his father committing suicide in Italy.

> *Mario:* I knew what my dad was going to do. I had a dream the night before he killed himself. I was trying to break him out [*i.e. of the car by breaking the glass*]. I told my mum about it but she wouldn't listen.

> *Dennis:* Was the whole event clear in your dream?
>
> *Mario:* Yeah. I knew it was going to happen. I knew it was going to go wrong. I told my mum something bad was going to happen today.

[Two cars collided outside and Mario saw this through the counselling room window. He wanted to go out and look at the crumpled cars at first, but then slumped into the chair and drifted into a dreamy state with glazed expression.]

> *Dennis:* Where are you now Mario?
>
> *Mario:* I tried to break in. The glass wouldn't break. I kept smashin' it as a hard as I could but it wouldn't break. There was no point; he was meant to die. I'd seen it in my dream.

If mother dies, in whatever circumstance, the emotional effects can be catastrophic, leaving the youngster insecure with no nurturing bedrock and with an unpredictable future (Lines, 2006). Typical stages of loss and bereavement and subsequent adjustment have been well documented (Kübler-Ross, 1982), but, for some clients healing may require a cognitive restructuring of metaphysical beliefs (Lines, 1999b; Nelson-Jones, 1996).

Big Life Questions of the unknown were asked of four boys undergoing bereavement group-therapy (Lines 1999b), which will be discussed more fully in Chapter 6. James (14), Phil (11), Matthew (12) and Clint (12) had each received sessions of person-centred counselling and cognitive-behavioural work before being brought together as a group. James had self-referred for relationship difficulties, and Phil, Clint and Matthew were referred by pastoral staff for behavioural reasons. Phil feared coming to school in case he 'might suddenly die like my brother!' When present, he threw tantrums in the corridors, was found sitting and crying on stairwells, and had often spurned teachers inappropriately with comments such as, 'You don't care!' Clint was the most intelligent of the group, but was confrontational towards teachers at times, challenging when being corrected, then reduced to tears after the crisis was over. Matthew refused bluntly to do PE, claiming that he should not be made to do sport since losing his mother. In a note to his PE teacher, he wrote: 'My mum was a PE teacher and she's the only one to teach me PE … I wish I was dead!' During one session, the group interview was recorded without me being present and each of the boys was asked to prepare a question. With permission of the boys and their guardians, I present the following discourse.

In the introduction of the group (un-facilitated) session, each of the boys gave an account of their loss:

> *James:* I lost my dad first after he went into hospital with stomach ulcers, and it caused a disease that destroyed his liver and kidneys. Several weeks later my mum died of an accidental overdose on paracetamol. They both died around the same time – my dad died in the February, my mum died in

April … My dad always said to me 'When its time to die it's time to die. You can't stop it.' So, I just think, well, that's it, they're gone, can't do anything to change it, and they wouldn't want me moping around for the rest of my life … So, I try and do the best I can, not just for me but for them as well … And in a way I still blame myself because she called out to me at six o'clock in the morning, but I was groggy … I didn't know what was wrong with her, and I couldn't understand 'cause I was half-asleep. So I went back to sleep, like. I woke up in the morning … Her bedroom door was closed … So …

Phil: I lost my brother about two years ago. He died of a heart problem 'cause I was in junior school, and my mum's friends came and told me that my brother had died on the way home from school. I started crying and I went home and saw my family crying … We didn't want to sleep upstairs 'cause we was scared. Just in case we saw a ghost of him.

Clint: I lost my dad not so long ago when we broke up for two weeks. It was on the day that we broke up when he died. He was actually in hospital at the time when he died, and he died of a blood clot on his lung, even though on the day he died he was diagnosed as having cancer, he died of a different thing. We had, sort of, had good times when he was alive [*voice breaks up, chokingly*], and seems as, it seems a bit boring [*Clint breaks down*] … now that he's dead.

Mat: I lost me mother in 1992. She died of a heart problem. Every time I try and talk to my dad about it he starts being upset as well.

Each of the boys suffering bereavement had a pressing, unanswered, question that not only confounded them but in some sense hindered the healing process, and, without planning, each question was raised in session. James, the leading character, asked early on, 'How do you think you're coping?', and in spite of his Stoic outlook his natural insecurity in having lost both parents was hidden behind a mask of appearing resilient before his younger peers. Phil asked James, 'Where do you reckon heaven is?' He had a curious notion that he might see his deceased brother as a new star in the evening sky, and his question prompted the spiritual theme at the close of the session (Chapter 6). But Clint's question was more tentative. As a means of coming to terms with the shock announcement at school that his father had died, he asked Matthew, 'Do you think it was, like, better … to find out when you were at home with all your family … ?' Matthew asked, 'What things do you have in common with your parents?'

When first hearing the audio-taped session, I was impressed with the stark, direct manner of communications over personal tragedies. I wonder if you noticed how each of the boys used the toned-down term of 'lost' before the equivalent of 'died'. Each narrative of loss was brief, but in later extracts – when confidence had grown to express feelings more openly – the boys not only gave fuller accounts but were determined to hold the floor. As will become evident in Chapter 6, each of the boys was keen to test *emergent belief-systems* as cognitive hooks upon which to hang their emotional insecurity.

Overcoming Obstacles in Relationships

There are occasions in all forms of counselling and psychotherapy where clients become stuck for reasons that they sense an overpowering weakness to achieve a task which for them is essential to their social relatedness and integrity of being. In western culture, where an individualism stemming from the Enlightenment mentality has stifled a relational sense of Self, a significant number of clients come for counselling because they feel utterly alone and alienated from others. Whatever richness of family and friendship bonding existed in their past, their present is characterised by intense boredom and social isolation.

Some have become wholly alienated from family, and others have cut all ties because of bitterness or feuds emanating from past quarrels where burying hatchets has not occurred. If we are by nature relational creatures (Mearns and Cooper, 2005), then something may have been lost or never cultivated. In order to 'get back on track', or 'discover within Self something that had been missing', or to 'become a social Self', there may be a requirement to identify that innate yearning for social connectedness through spiritually-centred counselling. I have written extensively on the relational tasks of young people moving from adult to peer group dependence (Lines, 2006), following Erikson's (1968) observations of role-confusion and identity crisis, particularly in regard to school bullying (Lines, 1996; 1999a; 2001; Luxmoore, 2000), but here I wish to discuss the spiritual dimension.

Customarily, person-centred therapy, with its stress on personal relating through the medium of a therapeutic relationship has been indicated for such difficulties, but there is always the risk that whatever the gains in counselling have been with an empathic therapist skilled at this level, it may not be generalised out of the counselling context and within the broader world where persons are not nearly so patient and self-giving (Masson, 1988: 232). The aim in all successful psychotherapy is empowerment. I invite you to examine the benefits of enlarging your practice by utilising spiritually-inclined interventions with cases similar to those that follow.

Leanne was referred for counselling by an adolescent mental health centre after she had taken an overdose. She was seventeen and had been brought up in fractious family circumstances. She had a younger sister two years her junior, whom she despised. During childhood she had been abused by her grandfather, who had been sentenced, but her father was so troubled that he took his own life. Leanne had never recovered from this, and there was continued anger over her mother continually siding with her sister instead of her. The final blow was the discovery that the person she had called 'mother' was not her biological parent. She felt totally alienated and unprepared to face the world alone. She had returned home to find her mother had given her bedroom to a lodger, and this had left her in temporary hostel accommodation. She had lost everything and was fearful of the future.

Dennis: How are things in the hostel, Leanne?

Leanne: I don't know how I can carry on. There's been a nagging feeling to go back and *creep to my so-called mother!*

Dennis: Is that what you want?

Leanne: God knows what I want. *I* don't even know what *I* want; who cares anyway … I have to break away; there's nothing for me there. The social has promised me independent living but *I can't do it.* I know *I can't do it.* I'm scared, really scared, and I'm not ready … [*Leanne begins to cry*]

Dennis: Leanne, what do you want to happen?

Leanne: I want to leave and make the break from home and find someone just for me, but I haven't it within me. I'm a coward, aren't I? … Do you think I can do it, leave home, I mean, and find someone, somewhere?

Dennis: Someone and somewhere are two different entities; I'm not sure which should come first.

Leanne: Mm …, somewhere really.

Dennis: I think you're very brave, and what you have to do will take a lot of courage. I think you can make the step. I believe you have a very strong spirit.

Vicki was 21 years old, single, lived with her father, and had been referred by her GP after being raped in a car by her first 'boyfriend'. She spoke of a recurrent nightmare of continually reliving the rape, of being held down on the back seat, of screaming for help as he laughed and fondled her body with no-one coming to her aid, and of feeling 'dirty and defiled'. The stimulus for the dreaming horror was obvious and there was no need for any in-depth Jungian analysis of archetypal significance, or Freudian exploration of the unconscious for insight of inner-conflict. I felt a cognitive style of therapy (REBT) was indicated for the following reasons:

1   Vicki's nightmare had become exceptionally powerful and there was need to exorcise its hold through imagery techniques and a programme of desensitisation.
2   her father had become too dominant in her life and she needed to break as free from his control as from the hold of the image of her violation.
3   she needed to discover new courage to engage socially since she was keen to have a relationship in spite of what she had suffered, and with this task *in vivo* trials of social engagement seemed appropriate.

The therapeutic programme was progressing nicely, but then a spiritual course of therapy became necessary after the following discourse.

Vicki:	How can I be sure if I go out with someone that the same will not happen? Are all men not the same? Are they only really after sex?
Dennis:	Has this been your experience generally?
Vicki:	I can't really say: he was the first person I'd been alone with.
Dennis:	It's understandable that you're going to be unsure after such a nightmare as that, yet you appear to be saying that you still want a relationship and a little romance?
Vicki:	I do, I do, but how can I be safe. Even if I go out with my girlfriends there will always be that time when we get spilt up by the predatory bastards.
Dennis:	I don't know what to say; I can see your dilemma: you want a relationship, yet you know firsthand that the risks are all too real.
Vicki:	I know you have only supported me for a short while, but do you think I can take that risk and have faith in people, have faith in life?

In both case examples, clients moved into the therapist mode of asking the question, and in each case the question was not rhetorical but was designed to draw from the therapist a judgment on the personal resources to complete a relational task, a task requiring great courage. It is not difficult to see the inherent dangers in heeding each of these requests by answering in the affirmative. Was my closing remark to Leanne naïve, over-optimistic, or potentially risky in endorsing a move toward autonomy before being really ready? Should Vicki be encouraged to be more cautious before risking encounters alone with men, or has she to learn that facing life involves taking risks?

Responding positively to client questions of competency in psychotherapy not only has the potential to place novice clients in hazardous situations, it draws the therapist to express judgments, which, apart from narrative and solution-focused therapists, practitioners generally believe they should avoid. The judgment in both cases is guided by my compelling confidence in the Rogerian belief in human potential for growth and healing, the Darwinian struggle to survive within a social nexus, and a compelling trust in the numinous spirit of life emerging from rich relating: becoming evident in Leanne's unremitting biological drive to break from family and find new friends, and in Vicki's desire for relationship and for human connectedness. I will have cause to reason later that there is a biological drive in life that compels us to relate with others, in spite of the risks (Mearns and Cooper, 2005).

Discovering Inner-Self

The notion of inner-Self has been introduced and its psychological basis will be discussed later. Inner-Self is understood through analogy and poetic metaphor rather than anatomical location. An emerging sense of Self caused Billy Elliot to suffer humiliation and teasing from friends and family, 'You look a right wanker, if you ask me, Billy!' said one acquaintance watching him dance. When discovering inner-Self, he described what it felt like when dancing:

> It sort of feels good. When I get going then I forget everything, and I, sort of, *disappear*. I can feel a *change* in my whole body. Like there's a *fire* in my body. Just *there*, like a bird, like *electricity*. Yea, like *electricity*.

Clients occasionally draw attention to their inner-Self in discourse. Sinita was 15 and she had approached me for support over constant worrying about her older brother and his addiction to heroin. Anxiety was draining her energy to live productively.

Dennis: When you think of Delroy now, when you close your eyes, what do you see?

Sinita: Someone who looks like a skeleton with a skinny face and sunken eyes, shiny brown.

Dennis: The shiny brown eyes still speak to you?

Sinita: Yea.

Dennis: Have you ever seen him actually taking drugs?

Sinita: Not actually taking them. I walked in once and saw him there and I just walked straight out again.

Dennis: So your way of dealing with this is not to watch him, not to look too hard?

Sinita: I couldn't watch him. If I had have seen him I would have flipped. I didn't give myself chance to see. What I can't see can't hurt me.

Dennis: So there's part of you that does not want to know too much?

Sinita: I don't want to know anything really, but because I know it all it just hangs over me all the time. If somebody tells me he's going back into jail it brings a sigh of relief.

Dennis: How is that?

Sinita: He's not in my way; he's not holding me back from living my life; I don't have to think of him; I don't have to keep checking on him any more. If he's inside, I don't need him there [*Sinita places her hand over her heart*] …

Dennis: How close are you?

Sinita: Too close. You know when you grow up with someone that's so close to you, then you know in the back of your mind that it will all end, that's how close we were … He was like my diary; I would tell him everything, day in day out. He would know everything. He was my diary … I am sick and tired of being hurt by him. All I've got left now is the memories. You just know it's never going to happen, I have to move on. Inside my heart I've got a part for every

> member of my family. There's a part for my mum and my dad and my other brother, but there's now a gap where Delroy used to be. Now, Del's gone, it's like a hollow in there and I'm trying to move everyone around to fill that space, but somehow I just can't.
>
> *Dennis:* I wonder if we could find a way of helping you fill that space with more of you?

It never ceases to amaze me how resourceful and adaptive young people are. When I ponder the lifestyles of many of my young clients and consider what they have gone through from my 'comfortable position' of having had a secure upbringing, having a fulfilling career and sufficient prosperity to bring me contentment, I am left bewildered over how they appear to come through with relatively few scars. It seems that the biological mechanisms of being human stand them in good stead to make the most of adversity. In spite of having faith in human potential and the human spirit, I come across youngsters who appear stuck and thwarted in the process. In such cases, the integrative youth counsellor may step-aside from his brief models of solution focus and pragmatic goal-setting to engage in a form of spiritual therapy aimed at reaching the inner-depths of personal resources, and Sinita's narrative suggested that she was ready for this constructive diversion.

Tony attended an Anglican Church in youth, and his parents said their prayers with him 'every night' until he assumed that responsibility for himself. He took part in the choir and rang the bells. He joined a Pentecostal Church, along with his wife, when in their thirties and had very different experiences. When reflecting on his father's religious commitment, he said, 'I didn't really feel that he was particularly what I would call an active Christian.' Personal freedom was of particular interest to Tony.

> *Dennis:* At what point did you feel there was freedom for you not to pray, or not to go to Church? [*A clock chimes and Tony smiles*]
>
> *Tony:* That's me ringing the church bells; that's reminded me of that. I used to ring the bells before the church service; it's funny bringing that memory back.
>
> *Dennis:* Yea.
>
> *Tony:* I think I do remember myself lying in bed, almost taking it on for myself in terms of speaking to God and feeling different. There was a point, however, where I felt something; I couldn't really put that into words but it was a spiritual experience …
>
> *Dennis:* How do you now review those experiences in the Church?
>
> *Tony:* *I actually felt saved by leaving Church* and the way that religion was experienced within the church environment. I left that particular church following a structural re-organisation. I felt,

Dennis: don't ask me to explain what God is, I don't know, but I felt
it was a healthy experience – leaving the Church. Now I can
find God, or perhaps God can find me. At the time it was
actually quite a painful experience from a social and a spiritual point of view, in terms of handling guilt: 'are you doing
the right thing'. I genuinely feel more spiritually mature and
more saved as a result of being free of Church expectations.

Dennis: What does freedom mean?

Tony: For me it is the freedom to be yourself; to be loved without
a sense of judgment … Did that make sense?

Dennis: Yes. It almost implies that you have some way of measuring that community by a standard which shows that something isn't right.

There was much Tony was teaching me through this session. His experiences of Christian life were of non-committed conformity and charismatic enthusiasm, and in both cases there was an inner-reference by
which he might measure religious shallowness and spiritual sentimental-
ity by humanistic values. Tony's narrative had a spiritual intensity and it
seemed as though he was growing out of religion.

Growing out of Religion into Spirituality

Many clients coming for counselling have unresolved religious issues,
and for these spiritually-centred counselling is particularly appropriate.
Some clients might prefer a therapist belonging to the same 'household of
faith' as their own, yet it is clear that many do not (West, 2004), particularly if doubt forms the substance of their questioning (Lannert, 1991;
Richards and Bergin, 1997). When the senator dines with the bishop of
Digne in Victor Hugo's (1980) novel, *Les Miserables,* he opens the table discourse with sentiments which echo the secular worldview:

> So where does the Eternal Father come in? My dear bishop, I find the
> Jehovah theory very tedious. It produces nothing but lean men with
> empty heads. I want none of the great All, which irritates me; I prefer
> the great Nothing, which leaves me untroubled … Life is all we have …
> The man who has nothing else has God. It's better than nothing and
> I've no objection, but for myself I stick to realism. God is for the masses.

The bishop clapped his hands and said, 'An admirable discourse!' He
offers no apologia in defence of the senator's rhetoric, and speaks only by
good works – 'It was the heart that inspired this man', not fancy words or
incontestable logic.

Before engaging in spiritually-centred conversation with Sam, she sent
me an email which described her present outlook. With her permission,
I present her account:

C. S. Lewis uses the idea of going through the back of the wardrobe to get to the other world of Narnia, and it struck me that in many ways the 'spiritual life' that I have now, but which was once a lot more vigorous, is a bit like a wardrobe of clothes. The fur coat is in there and also the evening dress, but they are not worn everyday, or even often. For those of us (you and me and others) who decline what is called the 'communion of saints', this is how the spiritual life goes on, it hasn't gone away; it's just put away, and got out when the need arises.

To me it seems that a great number of people *actively avoid* the questions about the interior world or the spiritual world and are (like me) incredibly incoherent when trying to *say* what it is they feel or think or know. The spiritual therapist in a way opens up the wardrobe door for people so they can try on the different solutions, to see what fits, what makes them feel right.

Sam: Inside my head the conversations go on, and no one that I can yet find has any interest at all in going, in some sense of knowing that there is a God. I suppose it's a bit like knowing you have a parent as a grown up, that part of me declines all your rational-speak, all your conditioning theories, and shrugs and says, 'OK if that's what you want to think'. But the bit in my head is inviolable, and I like to have it, like keeping love letters hidden away somewhere.

There is a certainty expressed by Sam that defies rationality, which reminded me of Jung's comment that opened Chapter 3. Sam revealed an ambivalence often experienced by many of seeing value in the Church yet feeling estranged from it in later life. For some people, such as me, the experience of growing out of religion stems from an ideological conflict with the belief-system (reinforcing Freud's prediction), for others it results from apathy or being over-swamped with life-demands (reinforcing Mother Teresa's view), but for Sam it was a feeling of not fitting in with the pretentiousness of people who are uncommitted to genuine Christian living. Sam's formative Christian experiences were in different denominations of the Church (Anglican, Baptist and Evangelical). Spiritual ambivalence is shown in these two extracts:

Sam: I would not like to be like a man I know who does not believe in God. I could not understand what there would be left in life. If you said to me, 'There is no God, there is no ultimate hierarchy, there is nothing, you don't have to be nice to people, there isn't any compassion or concern, then all I would say is that then all that could possibly fascinate me in my brief life would be hedonism. In which case, I'll get myself as rich as possible and enjoy myself while I can.

Dennis: If you were to look back at those episodes in your life that you have so eloquently described, which of those experiences, do you think, inform the sort of person you are now?

Sam: The thing that is difficult is that you don't come to places overnight. For most people it isn't a road to Damascus, is it? It's a gradual evolution to a place. For example, when this guy set up the mission, he travelled all round the country and laid hands on people and they had missions. And there were consequently opportunities to be with him on one of those missions, and I went to one of those ... and when we were altogether I was being noisy and laughing and joking, and mucking about, and he actually said to me, 'Be quiet and sit over there!' So, I thought, there's *no room for me here, and I am pretty moderate and in favour of all this gear,* and so there's no room for me, there ain't going to be room for the others; not the people outside – 'Be quiet and sit over there!' So, I suppose what I'm saying is that those different things have brought me to the point of not doing it any more.

Sam's stronger views on religious hypocrisy were poignant and are articulately expressed in this more extended narrative.

Sam: In the Anglican Church there was a rector who had lost his faith completely because his son had died from leukaemia. So, although he took confirmation classes, he would tell you quite openly that he could not hack it anymore; he'd lost his own faith through losing his son.

Dennis: And he voiced that to the group?

Sam: Yea. So he would basically say, 'This is the theory and this is what I did believe, but I am old now' [*sigh*] ... and it was horrible!'

Dennis: Did you ever want to cultivate a personal relationship with God through the medium of these people and this place?

Sam: Yeah, I think everyone was involved in that. At that time there was a great flurry of excitement about having hands laid on, and going on in the Spirit. Twelve left university and actually gave a year of their life going around doing that full-time instead of just doing it for two weeks while they were at university ...

Dennis: Was there any sense of mission growing there for you?

Sam: If I was honest with you, I don't think I have ever done anything where I have fitted in. I didn't fit in there, and I think it's because I have never really managed to put all the questions to one side ... I went to the church at Beacon Hill, and what I found there was that I just can't sustain life in the Church, because they require, not that you have a relationship with God, or that you even believe in God – they don't actually require that. They require that you behave in certain ways and can tolerate certain social groupings within the Church, and I just can't do it.

Dennis: I can sense a concern about hypocrisy over what was expected of you, and I'm wondering whether you've felt this from an early age?

Sam: Yes, I would say so. There was an issue over a person in the Church where someone married a girl, or got her pregnant; not absolutely sure. Anyway, to cut a long story short, their boy was born with a deformed foot, so he had to wear one of those big shoes. I don't know whether it was actually said but it was implied that because he had contravened God's law he was punished with his little boy's foot, and the marriage broke up. Now, for me, that's just tosh … I believe in retribution from God but I wouldn't believe that they then should punish, or should have the right to chastise that boy, be unkind to that child, or to his mother, which I think they were. You just know that's not what they should be doing …

Dennis: Is there a moral order higher than that presented by the Church?

Sam: Another guy caused a huge furore in the church because he said, 'You're always talking about love but you don't animate it; you never put it into action'. And he said, 'We're supposed to have everything in common, we're supposed to share everything. Now what I'm asking you guys here is, now let's just ask you straight, "Would you lend Graham your car?"' And there was like total hush in the Church because the answer was, *no they wouldn't*. Now Graham was the best and they still wouldn't lend him his car … I got into trouble myself. I remember at a prayer meeting on a Tuesday night. We were all sitting in rows like we were on a bus, and it was an open prayer to God, and you could basically dish-up your requirements and pray for this, and pray for that; so-and-so needs getting well etc. I don't know what annoyed me about it, but I just said, 'I really don't think this is normal. We wouldn't sit like this in company; we would just sit around and look at each other and make eye contact and things like that, but we're sitting on a bus. *Why are we doing this?*

Search for Meaning

Searching for a meaning in life has been a common need for mid-life clients seeking out a therapist. Viktor Frankl (1959), in *Man's Search for Meaning*, has become an authoritative voice on life meaning and curiously turns the question upon its head by asking what life expects of us, as though life itself is the 'critical parent' sitting upon our shoulder beckoning. Perhaps, this is a harsh image to use in amplifying what Frankl meant, but when recalling two cases where Jewish Holocaust inmates were contemplating suicide in the camp, and who reasoned that, characteristically, 'they had nothing more to expect from life', he writes: 'In both cases it was a question of getting them to realise that life was still expecting something from them' (1959: 87). For one inmate it was a child, but for Frankl it was the hope of seeing his wife again, and a compulsion to complete an unpublished manuscript which a guard had torn up before his eyes. For many clients disillusioned with religion, life itself is the authority, the *libido*, the energising spirit for growth and healing in bringing form from formlessness.

Many people reaching retirement find the adjustment from beaver-like activity to domicile existence of unscheduled routine quite difficult, particularly if they have not planned for retirement, and if they have few interests or social contacts. It is likely with many retired folk that their parenting roles would have ceased to such an extent that the curtain of the final act is felt to be falling. Pauline was referred for counselling by her GP for reasons of depression (being prescribed valium) and physical symptoms (irritable bowel syndrome, and panic attacks) that were thought by her to be due to psychological adjustment for having retired from lecturing at FE College, and for a diminished role as a needed parent. She was brought up within a close-knit Methodist family, but her failed marriage, her independent-minded children, her deceased church friends and her sensitivity for 'no longer being needed' left her with no meaning in life or reason to carry on. The integrative counselling style was taking on a cognitive emphasis, since Pauline had a tendency to 'catastrophise' (Dryden, 1991; Ellis, 1989) her situation and have unreal expectations of health and retired life (Nelson-Jones, 1996), when her search for life-meaning suggested the need to move into deeper spiritual therapy:

> *Pauline:* Why should God have not helped me over my illness? There seems no point in going on now, in making the effort; I may as well roll over and die like my friends for all my children care!
>
> *Dennis:* You appear to want the improbable.
>
> *Pauline:* I know my son and daughter have lives of their own now, with no grandchildren in prospect. I know teaching has finished and going to Church is pointless. I feel as though my life has been a journey coming to completion. You have been like a friend over these last months, helping me make sense of the past and in seeing that in a new light. You've helped me understand that I've probably been expecting too much. I now realise that my life consists of positive and negative events, not just negative ones. The panic attacks are not so prevalent and although I sometimes get fed-up and have some 'off days', I realise that this is unfortunate but not the end of the world … It's the same for everyone … I would love to have given up valium but this will be a longer-term thing. But what has life to offer me now?

This last question was not rhetoric, or a request for feasible options for one in her position and stage of life, but an invitation to become a different 'companion' in helping the client philosophise on personal meaning and future transpersonal possibilities.

Ben also was referred by his GP for depression. He felt his life was closing down and he had regularly contemplated giving up. His wife had died quite suddenly from a brain tumour and his business had collapsed. At the age of 52 he became doubtful of finding employment but fortunately he was not in debt. His two sons were in their late twenties and showed no signs of wanting to leave home. Being an ex-police officer, he had to overcome great personal resistance to come for counselling – 'I'm not a feelings kind of guy, and I must admit to finding this difficult.' In spite of this confession, the early sessions were punctuated by ceaseless sobbing:

> *Ben:* Not even my closest friends know how I feel; they think I'm coping. My sons are not communicative, but we are close.
>
> *Dennis:* You're clearly upset about the loss of your wife, but you appear also to be angry.
>
> *Ben:* I'm angry when my friends patronise me by saying 'some good will come out of this.' They see me as tough and a fighter – if they were to see me now!
>
> *Dennis:* And all this has led you to think about taking your life? [*Ben sobs again*].
>
> *Ben:* Have you ever thought of suicide and giving up?

Here was an invitation to share my feelings of despair when life had once held no promise.

Confronting Non-Being

Clare came for counselling initially over the bereavement of her partner. She was an elegant lady who took pride in her appearance, and looked considerably younger than her age of 68. In session she spoke at length about her fitness routine, her cosmetic surgery and her *need to keep young*. She had a pressing desire for another partner, but a much younger person. At one point, she began disclosing an anxiety about death and non-being.

> *Clare:* People ask me how I'm coping after losing Jack, and I know it seems selfish but I cannot live on my own. I want to stay youthful. I *need* to remain young.
>
> *Dennis:* Does death trouble you Clare?
>
> *Clare:* Oh please don't ask me about death! I dread even thinking about it.
>
> *Dennis:* How did you cope when you lost your parents?
>
> *Clare:* My parents were respected members of the Elim Pentecostal Church and they were serenely positive about their own departure, but I cannot accept it all. Religion has no meaning for me … My parents were staunch believers, but my brother and I stopped going when we were older.

Dennis: Do you envy your parents in any way?
Clare: I envy their certainty about things, about life beyond, but I
         don't think you can will yourself to believe, can you? I dread
         the day I get old. I cannot even think about my end – *to think
         one day I will not be here* [*heavy sigh*]. Can we get off the subject?

Joyto requested counselling shortly after immigrating from Delhi because
she was off work with depression. At the point of reaching 39, she felt her
children had less need of her and her business partners were considering
selling up. But what had led to her depression was her mother's 'untimely
death', not that she grieved over the loss but more that an opportunity had
slipped away to vent her extreme anger. Much has been written about the
pros and cons of cathartic expression and opinion is in no way settled (BACP
represented the debate in 2004). My judgment is to allow the client to decide
whether healing will come from discharging tension by 'clearing the air'
with 'powerful figures' (like parents), or from encouraging a forgiving spirit
to move on (Boorstein, 1996; Richards and Bergin, 1997).

Joyto: I pleaded with my mother not to enforce the marriage in
         India, but father was insistent. I knew it wouldn't work right
         from the wedding. My husband refused me contraception.
         My parents then moved to England to remove themselves
         from our faltering marriage – she was in denial ... She's
         robbed me of an opportunity to tell her what a terrible mar-
         riage she'd planned. I can't go on till this burden has gone.
Dennis: What is this burden you have to lose?
Joyto: I wasn't prepared by my parents for the 'outside cruel world',
         and was used as a sex-object by my husband. I didn't like him
         the moment we met. He was brutal ... He raped me. I insisted
         on an abortion ... was treated like crap.
Dennis: Like crap – like discarded faeces? [*Joyto sobbed – the image
         amplified her denigration*]
Joyto: ... Brothers said I should put up with it, mother ... [*pause and
         sobbing*] ... my mother ... she just turned her back ... as if to
         say ..., 'Just bloody well get on with it!'
Dennis: How does 'Just bloody well get on with it' feel? [*Joyto cries for
         a while and I took her hand*] ....
Joyto: When baby brother was born I pushed him away from lying
         next to mum. She never wanted me ... marriage was done for
         spite. I'm desperate to tell her what she's done to me ... to
         have her sanction the divorce. I was brought up to believe in
         reincarnation and the transmigration of the soul; now, I'm not
         so sure. I *have* to speak to her and have it out. Do you think
         that's possible? Can we communicate with those beyond?

An invitation is given by the client, as before, to expose my beliefs; this
time by enquiring into the Big Questions of the unknown. Pause for a

moment before reading on and reflect on what you would do, asking the question of what rationale informs your decision.

Many elderly clients, particularly those with terminal conditions or with an irrational dread of their own mortality, may enquire into their therapist's views of an afterlife, perceiving them as experts on everything. The counsellor from an approach that discourages self-disclosure, or which views it as counterproductive to personal awareness, will be left feeling impotent and unhelpful. There will be a discomforting feeling for deliberately not responding to a client's wish, of putting theoretical purism before caring, and of coming over as disinterested. Each therapist will need to reflect on such matters because spiritually-centred counselling requires the sharing of experience as a positive attribute, as we shall see throughout this book.

Conclusions

In light of our discussion to this point, it seems more appropriate to say that in certain situations and during particular periods of conscious life we either feel spiritual, or feel no sense of the spiritual at all, by which, I mean that we live by routine and commonplace patterns of thinking, feeling and behaviour with no reaching above and beyond; no search within and no guidance from transpersonal influences outside of Self. This chapter has asked the principal question that is imperative of all counselling and psychotherapy, which is, 'what do clients want from therapy?' The judgment is not so simple for some who may not know. Essentially, I have suggested that counselling practitioners might consider cases where their clients have disclosed particular needs which stem from unresolved or emerging spiritual needs. Indications for spiritual therapy have been illustrated through a range of clients, from pre-pubescent children to adults of post mid-life.

Spiritually-centred counselling is indicated for young people who have *paranormal experiences* of encountering ghosts and spiritual beings, and who may feel a need to normalise their experience with one they can trust. Some youngsters when *bereaved* of a close family member are left devastated, but unexpected loss does not always leave the bereaved permanently distraught, in spite of signs to the contrary. Loss prompts clients to search within their personal resources for new ways of adapting and living. Adolescents may draw upon spiritual resources of their person to *overcome obstacles in relationships*. Clients of all ages may need to *discover their inner-Self* when coming to terms with loss and worry in order to move on in their lives. A further indication for spiritually-centred counselling is where clients have *grown out of a need for religion* and where there is need to face the world with confidence and authenticity. Spiritual therapy is particularly appropriate when assisting clients to *search for meaning* when established roles and identities no longer have relevance or significance. Clearly, clients *confronting non-being*, whether coming to terms with terminal conditions, or contemplating their own mortality when near ones pass off the scene, will be assisted if the therapist has the skill and inclination to engage with them within the existential depths of human despair.

5

The Spiritually-centred Counsellor

Knowing others is intelligence; knowing yourself is true wisdom.
Mastering others is strength; mastering yourself is true power. If
you realize that you have enough, you are truly rich.

Lao-Tzu

What are the particular characteristics required of the therapist to move
into spiritually-centred counselling? This chapter addresses this question and opens with a discussion of the theoretical and practical implications when creating a healing relationship. I explain how spiritual
therapy differs from humanistic and pastoral work by presenting analogous guides for Self-discovery. The particular counsellor styles are a
question of how the therapist aligns himself with his client, how he
views his role and to what he likens spiritual therapy. Through some
casework, I hope to illustrate my work and invite counsellors from a
range of backgrounds and orientations to adopt the mode of spiritual-
orientation within their work.

All styles and approaches of counselling and psychotherapy require
suitable supervision to evaluate efficacy and to safeguard the interests of
clients, and spiritual therapy is no exception. In spiritually-centred therapy, however, developing an internal-supervisor as an ongoing requirement is imperative. The spiritual counsellor who is regularly in tune with
his client's presentations and deliberations will cultivate an internal dialogue as issues arise over how the material is affecting him, and how, in
turn, his own responses are affecting his client.

Unlike many therapeutic approaches which discourage the sharing of
personal material and self-disclosure, spiritual-oriented work requires the
giving of Self, since both parties are aiming to grow from collaborative
work. Inevitably, issues of congruence, transference and countertransference will be crucial, albeit in need of modification if neutrality in status is
required.

Spiritually-centred Therapists

It may be helpful at the outset to describe the distinctive character of the spiritually-centred therapist since some practitioners engaged in humanistic and pastoral therapy may view what has been demonstrated so far as being illustrative of their own work and approach, which may not be viewed as being essentially spiritual. Various contributors in Boorstein (1996) similarly felt the need to draw parallels and distinctions between traditional and transpersonal therapy, and in what follows I draw further from their work.

Counselling in the pastoral context, as articulated by Lyall (1995), works principally within the particular 'household of faith' and is therefore restrictive and, in my view, not in line with pluralistic understanding. Religious counsellors engaging with clients within the same faith tradition address similar topics as non-religious therapists, but when religious topics arise there will be a tendency to encourage the person to live out their calling rather than reflect on the validity of their personal beliefs. Our task, therefore, is to consider spiritually-centred counselling in a broader context.

Summarising our discussion to this point, I think the following propositions may make the distinctive character of the spiritually-centred therapist a little clearer:

- Whilst constructing general working definitions of religion and spirituality, there can be such an overlap in the way these terms are understood and used that we cannot judge what is specific to the experience underlying each term in an absolute sense.
- Religion and spirituality have historically been evident in a sense of *transcendence*, *immanence* and *relationship* according to their cultural manifestations, often creating an ethic of parochialism, tribalism and community, or a sense of connectedness with the sacred, the natural world or the cosmos.
- Of the two terms, spirituality rather than religion has become more pluralistic and fitting for secularism. Current (perhaps pejorative) discourses, such as 'the decline of religion' and 'the spiritual revolution', underlie preference for spirituality. An anthropological/history of religions perspective suggests that people have held beliefs in a spirit world long before becoming conformed to organised religious practice.
- Religious and spiritual people recognise the place and importance of the sacred or the numinous – whether through holy objects, shrines or divine theophanies.
- The *spiritual Self* is understood loosely as that intuitive, inner-sense of being that relates to the numinous, but it is unlikely that we shall be able to identify specifically the spiritual ingredient within human makeup that is distinguishable from the emotional, cognitive and behavioural aspects of the person. In a similar (but different) sense, 'the psychological' may not be separable from the emotional and cognitive – in the interests of holism we may only have recourse to understand the spiritual nature of human beings through metaphor and symbol.

Regarding the last proposition, Gergen (1999: 107–12) has illustrated that 'emotions are culturally constituted' since the evidence points to wide variations across cultures. Is an emotion a possession of mind or a public performance specific to a culture? Whilst we may agree on the commonality of the emotion of love, or loving feelings, when love ends and anger begins at what point are the two distinguishable from each other? Further, where does the loving feeling end and the loving thought or loving behaviour begin?

Spiritually-oriented counsellors can be identified as practitioners working within the science of transpersonal psychology who feel confident and competent to work upon issues of religion and spirituality broadly conceived. They recognise the various dimensions of religion and spirituality and are not perturbed that spiritual aspects of the person are not reducible or contained within conventional psychological constructs. They are quite at home in working with metaphor and symbol, supra-psychology and the transpersonal. Spiritually-inclined therapists recognise and venerate the numinous within human experience and functioning, being neither embarrassed by non-empirical discourse nor afraid to share similar accounts of their own with their clients (Boorstein, 1996: 183).

Apart from Brian Thorne's (2002) recent call for counsellors to reconsider the mystical within person-centred theory and practice, humanistic therapists generally do not give public credence to the numinous in the manner of Jungian analysts or transpersonal psychotherapists. The spiritual within the humanistic tradition is translated to human spirit, which may be conceived as sporting prowess and human accomplishment, artistic expression, aesthetic creativity or extraordinary feats of heroism and endurance against the odds. Thus, human spirit is an essential *life-force* that vitalises human existence (Swinton, 2001). Whilst recognising this as a valid understanding of spirituality, the spiritual counsellor broadens the scope to include transcendent mystery, the numinous, inexplicable phenomena and the nature of consciousness (Wilber, 2000). A further extract of engagement with Sam illustrates the comfortable ease when conversing on the supra-psychological level of mystical consciousness.

Dennis: Have you ever met anybody you would regard as being mystical?

Sam: I don't now meet anybody who even talks at an interesting level about any of this stuff, and I'm not sure I would meet them in the Church either.

Dennis: Is there anything you find attractive about mysticism generally?

Sam: I suppose what you're saying is otherworldliness. Here's an example, everybody is living their lives and it's all going along, and then with the Tsunami disaster there is a groundswell, an occurrence somewhere else that impacts upon those people's lives. And you could say that empirically there has been a great earthquake, but in the scheme of things other things happened because of that. I sometimes think that these things happened in order to bring a greater good, or in order to give us an opportunity to battle, or demonstrate our worth. Now that's all tosh, and I appreciate that, but I like it like that because I couldn't just bear to live in a world where we were just …, it's a bit like, have you seen the film *Ants*? Right, OK, at the beginning he's struggling with the meaning of life, and all of that, and at the end he's still down in that little ant hole by the bin [*Sam and I laugh*] – but there's New York! …

Dennis: Yes. The wave was incredible in bringing about a universal effect of goodness … When the wave challenges people and we see graphically the tragedy and loss, particularly through the human stories of mothers not able to hold onto their babies and having to let them go, and all the guilt that that will invoke, and so on, there seems to be some kind of universal compassion released. It was a bit like Princess Diana, as well. Some things touch us universally.

Sam: Well that thing with Princess Diana was incomprehensible to me. I can see what you're saying though; nobody would have predicted that in Diana's case.

Dennis: I pulled a muscle in my shoulder and went to school, and two people I spoke with had had the same experience. Uncanny! Jung talked about a phenomenon he termed synchronicity, as though there are similar things that mirror an archetype …

Sam: Yeah, that draws one thing to another.

Dennis: I can't give meaning to such coincidences, but …

Sam: No, you can't predict them either, can you?

Dennis: It's as though there are some experiences that seem to hit people simultaneously in different parts of the world with no obvious connection.

Sam: Yeah.

When writing the last chapter in *Brief Counselling in Schools* (Lines, 2006), 'Life Meaning and Spiritual Emptiness', I was conscious of composing a working style that was anything but brief and pragmatic, and one reviewer commented on this positively. In that work, I outlined five therapeutic assumptions that guide my work, and these I restate below because I have not had course to move very far from them:

- I assume that all people have a capacity to be spiritual and to think spiritually, just as they can be emotional in their being and can function emotionally, that spiritual growth is a universal phenomenon (Hay, 1982; Lines, 2000; 2002).
- I assume that brief work can be conducted by showing clients signposts for spiritual thinking, by suggesting possibilities for experiencing and for exploring pluralistic accounts of life from spiritual perspectives.

- I assume that the process of spiritual awakening occurs through Anderson and Goolishian's (1988) conversation metaphor. Life meaning for two people constantly develops through the interchange of ideas that are expressed in an explorative manner. It is not merely the information sharing that gives meaning, but through the conversation meanings are created from how various nuances are selected and worked upon.
- I assume that in order for effective spiritually-inclined therapy to take place, the counsellor must take the one-down stance and engage in dialogue, not as expert but as collaborative fellow-seeker (Gergen, 1999).
- I assume that the process of client self-discovery is enhanced when counsellors begin to disclose material about their own uncertainties (Mearns and Cooper, 2005). There is no hiding behind masks and no pretence of knowing all the answers. Spiritual counsellors in search of their own life meanings will bring their unresolved questions to the surface with clients, along with personal paradoxes and inconsistencies in thought, since both parties are engaged on a pilgrimage of self-growth.

Figures of Comparison in Client Alignment

Working under these assumptions, I see the spiritually-oriented counsellor as adapting a style to the particular situation as need arises to become as if a fellow traveller, a spiritual master, a collaborative mini-philosopher, an intuitive enabler, and a spiritual narrative therapist.

Fellow Traveller

Many of us enjoy strolling through the countryside on hot sunny days amongst friends under no pressure of time. The spiritually-inclined therapist takes up a pose of psychological equivalence. Sometimes we take ordinance survey maps as a guide when trekking across unfamiliar terrain to find a particular location – I recall trudging through peat bogs on the Pennine Way, in mist with only a compass and map as guide, and of enjoying a pint when reaching the pub. Children relish free play and exploration, particularly by getting lost and found within a safe boundary. We understand how they experience their world and social relationships through games. So, it would seem that whether young or old there is something archetypal about exploring unknown territory, especially with friends and companions.

Whilst some individuals prefer to be alone and to travel the world with nothing but a backpack, moments of human connectivity can occur on spiritual retreats in group fellowship where individuals are considering the Big Life Questions of human existence. I was not envious of Ellen MacArthur sailing around the Capes in 71 days, or of Steve Fossett's world flight in 67 hours, largely because they *travelled alone*, but when Ewan McGregor and Charley Boorman (2004) crossed continents on a motorbike, *together,* that for me would be magic. Apart from companionship, they met such interesting people – a Mongolian herdsman so impressed McGregor that he gave him his binoculars to magnify the mountains: 'I want you to have them; you'll make better use of them than I ever will' (2004: 202). And when meeting the people of Kazakhstan, he said, 'I feel I belong here, on my bike, in the here and now'.

As fellow traveller, the therapist aligns himself with his client on life's journey. I was struggling to find a metaphor that might lift Sam from her sense of boredom, fittingly expressed as being caught up in a gerbil wheel – I suspect most have watched the gerbil frantically in a spin but getting nowhere. She needed the stimulation of *being with* reflective people of the same quality thinking as herself:

> *Sam:*   If you ask, 'Where are you now?' There is a momentum given to what you do by being on the gerbil wheel. So, work gives you positional power, gives you ego operation, a sense of place; it gives you lunches and breaks; it gives you a reason to go out.
>
> *Dennis:* And it gives you an opportunity not to reflect?
>
> *Sam:*   Yea. It also has a momentum so when you're on that wheel it goes fast, it goes slow, but it's still going. When you stop, like this and look all around you're just bewildered.
>
> *Dennis:* Would you regard yourself now as being within a forest?
>
> *Sam:*   I don't know about the metaphor really. Where I am at the moment is that I have a choice: I can engage on a superficial level, on a transactional level, with people if I will initiate that engagement. If I don't initiate it, I don't see anybody from one weekend to the next. So, I suppose you'd say that I'm lonely … So, no, there's no intimacy with people who may enquire inside my head; there isn't any more. So, I wouldn't say it's a forest because a forest implies a dark, gloomy place, overhung, and all of that.
>
> *Dennis:* Forests are amongst beautiful surroundings, though; often with no path; there's just …
>
> *Sam:*   You?

I had failed to connect with Sam's sense of aloneness resulting from refusing the wheel of work-engagement. By offering a metaphor that suggested for me peace and tranquillity, I had missed the point of her dilemma of disengagement, and Sam was quick to draw my attention to it. The therapeutic engagement offered an opportunity for companionship on the journey, but, as David Mearns (Mearns and Cooper, 2005) illustrates in therapy with Dominic, clients rescue their therapists when uncertainties and vulnerabilities are exposed. Sam's gerbil wheel was her symbol of engagement, 'warts and all', whilst my metaphor of forest suggested for her gloom and darkness. Sam's ambivalence was over the extra packing she would have to carry by re-entering the gerbil wheel. In spite of losing direction with my misapplied metaphor, the spiritually-centred discourse gave us both a brief period of companionship to continue searching for new senses of relational being, since I too am travelling a journey of altering terrain.

Spiritual Master

Therapy as *co-construction* weakens the binary notion of expert/novice, the typical model of isolating 'the problem' to 'be corrected' and the contention that the task is to 'lead the way of knowledge' (Gergen, 1999: 170), a paradigm which is as applicable to science as to religion. Prophetic visions have been *the authorisation* of religious initiates – seers, prophets, priests and priestesses, wandering sadhus, gurus and aboriginal shamans. They are recorded in all scriptures:

- monotheistic faiths – the Torah, the New Testament and the Qur'an
- polytheistic religion – Bha-gavad Gita
- naturism – Eight-fold Path, African and North American folk lore

Elijah, Amos and Hosea spoke under the influence of the Spirit of God and saw visions that for them were authoritative (Lines, 1995b), as indeed did Mohammed when speaking with Gabriel, and the Buddha under the tree. Mystical auditions authorised the prophet in ancient times, and there are some secular claimants and fundamentalist initiates who profess to speak under divine inspiration even today (in spite of there being no guaranteed means of authentication). Some clients appear to need a counsellor or psychotherapist who speaks with the authority of a spiritual master.

In Indian tradition, a guru had a significant role as a holy teacher bringing persons into union with God, and wandering sadhus have a prominent role as spiritual masters. They follow Vishnu (the preserver) or Shiva (the destroyer–rejuvenator) by renouncing their worldly life and material possessions to live a celibate life. They have a distinctive, half-naked appearance, wearing orange turbans and being covered with ashes. They smoke hash mixed with tobacco in clay pipes and enter intoxicated dreamy, non-rational states of consciousness – in this respect resembling North Americans drinking peyote mixtures, or Rastafarians smoking marijuana. As a rite of passage, youths are attached to a wandering sadhu and leave the family home for the wilderness on an inward journey. It is common for adolescent boys to look for a secular counterpart of the spiritual master as a right of passage (Biddulph, 1998), and effective youth counselling is inadvertently reinforcing attachment principles (Lines, 2006).

There has occurred considerable interest amongst celebrities to live amongst communities with sadhus and shamans as spiritual masters. They appear to have a New Age quest for inner-wisdom that is perceived only to be gained through initiation rites and altered states of consciousness.

Apart from early psychoanalytic practice (where hypnosis formed an essential part of practice), and various strands of transpersonal psychotherapy (Tart, 1996), altered states of consciousness do not figure largely in therapeutic practice.

West (2000, 2004) draws close parallels between shamanism and psychotherapy that are worth considering (Ellenberger, 1970; Strupp, 1972). The shamans of aboriginal societies are traditional healers, and the link is made by West because modern psychotherapy (neo-shamanism) has many similarities, including the common experience of a creative or initiatory illness prior to taking up an existentialist role of healing. To establish the point, West traces the biographies of key psychotherapists, Freud, Reich, Jung, Horney and Rogers.

Readers of West may or may not agree that an initiatory illness, as featured in the lives of the distinguished figures above, is the common antecedent of taking up the office of counselling, but for me it sets a worrying precedent similar to that occurring in Evangelical Christian groups where there is a possibility of feeling inferior for not having tangible evidence of receiving the Spirit. I would further add that my spinal injury in mid-life (Lines, 1995a), which required social adjustment, was not judged by me to be a signal to commit myself to counsellor training.

Collaborative Mini-philosopher

The shift from expertise to collaboration is the preferred style (Gergen, 2001) since the latter opens up the possibility of a broader expanse of meaning-making through joint interpretations rather than through predetermined theory (Anderson, 1997). The case for the spiritual counsellor to be a collaborative mini-philosopher has been argued elsewhere (Lines, 2002), and the first chapter was written to keep you abreast of some of the major issues that have informed the modern philosophical and religious outlook (Howard, 2000). It seems to me that the spiritual counsellor should have a genuine interest in philosophy, religion and particularly spirituality on a broad front. I consider he should be committed to a tolerant position of open-ended enquiry about divine dealings with humankind through multifarious traditions, some of which may not be ostensibly religious (Lines, 2002). The counsellor is not likely to be a philosopher of religion, since few psychology training courses cover spiritual issues (Lannert 1991; Lukoff et al., 1998; West, 2000), yet there are many problems brought to counselling that have spiritual elements and themes that require a therapist who is well versed in such matters.

This is not to imply that spiritually-oriented therapy is merely a cerebral activity of two philosophers engaging in platonic dialogue. It is not concerned with deductive logic or coherent reasoning, but is primarily interested in existential questions of life meaning and human destiny, the sort of questions that have occupied the religious as much as the philosophical mind. Rational emotive behavioural therapy (Ellis, 1962) and cognitive therapy (Beck, 1976) utilise Socratic questioning as a means of modifying irrational beliefs for their clients to function more productively, but spiritually-centred counselling is less language-dependent and more concerned with an inner-world experience as influenced by feeling as by cognition.

Religion has bad press in the secular age, which is unfortunate, particularly the position of Islam in the light of recent events, and this topic became important to Ibn:

Dennis: What do you feel about some of the criticism that has been levelled against Islam, particularly since the bombing of the trade towers and the war in Iraq?

Ibn: Well, this gives an opportunity for non-Muslims to criticise not those Muslims but Islam, which is the wrong way of doing it. They should be criticising those Muslims, or so-called Muslims, but I don't think there is any criticism of Islam that is justified.

Dennis: Does criticism of Islam disappoint you?

Ibn: Oh yes. I don't feel that they understand what they are doing. Somebody who is a proper Muslim should be living his life in submission to the will of God.

The political dimensions of religious conviction become important issues for clients in the light of current events, and the spiritually-oriented therapist must not dodge this difficult terrain if this is what emerges in session. Spirituality is not so nearly tainted in the modern psyche. Whether we ask the Big Life Questions in the name of religion or spirituality matters little so long as clients have an opportunity with their therapists to enter such dialogue. Along with Jungian analysis, spiritual work 'amplifies ideas and raises questions rather than reducing concepts to final answers' (Brookes, 1996: 76).

The Big Life Questions may appear overly philosophical and peripheral for those seeking fulfilment in deeper inter-personal relations – in such cases their inner-spiritual depths may be more efficaciously reached within the experiential group dynamic, such as psychodrama or Gestalt group therapy – but for others who reach for meaning beyond the transitory, in-depth spiritually-centred counselling may be indicated.

The credo, *the just shall live by trust* is a vestige that has merit, and is the framework within which deep questions are asked in the new spiritual paradigm (Lines, 2002). Religion devalued this by applying it to the blind acceptance of articles of faith, rather than prescribing it as the stance of committing oneself to the great unknown. I asked Tony Big Life Questions about a final judgment and existence beyond mortal life:

Tony: I tend to think there won't be a judgment, daft as it may sound. I've really put it out of my mind, to be honest. I was brought up to believe in a judgment and the fires of hell etc., but my instinct tells me everything will be OK. God is bigger than conditioned responses ...

Dennis: Do you think there is a life hereafter?

Tony: I don't ponder that, probably because it's too difficult to ponder really, but I think I have a sense of trust that things will be all right, not obviously all the time, but I do have a sense of trust, and that I'm looked after and things will be OK. Now, where that comes from is also very interesting, but I think it's quite real.

Intuitive Enabler

There is considerable mistrust and scepticism of unbridled intuition by secular-minded empiricists. This is due to the fact that it is a human trait largely beyond verification and objective measurement. Nevertheless, intuition represents an authoritative discourse for many today, particularly those who attest to the validity of their 'gut reaction' having a positive outcome – *call it a woman's intuition, if you like.*

Whilst many recognise this inner judgment as commonplace, some initiates have induced intuitive judgments by use of sacred symbols (*Urim* and *Thummim* stones of the Jewish high priest's breastplate) or through intoxicated states (sadhu and shaman). Although Paul attempted to regulate Spirit gift exuberance in the early churches, *glossolalia* (speaking in tongues) was a regular feature of communicating within a divine realm. These semi-trance states of ecstasy had the effect of loosening guttural control to conform to communal, imitative worship (Lines, 1995b). Social anthropologist, Bruce Parry, achieved an intuitive state of inner-self examination amongst the Babongo people after pricking his tongue and chewing roots of a local plant. He hallucinated and experienced visions which were claimed by villagers to stem from the realms of the dead. He experienced a three-day trip of altered consciousness, which had the effect of seeing different orders of reality (similar to LSD in the 1960s) and of stimulating a purging of past mistakes (BBC, 24 January 2005).

Carl Jung spoke of a common phenomenon called *synchronicity*, or meaningful coincidence (Jung, 1952), mysterious happenings or waves of thought that mirror archetypal patterns of the collective unconscious. Whether or not this is accepted it does seem intriguing and thought provoking that coincidental events take place, as I discussed with Sam in an earlier extract, and such events occur irrespective of time, culture and place.

West (2004) cautions against a too elaborate attention to paranormal phenomena, but transpersonal psychotherapists are more ambitious (Boorstein, 1996). Within these differing authorities, perhaps a question of balance seems sensible. 'There are instincts which respond to all the chance meetings in life', wrote Hugo (1980) when shaping his narrative of Jean Valjean's encounter with Cosette. Chance meetings are mysterious phenomena to which I can relate, and which I regularly find my clients speaking of. Such providential encounters are significant matches with others which conform to a principle of *need* meeting *provision* in a mutually complementary sense. There are risks of abuse here, of therapists exploiting vulnerabilities of their clients in power games, but equally there are risks of therapists having their ears closed to their client's intuitive promptings of spirituality.

Pierre Teilhard de Chardin wrote a series of books (1955, 1957) to illustrate the emergence of consciousness (*noosphere*) within the evolutionary record, and Wilber (1998, 2001a) has developed the notion with a model that traces the evolution of Spirit from egocentrism to transpersonal consciousness. De Chardin was not a pantheist in seeing God *as* everything in the natural world, but as a mystical Catholic priest he combined the two realities of empirical science and mystical theology, by seeing God *in* everything. The idea of God being immanent, as the Spirit within the natural universe, recalls the popular lyrics of songwriters like John Denver and poets like Wordsworth and Keats.

Eastern religion, Zen and Chinese philosophical systems of thought, have recognised Spirit in the natural world, as an existential reality which is as convincing as the empirical reality of recent western thinking. Taoism and Zen serve as two examples of intuitive Spirit with no propositional content:

He who knows others is learned. He who knows himself is wise.

The way to do is to be … To know you have enough is to be rich.

Do not conquer the world with force, for force only causes resistance. Thorns spring up when an army passes. Years of misery follow a great victory. Do only what needs to be done without using violence.

When spring comes the grass grows by itself.

> Sayings from *Tao Te Ching* (Lao Tzu, 1997)

The *Tao* has obvious parallels with other religious and philosophical terms (*Logos* in Hellenised Greek thought, *Wisdom* in Jewish writings, *The Way* in Christianity). The fundamental assertion of Taoist philosophy is that there is an important reality, prior to heaven and earth, and this reality is *Tao*. The *Tao's* image is female, and there is no clear answer to what gave rise to the universe, apart from Chapter 42 where it is said: '*Tao* gave birth to the One; the One gave birth successively to two things, three things, up to ten thousand.'

Most Zen teachings derive from a monastic tradition far removed from the everyday world of the twenty-first century, a world where monks dress in black robes with shaven heads and where they still engage in regular sitting and traditional monastic ritual. They live an austere existence of spirituality. Zen has become popular in the West, however, but in a more secular and pragmatic form of philosophy. Popular writers (Tolle, 2001) and teachers (Joko Beck, 1997) have applied Zen in everyday western settings, and, as Gergen (1999: 236) says 'we are encouraged to ask about the positive implications of the concept of no mind, and its associated practices.'

Most counsellors and psychotherapists would not go to such extremes of inducement, but would claim, nevertheless, an intuitive skill to read their client's inner-world. In the next two chapters, *Spirit in life* is considered a reality discourse for clients by demythologising the somewhat personalised Holy Spirit of New Testament teaching, and by re-viewing the world of human experience through a lens of *believing is seeing*.

Spiritual Narrative Therapist

There are two significant features of narrative therapy that are appealing to the integrative therapist who wishes to engage in spiritually-centred counselling. First, there is recognition that we define ourselves and our lives through stories. Our client's stories occupy the major part of counselling discourse. In addition, there are cultural narratives that have an overarching influence on self-understanding. Religious traditions, as we shall see in Chapter 6, are reinforced through stories and grand narratives. Secondly, the typical style of the narrative therapist, as Payne (2000) illustrates, is of a yearning to learn more and more of the client's world through repetitive questions along the lines of 'Can you tell me a little more about that?', and from an initial position of complete ignorance: how can we really know the world of another?

> Stories can invite *fuller audience engagement* than abstract ideas. In hearing stories we generate images, thrive on the drama, suffer and celebrate with the speaker. Finally, the personal story tends to *generate acceptance* as opposed to resistance. If it is 'your story, your experience' then I can scarcely say 'you are wrong'. (Gergen, 1999: 158–9)

Through spiritually-centred counselling, questions are aimed at assisting clients to realise who they are, at reaching that inner intuitive Self:

- I wonder what spiritual experiences seem to resonate with your being?
- Did you feel at home with the religion of your youth?
- How do you feel your formative religious and spiritual experiences have informed the type of person you are?
- Can you tell me a little more about why you felt at one in that place?
- How do you spiritually differ from members of your family?
- What are you doing when you are completely in-tune with who you are?

When attempting to help clients to transcend their normal boundaries of existence, a different range of questions is asked. The miracle question, as employed in solution-focused therapy and other integrative styles, is a good example:

- Suppose you woke one morning and a miracle had occurred, and the world was different. Everything was happening in just the way you wanted it to. What would be happening? What would you be doing that you are not doing now? What would you be thinking? How would you be feeling different?
- What has to happen for you to be the sort of person you want to be?
- Can you describe what needs to change to become your dream Self?
- Are there occasions when you have felt uplifted to a different plane of reality?
- What do you consider the ultimate level of your capability? Now tell me what gets in the way of you reaching higher? What agency of support could assist you to transcend your natural potential?

Spiritually-oriented therapy aids the person to reframe nihilistic dreads with modified or re-authored narratives (Epston et al., 1992; White and Epston, 1990) or through discourse to create new meaning through metaphors and repertoires of well-utilised narratives that describe the way things are (McNamee and Gergen, 1992). Mythological stories and symbols form a constellation of our own archetypal energies and give clients a deeper awareness of their inner world (Jung, 1978 [1964], 1969).

With the biblical myths, the essential power lies in translating their messages in everyday living, for example, the Creation story teaches of a divine Being bringing order out of chaos; the Son of God exorcising the demons figures the return to sanity of those overwhelmed with ill-fortune; and the empty tomb figures the divine Spirit superintending the natural world. Life, according to the new paradigm, recognises the creative Spirit; it is not a mere struggle to survive, a shallow sex drive to propagate the species, nor is it a return to superstition or euphoric detachment, but it is a spiritual journey through and within life (Lines, 2002).

An unfortunate aspect of religious orthodoxy has been a tendency to stifle the Spirit of intuitive reasoning and creativity. For those clients stuck in their religious ideologies and practices, the spiritually-inclined therapist will encourage them to reinterpret phenomena through new stories of who they are in order to free them from 'dominating grand narratives' which tell them how they should be.

Dennis: Can you describe what needs to change to become your dream Self?

Rachel: My problem is I can't surrender this 'dutiful daughter' bit even though I know it's ridiculous and out of fashion. I'm not a feminist, but why I should run around after my manager when he irritates me and deserves no respect, I cannot imagine?

Dennis: It's funny how these grand narratives have such power over us. I was brought up within a household that valued industry and hard work, and, although my father never read anything but newspapers, he was so influenced by the Protestant Work Ethic, and certainly so drilled it deep within my unconscious, that I still at the liberated age of fifty eight feel guilty if I sit for too long and relax, doing nothing.

The Internal Supervisor of the Therapist

Supervision is a requirement of all counselling models in line with the BACP *Ethical Framework for Good Practice in Counselling and Psychotherapy* (2002). In addition, most therapists, I hope, reflect long and often about their counselling interventions, strategies and inner motivations. But when does spirituality become a serious consideration in supervision? David Lyall (1995: 69) presents helpful suggestions on the organisation and planning of supervision, and West (2004) offers useful tips and guidance on supervisor selection in terms of spiritual sensitivity, but in what follows I draw attention to the need for each spiritually-oriented therapist to develop his own internal supervision.

Customarily, counsellors will record sessions of their work and bring a tape for analysis to their supervisor. Student counsellors commonly have an assignment on therapy analysis for their tutor to assess. I regularly find recorded sessions of my own work illuminating, in that replaying the session over and over again reveals different insights and meanings of my clients' deliberations and of the suitability (or unsuitability) of my interventions. Discourse analysis is a developed science with a range of sophisticated tools and methodologies designed to interpret inflexion and pausing and the structure of spoken discourse. Over-analysis, however, can distort meaning by moving the discourse further away from the subject. I find the narrative begins to develop new life and meaning as I unconsciously interject meaning that may be foreign to what is said, and the writing of transcripts can further extend the distance from intended meaning. In spite of these reservations, listening to one's practice is a useful exercise in developing technique in internal supervision.

Gordon Lynch (2002) is keen for pastoral counsellors to evaluate their values through techniques of Inter-Personal Process Recall (Kagan, 1990), by watching or listening to recorded conversation in order to 're-live' the conversation and ask what the practitioner was thinking and feeling at certain points. He calls this 'Theories-in-use' and believes that values assessment through internal dialogue is an essential characteristic of the spiritual counsellor. David Mearns (Mearns and Cooper, 2005) commends the same.

I illustrate this through my therapeutic involvement with Jim, a 13-year-old client who, as counselling came to a close, became a loyal supporter of me in my disability. The case vignette illustrates the inner questioning state of reflection, which, in this case, had to take account of professional boundaries, therapeutic roles, child protection, legal accountability within the counselling setting, and the risks of power-positioning in and out of therapy.

Internal Supervision with Jim

Jim was referred for counselling by his father and his Head of Year for a series of fights in school during his second year in secondary school. He was regarded by teachers as a boy of above average intelligence and as a person with a lively sense of humour. His major difficulties stemmed from considerable environmental influences. The counselling was going along quite well since Jim was committed to explore how he might avoid being excluded as had happened with his older brother. We were working collaboratively using the Egan three-stage model in brief therapy (Lines, 2006), but then a feeling of *presence* (Thorne, 2002) occurred that indicated a need to divert from the main programme and to attend to something much deeper and more intuitive. It indicated, indeed, a requirement for spiritually-oriented therapy.

We were discussing an apparent discrepancy, often observed by me and by others close to Jim, that there seemed to be a tension between two poles of his character. In one sense, there were clear indications that he was a sensitive boy with genuine altruistic tendencies, and in another there were other indications of a need to develop a self-concept to survive in his social world by becoming violent and aggressive, almost to live up to the expectations of his older brother and father. Circumstantially, his mother could recall a time when Jim was threatened and manipulated by much more powerful boys to the extent that he would often run home crying, and yet the dread of appearing weak and inadequate amidst a family of strong and dominant male role-models who were feared and renowned as people one does not mess about with was more than he could take. The question before us, then, revolved around two beliefs of Self emergence: an innate Self, or a socially constructed Self? Certainly, there was sufficient evidence for both theories of Self to appear plausible if not correct. Does spiritual therapy work to reveal Jim's innate Self from that adapted to survive his current social situation (Being psychology), or to create a new, pro-social Self for future economic independence and personal happiness (constructionist)? The question before Jim and me was how to give voice to two theoretical realities.

Power-positioning   One question formulating in my mind was how Jim might wish to be viewed by me, a male counsellor sitting before him – how would he want me to *see* him? Having a disability might suggest to him that my physical weakness might allow him to freely expose the sensitive side of his nature without fear that I might prejudge him as weak; that I may contain his feelings of ambiguity. However, it could not be assumed that Jim would find it easy to sit beside a counsellor, such as myself, having achieved a reputation as being mentally strong if physically disabled. My personhood presented a different model of male power, where, paradoxically, I could provide him with an opportunity to 'be himself' within a safety zone. There would be no need for pretence and façade. I felt it was not necessary for me to expose this surface contradiction between his cowardice in the past (according to his mother) and a felt need to respond to the pressure of his father's expectations of him as a feared male. Michael Toolan (1988) speaks of a tendency for young people to presuppose the required answer in the manner in which questions are framed so as to elicit a response that will curry favour from the interviewer. My question therefore required careful thought.

Daring to Risk Self

Dennis: I am wondering, Jim, what sort of person you really wish to become when you are older? [*Jim smiled and made fixed eye contact*]

Jim: I dunno; never thought about it.

Jim momentarily turned his head away in a pose of reflective thought. I kept my eyes fixed firmly on his, and he turned again to look at me and smiled.

Jim: Who helps you after school get into your car?

This response could indicate an overestimation on my part of his cognitive ability in having to answer an abstract future-oriented and highly speculative question. It could also indicate a subtle manoeuvre by him to draw me away from challenging material. The statement was incongruous to my question, and in many respects with young people this could be an interpretation that the counsellor may draw too hastily. The question in my mind was 'What lay behind this response?' Thorne (2002) rightly, in my judgment, presses person-centred counsellors moving into the spiritual sphere not to allow their theoretical principles to override the need to be a genuine, caring person; not to allow their practice to prevent them from responding as a human being before another in need. Cooper (2005), from an existentialist background, views receptivity as a reciprocal engagement, and commends therapists to 'breathe in' their clients through 'holistic listening'. Young people and adolescents, not least in a secondary school, have a desperate need to be valued and needed – was I to allow Jim to enter my personal domain?

I checked personal feelings within my professional boundaries before attending too promptly to his question.

Dennis: Sometimes kids help me after school if they just happen to be around, sometimes teachers help if they notice me making my way to the car park, and sometimes cleaners come to my assistance ...
Jim: Can I help you?

His response was immediate and unpredictable, yet natural and genuine. But what lay behind it?

Professional Boundaries and Being Human   Young people often develop sophisticated skills in interpreting body language and facial gestures – particularly with close loved ones – to supplement their inadequacy in expressing themselves through language. They often lack confidence to say what they actually feel. If they look up to someone, they will not risk miscalculating situations by ill-thought-out statements which potentially fail to convey what they genuinely feel – better say nothing than get it wrong! They are biologically predisposed to draw adults towards them in order to be loved, cared for and parented, just as adults and caring professionals are biologically predisposed to look out for and care for needy children. There is often much unconscious projection going on. In other words, Jim was not thrown for one moment by my attempt to feign a growing bond that was growing between us. He had intuitively picked this up and he was drawing me to like him, not only to his own but to my advantage as well. There was no hesitation; he saw an opening and had no reservation in asking a pointed question directly.

Next our conversation moved towards the practicalities and the necessary parental consent of Jim giving me some assistance after school. In many forms of counselling this would be judged to be inappropriate and unprofessional; it would be surmised that assisting a disabled counsellor personally would be a dangerous crossing of a professional boundary of distance between counsellor and young client. I do not feel, however, that the counsellor wishing to engage in spiritually-centred counselling in depth, in relating to the client as an encounter of relational depth (Buber, 1958; Mearns and Cooper, 2005), should need to be wholly guided by such an apparently cold professional requirement, so long as potential hazards are recognised.

Professional Boundaries and Child Protection   Obviously, in such a power differential, child protection and the need for safe caring practice is fundamental and must be held as a high priority, not least within a secondary school (Lines, 2006). In spite of child protection protocols, if the counsellor is to help a young person to understand and make contact with that innermost prompt of his being it may be necessary for the therapist to reveal his Self in a mutual exercise of love and caring.

> *Dennis:*   Jim, if you would like to help me after school I would like that very much.

Jim has responded to me not as his professional guide and therapist but as a person with whom he wants to make an emotional and spiritual attachment, and in further work we attempted to articulate that inner nature of altruism coming to form within a social context.

> *Dennis:*   Have you ever helped people like me before?
> *Jim:*   When I was younger I watched old people crossing the road, and looked at disabled people carry their shopping. I always wanted to go over and help them but my mum wouldn't always let me.
> *Dennis:*   Really?
> *Jim:*   Yeah. There's this man about two doors away from us, an old man, and he struggles a lot, but me mum lets me go and help him. His name is Jack. I do his gardening sometimes, and help him wash his car. Me mate sometimes takes the Mick, but I ain't bothered.
> *Dennis:*   I guess, Jim, this is part of your nature, who you really are. I wonder whether the need to fight and to come over as tough is just for you to survive without being put down. I wonder when you're grown up you will be 'Mr tough guy', like those around you, or be a sensitive, caring human being.

In this extract there is the emergence of a spirit of self-confidence from a lad who, according to other statements he had made in therapy, was preoccupied with self-image, as befits many teenagers of his age. Not only so, he has sufficient confidence to 'be himself' within the street of his neighbourhood. It may be, of course, that both Jim's parents would have been proud of their son and of his unselfishness in helping a needy neighbour and that such an attitude might not contradict a self-concept of being tough. Being 'hard' and not a wimp, or a 'pussy', as Jim would say, is not incompatible with a kind and generous spirit, but it would involve risks for Jim in following his natural altruistic impulse – his 'true nature'. Such behaviour towards others might be judged as being soft and 'wimpish' when there are far more masculine (*sic*) things to do like following his mates in the gang who engage in 'roughing people up' or 'nicking motorbikes to ride across the fields'.

> *Dennis:*   There are some people, Jim, who believe that the way we truly are is not the same as when we have to become someone different to survive. [*Jim looked at me puzzled*]
> *Jim:*   What d'you mean? Like what I want to be?

Dennis: Yes. A boy I fostered once had to go from me for a short time because I found him really difficult to manage. His social worker asked me to take him to a children's home. When we walked down the drive and saw the tough guys hanging out of the windows, he became a different person. I saw him become someone I didn't recognise, even though we'd lived together for four years. He said, 'Alright man. How ya doing?' He had to become tough to prepare himself to survive in that situation; he didn't have to be like that with me – in the event he didn't stay there.

Jim: I see what you mean; that's a bit like me.

Self-disclosure   How could the difference be explained between the innate-Self and the Self-concept for a 13-year-old lad? What sense could he make of the social and emotional impulses of his development whilst undergoing the process of puberty and role confusion (Erikson, 1968)? I decided upon a response of self-disclosure (Cooper, 2005), and shared with him something of my past, when I felt vulnerable and inadequate as a foster parent. Self-disclosure, again, is considered a violation of appropriate boundaries and is frowned upon in many schools of psychotherapy and counselling.

Traditional psychoanalytic models encourage therapists to minimise their affective involvement, to offer themselves as blank projection screens, and to put aside their own material, life experiences and personal growth for the benefit of the client. The transpersonal orientation offers another perspective: the therapist may serve the client best by viewing the therapeutic relationship as karma yoga to foster his own transpersonal growth through consciously serving the client, similar to the Christian concept of self-giving (Walsh and Vaughan, 1996).

The therapist models an openness and willingness to view therapy as a process of learning through service. Boorstein (1996: 183) discusses his personal dilemma of a felt need to self-disclose within transpersonal psychotherapy that is in tension with his former psychoanalytic training of self-disclosure which is believed to distort the transference relationship. Since ego transcendence, rather than consolidation, is the ultimate aim, he believed it necessary to identify himself with people and life in general. The humanistic-existential model, however, has emphasised the importance of participation by therapists in all their humanity in the therapeutic relationship, opening themselves fully to the client's and their own reactions (Thorne, 2002; Cooper, 2005).

Dennis: When I was about your age I fell out with my mates because they were getting involved with things I didn't want to get involved with. I started helping this teacher after school run a table tennis club, and I discovered within myself that I really liked working with young people more than being with my mates. And I suppose my life has been totally taken up with young people, from youth clubs to running a children's home, to becoming a teacher and finally a youth counsellor.

Jim: I see what you mean. It's like me but with old and disabled people.

Dennis: Oh, thanks.

Jim: No, I didn't mean it like that [*I laugh and Jim laughs along*].

Countertransference

Shared Spiritual Tensions

The case of Jim illustrates the need in spiritually-centred counselling to self-disclose. Naturally, if self-disclosure is accepted ethically as an effective intervention, then sharing similar accounts of religious narratives will naturally occur in session without fear of countertransference.

Dennis: Do you think your children have missed out for not being brought up within a faith community?

Sam: Well, I don't know, you see, because I have found it too problematic for me to accept. So I couldn't inculcate it into them.

Dennis: If I'm allowed to share this with you, it has troubled me that of the many children I have fostered I have not been able to bring them up within a Christian or even a spiritual environment with integrity, particularly in regard to denying them of the social benefits of the Church youth group – camping in Wales, trekking over Snowdon, and the like. I can't find that spiritual environment any more.

Sam: I think that might be a generation thing as well. I think the Church has got lost in space. It had an application 40 years ago, but we're talking about when we were children 50 years ago. And 50 years is a long, long time, and also, all the values of that time they're not there anymore.

Dennis: Not even in the Church?

Sam: Not in the Church of England. They're giving the world away by a rate of knots. You would have to go and see, wouldn't you?

Thorne (2002) is critical of inflexible attitudes regarding transference if it is used as a justification for failing to be authentic or as a sophisti-cated device for preventing a true relationship. Through transference, the therapist defends himself against real involvement where the exploration of the actual feelings between two persons can take place. For devout religious counsellors, there are serious issues of countertransference to consider.

Religious Faith and Countertransference

Should a spiritual counsellor have had a genuine religious or spiritual experience, or be committed to a life of faith, in order to practise spiritually-centred counselling effectively? I have discussed this elsewhere (Lines, 2002), but summarising the points raised, I feel that this is not essential, but would add that if spiritual counsellors have had such personal experiences then this would form for them a backcloth and range of valuable perspectives for interpreting similar such phenomena in their clients' lives.

Religious and existential counsellors are familiar with and comfortable in dealing with spiritual themes and dilemmas (van Deurzen-Smith, 1984), but for some belonging to fundamentalist and exclusive communities of faith there will be issues around congruence. A regular feature of Evangelical Christian witness is the public testimony of declaring how God's Spirit has been active in personal life. A too-exuberant display of personal testimony (as we saw earlier in Sam's discourse) can be divisive and showy, leading to considerable scepticism for the secular-minded, enquiring soul. There is often a failure to evaluate 'spirit enthusiasm' objectively for the subject, due to the immediate payoff of self-aggrandisement.

If counsellors are under the influence of faith, then they may better understand the crises that challenge a life in faith of their clients. With clients belonging to religious communities, but who reach significant faith crises, a general understanding of the characteristics of the power of faith, its cultural and social aspects, its exclusive power of control or liberating comprehensiveness, its transforming potential or enslaving obligations, is a useful grounding for counsellors.

Religious affiliation, however, can be an obstacle to forming a therapeutic relationship. For clients feeling the need to break away from the faith of their upbringing, a religious counsellor may prove unsympathetic to their natural feelings of guilt (Lines, 2002). West (2004) illustrates this point in his own casework. Growth may necessitate a departure from a former religious denomination, or it may involve a new spiritual direction that produces familial tension (Lines, 1995a). In such cases, religious counsellors who have a mission to save people may find the work a threat to their own personal belief-system, and this may render their unconscious interventions unhelpful – the client experiencing a judgmental countertransference that forms a blockage.

Evangelical Christian counsellors are sometimes faced with an ideological conflict in this respect. They may find difficulty in viewing client's dilemmas neutrally, being committed to prescribe solutions within a 'saving faith in Jesus' framework. Whilst not wishing to undervalue the transforming power of Christianity, the modern religious world has an impressive gallery of saints and is rich in universal imagery to change peoples' lives.

Countertransference occurs equally with those therapists who project their own unresolved religious conflicts on to their clients (Lannert, 1991). Research suggests that clients will acquire the values and disbeliefs of their therapists rather than the other way around, and for such clients this may be less adaptive than their former neurotic functioning (Lannert, 1991; Richards and Bergin, 1997).

Conclusion

This chapter has attempted to define the integrative counsellor to clarify how spiritually-centred therapy may differ from humanistic psychotherapy or religious counselling within a faith or pastoral context. I have drawn parallels with transpersonal and conventional styles but have illustrated where they differ. Five assumptions underlying my practice were outlined, the chief being that all people have the capacity to be spiritual. Stances of the spiritually-oriented therapist have been portrayed through analogous figures – as fellow traveller, spiritual master, collaborative mini-philosopher, intuitive enabler or as spiritual narrative therapist.

A requirement of spiritually-centred counselling, I have suggested, is self-disclosure. I have reasoned that the therapist should willingly share related material where this is appropriate and where it may help to normalise phenomena for a worried client, or open up new paths for possible living for one who is enterprising. Amplifying common human experience with richer narrative may assist a client towards healing or growth. A discussion centred on regular internal supervision, where, along with mandatory supervision, I proposed that the spiritual counsellor might develop an inner-mental dialogue of how he is affecting, and being affected by, the client's deliberations on faith, religion and spirituality.

Self-disclosure not only marks spiritual work as being non-conventional, but runs the risk of crossing ethical and professional boundaries, not least with young clients, as was illustrated with an adolescent case vignette. Issues of congruence were finally addressed, and obstacles of transference and countertransference were examined for those counsellors holding strict religious allegiances.

6

The Process of Spiritual Healing

We know what we are, but not what we may be.

William Shakespeare

The sacred is everywhere; we need only to open our eyes.

David Elkins

In this chapter, I examine the emerging Self and the process of spiritual healing. The emerging Self and personal development have been the subject of much study, and this chapter will assess the contribution of transpersonal psychology. An all-too-important question in all forms of counselling research is what is actually going on in therapy in distinction to what is thought to be going on: assessing the client's view of improvement, the counsellor's evaluation, and the factors which might bring about change. We have to grapple with what may be happening for the client during spiritual therapy and this will depend upon an understanding of personal spiritual makeup and of the transpersonal process of change. One recognised difficulty in outcome research is the separation of complex interrelated variables of approach, relationship and intervention. In attempting to assess spiritual outcome for clients, I present for consideration an extract of four boys in bereavement group therapy without myself (as therapist) being present.

The process of spiritual healing in an activity largely dependent on two people in relationship will rest on an understanding of the dynamics of that special relationship that counselling is, but the therapeutic relationship is unique and private, and research consistently has been unable to penetrate the process to identify what precisely has brought about healing and recovery for clients. A contribution to resolving this research dilemma is given from a spiritual perspective. Change during psychotherapy and counselling is a form of spiritual healing, and this may occur when clients reformulate 'the solution' via a lens of enriched human-divine relating. I hope you will consider applying this rather speculative perspective of healing within your customary manner of working to see if it works for you and your client.

Biological Self – what is it?

In a study of spiritual healing we will ask the inevitable question of what it is that requires healing. Answers will depend on what we understand by the nature of Self. There are many models of human development (Freud's psycho-sexual progression through oral, genital and latent stages, Fowler's faith development model, Kohlberg's six stages of moral development, Erikson's eight stages of man, Wilber's Spirit-in-action through the evolution of consciousness, Rogers' fully functioning person, Maslow's self-actualisation), and writers of psychology and spirituality have catalogued them and have chosen those they feel are most convincing to them (Jacobs, 1993; Rowan, 1993; West, 2000, 2004). But it is Jung's theory of individuation that principally accounts for the realisation of Self (Heron, 1998).

Largely due to Persian and Hellenistic influence, religion has postulated a divided Self made up of body, psyche and spirit, or soul, to account for the broad range of human experiences, but anatomical science, holistic psychology and developmental studies have questioned this. The study of an *emerging sense of Self* has been of interest to psychologists.

Hartley (2004), in support of somatic psychotherapy, discusses various theories of an emerging sense of Self. Analytic theory states that various developmental tasks have to be completed at particular age-appropriate times, and that if these are not completed there will occur disturbance or pathology. These tasks are attachment, separation and autonomy. The object relations theorists further view the infant as beginning life in a merged state of symbiotic unity with the maternal universe before gradual separation and individuation (Hartley, 2004: 82). For Klein, the infant deals with fantasy before reality. In contrast, Stern (1985) proposes that an infant begins life with an *emerging sense of Self* in relation to others, where she constantly negotiates issues such as intimacy, autonomy, trust and relatedness throughout development. Reality, for Stern, occurs before fantasy, and pathology can have its roots at any time of child or adult development. Stern's (1985) developmental model proposes four senses of Self:

- Sense of an *emerging Self*, from 0–2 months
- Sense of *core Self*, from 2–7 months
- Sense of *subjective Self*, from 7–15 months
- Sense of *verbal Self*, from 15 months to the second year.

The core Self is highly significant for healthy development. Freudian theory of the origin of neurosis being due to oedipal relations is disputed by some theorists. Otto Rank, an early follower of Freud, speculated that birth-separation trauma might be the origin of all neurosis, and Stanislav and Christina Grof (1989, 1990) explored further this hypothesis. Grof (1985) believed that altered states of consciousness are natural phenomena essential for healing. He further researched the birth process and claimed that by reliving the traumatic birth experience the patient releases energy for transpersonal experience. Observations of foetal motility suggest for some theorists that an emerging sense of Self is occurring in the womb, yet Hartley (2004: 92) points to the genetic makeup of each individual as a variable factor in determining how one particular infant might respond to a traumatic experience compared with another.

Social anthropologists view the emerging and developing Self as satisfying evolutionary requirements (Darling, 1996). Evolution has furnished us with a range of sensory repression systems that save us from being overloaded by the minutia of our surroundings, and our belief-system carries out its own executive function of integrating a mass of data to produce a meaningful and coherent picture of reality (Darling, 1996). In other words, we are hard-wired to perceive reality within the environmental context of approving people. These are causal explanations of how our sense of Self emerges, however, which disregard any influence of external transpersonal agency.

Gergen (1999: 6) says that 'we inherit today over two thousand years of deliberation on and celebration of the subjective self, our sense of being reasoning and choice-making individuals.' But the modernist belief about the Self goes back to the Enlightenment, to Descartes, since this was the time where the Christian soul and Plato's 'ideal' were challenged by asking for the evidence. The 'reductionism' by science of human beings to little more than electro-chemical factories (or complex switches for one client – Chapter 8) that resulted was neither appealing to the masses nor convincing to philosophers who were interested in the nature of being. Self-determination was the ethic of the Industrial Revolution, a free autonomous mind is the goal of education and human volition is the hard-earned prize of the democratic state, but there is not only a cost to personal relationships, there are three conceptual problems with the presupposition of individual mind that are rarely addressed:

- First, my 'interior consciousness' assumes it can *know* the exterior world, but such a causal connection has never been proven philosophically; it is only inferred from a premise of dualism: 'To embrace the material view of persons ultimately turns the idea of free and conscious deliberation into cultural mythology' (Gergen, 1999: 9).
- Secondly, how do we as subjects acquire knowledge of the objective world? For the *empiricist*, the mind functions as a *mirror to nature*, sensing the world 'as it is'. Locke (*Essay Concerning Human Understanding*) proposed that the mind was a *tabula rasa*, a blank slate from birth that is filled from experiencing the world 'as it is', but Kant showed, as highlighted earlier, and as subsequent psychology has shown, that our world of internal reality is *an interpreted world*. The world is not pre-given but evolves and so must our worldviews, or as Wilber (2001a: 54) puts it succinctly: 'The problem with maps is: *they leave out the mapmaker.*'

- Thirdly, if we attempt to observe our mental states, what part of our mind is doing the observing? And what part is being observed? What is the 'inner eye' and what is the object? How does mood affect observation? Even if I might *think* I *know* a state like sadness in my own mind, can I be sure that that feeling equates with sadness as experienced by another?: 'Even though it seems self-evident that we can think, observe, desire, and so on, perhaps it is only self-evident because we don't question the supposition' (Gergen, 1999: 13). Wilber (2000: 174–187) denounces the exclusive attention to materialist brain study that dismisses the evidence of interior mind: when I say, 'My mind is fighting my body', I don't mean *my neocortex is in conflict with my limbic system! I mean my will is in tension with my desire.* Some of these assumptions have been challenged by transpersonal psychology.

Emerging Spiritual Self

Stanislav Grof (1998) has mapped the psyche beyond the biological and biographical features to highlight the transpersonal dimension – states which in other contexts are referred to as spiritual, mystical, religious, magical or paranormal. Grof and Grof (1989, 1990) think that adolescence is a process of *spiritual emergence,* whereby an individual experiences 'holotropic phenomena' – the sense of moving towards wholeness. Non-ordinary states of consciousness are signs of spiritual emergence and are characterised by transformations associated with perceptual illusions, intense emotions and profound cognitive insights, insights which 'reveal' for the individual extraordinary revelations of the natural world and the cosmos (Grof, 1998). According to transpersonal psychology, mental phenomena are not exclusively based in the brain, but are the product of a transcendent reality that bypasses our ordinary senses of consciousness to reveal sources of information that transcend the boundaries of individual cognition – they are *beyond Self* (Grof and Grof, 1990).

As illustrated in earlier case material, pre-pubescent and adolescent youngsters will at times experience auditory and visual hallucinations, disorientation, delusions and senses of dread, morbidity and, paradoxically, of immortality (Lines, 2006). Bray's study (2004) of adolescent boys of Maori and Pacifica backgrounds has suggested that paranormal experiences may be understood as developmental stages of spiritual emergency amongst youths experiencing loss. One boy living with his grandfather developed a reassuring bond with ghosts of his deceased father and baby brother, another wrote about dreams of visiting another dimension to make pacts with spiritual beings. A third lad felt an alien had entered his body after witnessing his father attack his mother with a broken bottle, an experience which left him with a divided Self and facial spasms (2004: 17–18).

When adolescents experience trauma or loss, writes Bray (2004), holotropic states are not symptoms of psychosis, but are biological processes of healing and spiritual emergence as the injured Self moves towards psycho-spiritual wholeness. Reactions to crisis are not psychotic conditions to be treated with drugs; they are psychological mechanisms of spiritual healing which require adaptive decision-making and transformational insight. Spiritual therapy should be centred upon affirming and normalising such experiences.

Wilber's (2001a) view of a spiritual Self falls within a comprehensive and elaborate scheme of the course of the Spirit's evolution from matter to life to mind to soul to spirit and higher states of consciousness (for a brief account see Wilber, 2000: 61–4). *Spirit-in-action* through evolution is manifest in four quadrants. His theory states that each evolutionary stage incorporates all previous ones and then branches into new forms. There are three levels to transpersonal development – Centaur (real Self), Subtle Self (soul) and Causal Self (Spirit) – and for each there is a particular counselling style or meditation recommended.

Critics of Wilber's model point to its hierarchal linear structure of development, which fails for many to match their spiritual experience (West, 2004: 61). Similar to de Chardin's vision of Christ being the Omega point, Wilber views the ultimate state as becoming One with everything, as being absorbed into Ultimate Being, following Buddhist teachings of salvation – the time for which all Bodhisattvas shed tears of longing (Wilber, 2001a: 307–11) – but this leaves many, like myself, feeling lost in metaphysical nihilism.

Healing Bereaved Self

The accounts of four boys involved in bereavement counselling were presented in Chapter 4. A further extract of discourse is now considered where paranormal and sketchy belief-systems were teased out and tested in group therapy. I have presented a discourse analysis of this joint interview elsewhere (Lines, 1999b) within the context of a therapeutic programme (Lines, 2006), but in what follows spiritual themes are presented to illustrate *spiritual emergence* through one still frame of the healing process.

In spite of James ridiculing 'pointless crying', he presents for the group an interesting perspective and psychological support by re-viewing bereavement not as extinction but as reincarnated existence 'through off-spring', a form of perceptive continuance, which Phil, at least, was keen to embrace:

> *James:* There's nothing there. Crying is not gonna do any help. It might help you feel better; it's not going to bring him back … But some people are more sensitive than others … But if you carry on living your life you're making them proud and you're living. They're living their life in you, if you

know what I mean … While I'm alive my dad will never be dead, if you know what I mean. So everyone's there. And I suppose it's the same with Phil, as long as he's alive his brother is not dead 'cause he acts like his brother, yea.

Phil: Yea …

James: Same with you [Clint], as long as you're still alive your dad's still alive – within you. Same with you [Matthew]; you more or less have the same things as your mum. As long as you're still alive your mum's still there – but in a different form …

Phil and Clint move on to offer alternative speculations of a post-death existence:

Phil: James, where do you reckon heaven is?

James: I don't think there's a heaven. I just think there's souls floating around watching us.

Phil: 'Cause, I reckon …

James: I don't believe in heaven, or hell, or God. I don't believe in any of that

Phil: I reckon that heaven is space and that, you know, where it's got all the nice colours and that.

James: … I don't believe in God, yea 'cause, erm, like, what's God ever done for me except the worst … If you think about it, my life has been *a total and utter hell*. I've been bullied and I've lost both parents; I've got nothing else to believe in but myself …

Phil: 'Cause I want to get a telescope and look at space, and I feel, like, if I look through the telescope I'm gonna see my brother.

James: You might … What do you think Matthew? Where do you think your mum is? [*sharp intake of breath and yawn*]

Matt: Now?

James: Yea now.

Matt: I dunno

James: Where do you think your dad is Clint?

Clint: I think he is where he wanted to be … I think when people die they go to their dream place, like.

James: They go to their ideal place.

Clint: Yea, like, what they really wanted to do when they were alive they do it when they're dead.

James: They do it, yea, like when, say, you wanted to go out on a Saturday night to a club; get to do all the wild things you never got to do.

Clint: Or something like that, yea.

James: They sort of float around, you know, like, watching us – a bit like angels but not, you know, with those stupid wings.

Clint: Yea [*group laugh*] …

James: And those goofy little halos.

Clint: Yea man.

Phil: I reckon they might go to another place, a new solar system.
James: Solar system?
Phil: 'Cause there must be different solar systems.
James: There is; there's hundreds.
Clint: Millions.
James: Space is ... do you know why they call it space?
Phil: Why?
James: 'Cause there's so much of it, like ... there's so much space.
Phil: But that ...
James: It's never ending.
Phil: But I think that's strange because it never ends.
James: Well I reckon it does end, in a way, I reckon, yea, it's like this. I reckon the solar system, well the whole universe, the whole of space is one big circle, yea, like a doughnut-type but you can't go out of it. You can't get out of it because every time you try to go out of it you can't; it's one big gynormous, like a million years each way. So it's impossible to end.
Phil: But, what do you think is out of the solar system – the universe?
James: I don't think anyone will know.

Client Change/Spiritual Healing – without the Therapist

During one brief moment, James expressed cathartic anger over divine injustice and in so doing surrendered his posture of the well-controlled, stoic leader. Phil's fear of seeing a ghost of his brother had partially been exorcised in session by James' rationalising and by teasing out his theories of astrology. His neuroticism about dying in the same manner as his brother became less acute after borrowing and reapplying James' belief to *re-view* his life as embodying his brother's being, and after entertaining Clint's view that the dead may *enter their dream place* and be doing all the things they had wanted to do when alive. Clint definitely became more conciliatory towards teachers managing him after *normalising* his experience through dialogue. Matthew, whose bitterness and tendency to 'punish everyone' was long-overdue, may have found solace in *re-viewing* his mother *in him* from James' theory, I cannot be sure, but, curiously he elected to take up PE after this session. In spite of acceptance of loss being gradual and non-formulaic, there was during the session evidence of healing.

Client's Assessment of Healing

Each of the boys was asked to speak on the benefits of the group session and to say whether it had helped. James said, 'I felt less isolated, as though I was not the only person who had gone through losing my parents.' Phil said, 'It was OK. I wasn't the only one going through it.' He also shared more sensitive material in individual work later on. He described how he thought he had become, for the family, his dead brother's replacement – perhaps this notion was developed from James' continued existence theory. Clint said, 'I found it helpful, yea.' Matthew smiled and said, 'Yea, it was good.' 'But how did it help?' I asked. 'You've got to get on with life', he replied. I asked him where that idea had come from, but he could not recall that it was from James. Matthew was much more outspoken in the next session of individual work and revealed information not previously disclosed, including that his mother had taken her life. Matthew came again for counselling to help build better peer relations and to learn 'to be happy' (Nelson-Jones, 1996) but, sadly, ceased attending school before work was complete.

My Assessment of Healing

There was clear (and understandable) evidence of James carrying guilt over his mother's call for help and his lack of response – 'And in a way I still blame myself because she called out to me … ' – but in expressing this he found an opportunity to explore the reactions of a non-critical audience. At one point, James, like a mini-philosopher (Parkes, 1986), found patterns in each of his peer's experiences – 'I think that the thing we all have in common is …' – that helped normalise his unique experience.

Phil was quite egocentric and insisted on not being dominated by James' control of the dialogue. He described the effects of his loss as first being scared at night in case he saw his brother's ghost and second as a sense of numbness (Kübler-Ross, 1982) – 'I felt I was dreaming.' Phil showed an interest in astronomy (astrology?) in the forlorn hope he might see his brother in some distant star or something (he did not specify), a naïve belief, authorised by James, which became a psychological hook on which to hold.

When James ridiculed crying, Clint did not agree and said he found crying a helpful release – 'It's not like that for me though. One day I can be fine, but then the next day something could happen' – along with other coping strategies, like voluntary counselling, talking to his mother and looking at photos to remember the good times. No one was able to contain Clint's brief upset – 'It's [life's] a bit boring now that he's dead' – though all had registered it, and in one sense he led the group with greater honesty and by integrating feeling with outspokenness.

Matthew was the most reserved and offered little in terms of support for the others, yet it was interesting to see how he expanded his account once prompted. He felt assured when considering a son-deceased mother identity, and said: 'To my mum, I've got the same colour eyes, the same colour hair, the same hearing problem and the same heart problem'. Seven years had past since losing his mother, but for Matthew it was as if it were yesterday. He indicated that his father was not coping and was unable to talk about his mother's death, and he was thereby having to parent his father (and younger siblings – picking them up after school, cooking their teas, etc.) when what he yearned for psychologically was to be cuddled and nurtured by a mother who had been snatched away unexpectedly.

The four boys illustrated different degrees of numbness, denial, anger and depression as they struggled to accept and to cope with their losses (Kübler-Ross, 1982). Clint was angry to be told at school about his father but was moving towards acceptance, whilst Matthew directed anger inwardly. With Phil, there was marginal evidence of numbness and denial. He oscillated between these and anger, but was a long way from acceptance (Parkes, 1986), and still dreaming.

Spiritual emergence was evident in the healing process through:

- Learning to cope philosophically
- Reframing unique experience within a normalising framework
- Drawing from as yet untapped resources to carry on
- Beginning to shed metaphysical beliefs without discarding a numinous presence – being watched over, bereaved person's presence 'through them', and knowing their dead loved ones were OK.

None of the group could handle deeply expressed sadness, and most of the coping strategies were philosophical in directing thoughts towards attitudes and beliefs that were accepting of what had happened. Normalising extraordinary loss-experience through finding commonality in their varied experiences assisted the boys in restructuring their thinking and behaviour to face their bereavement and to get on with the business of living. The shared discourses of optimism and basic pragmatism appeared mutually effective for the giver and the given alike. In spite of limited experiences of life, there was evidence in follow-up individual counselling with three of the boys that the process of narrative sharing and the phenomenological sense of group *connectedness* had fostered a deeper level of 'understanding of Others apart from Self' than was evident before (Rowling, 1996). Metaphysical beliefs were not rejected wholesale, since they served as emotional hooks, but they were modified through discourse to aid in the healing process.

Mystical Conceptions of Self

As outlined earlier, the monotheistic faiths promote a transcendental religiosity, whilst eastern religion and phenomenology (philosophy of perception – Edmund Husserl) are more intuitive and immanent. Jung saw meaning in the teachings of first-century esoteric sects of Gnosticism, particularly the notion of a 'spark' of divinity within each person which earnestly seeks to return home to God. Ireneaus (*Against Heresies*) was successful in branding Gnostic teaching as heresy, but for some Christian communities Gnostic motifs were not believed to be inconsistent with Christian teaching (*Gospel of Thomas* etc.: www.earlychristianwritings.com). Gnostic beliefs were synchronistic, and were absorbed within Hellenism, Judaism and Christianity. In each manifestation, there is the suggestion that we have a divine element within our nature, and this stands in contrast to Christian orthodox teaching of being 'filled with the Spirit', i.e. as an external agent given to the initiate. This is an entirely different emphasis of spirituality, as something within the person and, by implication, *every person* (Lines, 2002), and such an insight is more fitting to the pluralistic outlook.

In addition, eastern philosophies, Christianity, Judaism and Islam have rich traditions of mysticism and mystical thought. There has been much interest in Zen, mysticism and other less formal transcendent psychologies for the exploration of being in recent times (Lukoff et al., 1998). The cross-pollination of the world faiths has given rise to a more universal understanding of spirituality, with mysticism, intuitive knowledge and transpersonal psychology becoming popular in meeting clients' spiritual needs (Boorstein, 1996). Absolute mysticism promotes salvation as a detachment from social relationships and the real-life situation, but also involves self-surrender of cognitive control that leaves the gullible open to being manipulated by others, or to auto-suggestive processes that can lead to delusion and mental imbalance if not checked by philosophical reasoning, as highlighted in Sam's and Tony's experiences. But philosophical steering is the antithesis of intuitive knowledge. So, the therapist is left with an impasse. For those who seek esoteric routes for their own spiritualism, it is difficult to see what role the uninitiated spiritual counsellor can have for those clients who are committed to these paths of self-exploration, but mystical perceptions of life on a larger scale have value in the new spiritual paradigm (Lines, 2002).

From Otto, Jung saw spiritual experiences as numinous and direct and as originating in deeper levels of the psyche: 'they are associated with the feeling that one is encountering a dimension which is sacred, holy, and radically different from everyday life, and which belongs to a superior order of reality' (Grof, 1996: 517). Spiritual experiences are not only available at the higher stage of development (Wilber, 2000), however, and Elkins (1998: 277) maintains that spirituality is a this-worldly phenomenon:

> I have tried to present a new vision of spirituality, one that is relevant to the postmodern age. The essence of this vision is that spirituality is universal, that the sacred river from which we slake our thirst flows throughout the world … The sacred is everywhere; we need only to open our eyes.

Synthesis of Biological and Mystical through Human Relating

These contrasting visions of self may find synthesis through features of humanistic psychology. Maslow describes mystical moments as *peak experiences*, and others suggest they are common and indiscriminate occurrences of spirituality (Elkins, 1998; White, 1996). Thorne (1998) speaks of *magic moments* and suggests that the *mystical Self* can be reached through an intensity of relating with others in a group or in individual counselling, which is akin to Rogers' making 'psychological contact' (Tudor, 2000). Rogers has been portrayed as a mystic in his latter years by several authors (Thorne, 2002; West, 2004), with a challenge for person-centred counsellors to recognise the spiritual dimension in the existential encounter of therapy (Thorne, 2002). Clark (1967) promotes 'sensitivity training groups' for mutual self-actualisation, and for discovering a sense of *being-ness one with another* through prizing others in genuine experiencing of interdependence. Finally, Mearns and Cooper (2005) are pressing counsellors to engage in 'relational depth' from different theoretical backgrounds but with no mention of spirituality.

I have spoken elsewhere of the new spiritual paradigm where spirituality may be seen in the person (Lines, 2002). The central thesis is that the divine may be experienced through the human if the subject views encounter through a lens of *believing is seeing*. A prophetic feature in the history of religion is the phenomenon of *seeing*. This revelatory state of mystical initiates may be applied as a therapeutic tool in the counselling process. In the movie, *Loch Ness* (Bevan et al., 1995), a marine biologist sets out to dissolve the myth of the legendary monster. A little girl who claimed to have seen the creature reminds the scientist of a different paradigm of seeing and believing. Dr Dempsey explains to young Isabel that as a scientist he has to see the creature before he can believe in its existence, but she contests this with great certainty and counterclaims that he will need to believe in its reality if he would wish to see it.

In such an example, a child may see truths that are missed through an extensive training which conditions the mind into lateral thinking – *we see* what we want to see, or are conditioned to see, or believe we will see. According to Buber, 'We receive fuller knowledge from the child' (Buber, 1958: 40), and sayings in the New Testament, like other religious writings, speak of the profound, intuitive wisdom often found in children (Mark 9: 37; 10: 14-15 NRSV). Isabel might better understand, for example, the meaning of the myth for her community as well as the social implications of self-doubt.

Buber (1958) suggested that the divine Being could be viewed through every person with whom I enter into relation, be it my friend, spouse, partner, child, boss or neighbour. These worldly encounters are the means by which I address God: 'There are moments of silent depth in which you look on the world-order fully present ... . These moments are immortal, and most transitory of all' (Buber, 1958: 47). When the counsellor views the client in such a way, an extraordinary *soul matching* occurs in therapy (Lines, 2006). This sentiment has enormous social consequences:

> By declaring that man is responsible and must actualise the potential meaning of his life, I wish to stress that the true meaning of life is to be discovered in the world rather than within man or his own psyche, as though it were a closed system. I have termed this constitutive charac-teristic the 'self-transcendence of human existence.' It denotes the fact that being human always points, and is directed, to something, or someone, rather than oneself – be it a meaning to fulfil or another human being to encounter. The more one forgets himself – by giving himself to a cause to serve or another person to love – the more human he is and the more he actualises himself. What is called self-actualisation is not an attainable aim at all, for the simple reason that the more one would strive for it, the more he would miss it. In other words, self-actualisation is possible only as a side-effect of self-transcendence. (Frankl, 1959: 115)

Peak experiences of transcendence were traditionally understood within religious or aesthetic mediums, but may be re-viewed from a stance of seeing human social interaction as everyday spiritual encounters (Elkins, 1998). The experience moves on from the vision of Elkins (1998: 63): 'Our problem is not that the sacred has ceased to exist, but rather that we have lost our connection to it.' For it is not merely a 'taking note', or a 'making contact' (Boorstein, 1996: 187), with that which was formerly hidden or lost in tranquil landscapes or naturally drawn friendships, but an engage-ment with another through a perception of their special importance in relation to me. This engagement draws and gives energy within a numi-nous, this-worldly, encounter – *the knitting of being with being*. In essence, this spiritual insight is a synthesis of the divine and the human, a spiritu-ality that involves an attachment to life for deeper human contact, and a viewing of human attachment as a visible form of invisible transcenden-tal experience (Lines, 1995b: 172–3). There can be few richer experiences of making human contact than in the special relationship that grows through the process of counselling and psychotherapy at its most effective and genuine interface of encounter of being with being.

A Therapeutic Process of Spiritual Healing

Counselling for orthodox religious and spiritual difficulties are covered in the literature (Richards and Bergin, 1997), but if non-ostensibly religious difficulties that threaten clients' senses of being and personal meaning are addressed through the human-divine lens, then a broader scope of work opens up. The counselling process required for the new spiritual paradigm (Lines, 2002) consists of three interconnected elements:

- Seeing the spiritual in the person
- Validating mystical experience as numinous moments for growth
- The decision to view personal and counselling relating within numinous constructs.

Existential and spiritually-inclined counsellors might consider help-ing clients to explore their higher selves through their own social and familial attachments, and to view their personal *peak experiences* as much in intense, *magical moments* of human interaction and *connected-ness* as in divine experiences of the former, conventionally religious, paradigms. Whilst some reach their spiritual depths by an absorbed, undifferentiated meditation upon a religious icon or holy Being, others claim that the mediums of art and music are equally effective (Elkins, 1998). But there are those who discover their depth of being through human relating.

Clients may recognise *moments* in their lives where they have had tem-porary *peak experiences* in human interaction in which they have experi-enced a heightened element of their being, a state of peace and of well-being. They may not describe the experience as being religious, but may well view it as spiritual, since it has enhanced their capacity for loving and increased their motivation for the greater good that is above egocentricity (Kelly, 1996). Often there is a purging of the soul, a creature-consciousness, a good feeling and inner peace for having had the experi-ence, together with a vow to become more dedicated to something or someone. Wilber (2001a: 138) judges a *peak experience* as a 'peek' experi-ence of a higher dimension of transpersonal consciousness towards which the 'Spirit in the Kosmos' steadily unfolds.

The intention of speculating on this sense of *connectedness* is not to reduce the spiritual to the mundane (Eliade, 1961), but to see the spiritual in what is encountered in the natural, and in the here-and-now. In the new spiritual paradigm the counsellor views an occasion in the counselling process itself as a captured *moment*, as a one-off unrepeatable experience, and as a relational encounter of transcendence. The perception of the new spiritual paradigm is not to view the client as a mere person amongst the many, but as a very special person with whom I have the privilege to be in relation. The human-divine vision I am promoting endorses McGuiness' (1998) sentiment of seeing the individual as having an invio-lable core of dignity. If I view my client as the sum of everything I value and hold most dear, and if I view our engagement as a *peak experience* having the potential for *moments* of transcendence, then the possibility exists for the Other to experience the same (Lynch, 2002), and for us both together to begin a soul journey of relational being through a collabora-tive style of therapy.

In my late twenties, I went on a spiritual retreat in a Roman Catholic monastery and, apart from a brotherhood bonding that had grown amongst the group through the spiritual teaching and open expressive worship, I grew very fond of a fellow student. She was beautiful and had an attractive smile and manner of giggling that I found enticing. I fell in love with her and thought about her nearly every conscious moment. I rushed into the conference hall to sit as close to her as possible and peered at her throughout lectures consistently. The relationship of intense affection was only in my mind, since I knew she had a boyfriend in the college, and I felt I should not violate her relationship with him by being presumptive or by pressing a question in his absence that would put us both in a compromised position. As a dare, our group slept on a mountainside all night long and I slept alongside her and talked into the early hours till falling asleep. On a crystal clear night, with stars twinkling high above our heads, I felt I had entered *heavenly places* (Ephesians 2: 6–7) and was in tune with the universe.

I wanted to be near her and to talk, and the sense of presence in being together (Thorne, 2002) left me feeling a 'transcendent awareness of the unity of the cosmic system' (Rogers, 1975: 6) through being close to a very special human being. I wanted to share my life with hers and to learn as much as I could in the brief moments we shared together. I felt an inseparable bond and a sense of *connectedness* with another person as though my finite boundary of individuality had merged with the cosmos and all life – but we did not touch. In Chapter 5, I discussed my soul-mate feelings of bonding with Jim as an example of 'having thoughts of another human being coming regularly to mind' (Thorne, 2002) – and of having all the intensity of being in love – and in the case vignette which closes this chapter, I try and articulate this counselling process of *spiritual connectedness*.

Caroline was in her mid-thirties, lived alone and had recently before coming for therapy broken away from her dominant father, who held an esteemed position within the Methodist Church. She found this newly acquired independence threatening since her father had been diagnosed with a terminal condition and had foisted powerful feelings of guilt on her for moving out. The early sessions centred on dealing with induced guilt through cognitive styles after assessing this to be her need through a Multi-modal Therapy Assessment Questionnaire (modified from Lazarus, 1981). Part way through the fourth session the therapy took a distinctive spiritual turn after Caroline had questioned who she really was.

Caroline: I can never know who I am because of my father's brainwashing. He makes me feel dreadfully guilty for leaving, but he can cope without me. I know he runs me down when he preaches. He makes me feel as though I can't be trusted to know who I am by quoting the Bible.

Dennis: What scripture does he quote?

Caroline: Oh, his favourite passage, apart from 'Honour thy father and mother' and 'Spare the rod and spoil the child', is 'Before you were formed in your mother's womb I knew you', to show how God and him know me better than I know myself.

Dennis: These references are from a part of the Bible that was formed in a cultural setting very different to our own, and the second, particularly, within a family context of younger children. The third passage is a curious text to present before you. I'm left unsure why it should have relevance to you.

Caroline: I know exactly why he throws it at me; it's to undermine my self-confidence and to leave me doubting my own certainty. You see, my dad rejects all psychology unless it suits him or it can be found in scripture. He thinks that all we need to know is there in the Bible; that science and unbiblical knowledge is worldly and ungodly. Isn't it pathetic? He benefits from 'worldly, twentieth-century comforts and medicine', but he just can't stand it when I tell him I don't believe in any of the religious stuff; that I can get along quite nicely without God, and that the universe doesn't collapse when I turn my back on Methodism. But what boils my blood is when he tells me that I don't know myself, and that I'll soon come round to his way of thinking.

Dennis: Do you see yourself as a spiritual person in any way, as having spiritual needs within that are outside conventional religion?

I was beginning to feel deeply for Caroline, as an entrapped person trying to escape her father's fundamentalism. I wondered whether this bonding was a felt need to 'save her' (in becoming a further 'authority' through cunning theological exegesis), or to move towards her in a more personal, less professional relationship – my feelings intensified with continual thoughts about her between sessions and of feeling I couldn't wait till our next meeting.

Caroline: My spirituality lies in loving to be with people, not religious people who seem to live in a time warp, but I become excited when meeting interesting people ... Oh, and I love to walk in the Lake District.

Was this an opportunity to share my passions about nature and the countryside in a covert and subtle manoeuvre to form an extra-therapeutic relationship by kidding myself that I was only interested in helping Caroline explore her own spiritual needs?

Dennis: I wonder how it is for you that you become spiritually excited when meeting interesting people, and by being within the Lakes?

Was this response an unconscious hope that Caroline, who was clearly interested in psychology, might find me an interesting person; that she might long to be with me as I with her? And what was it about walking in the Lakes that she considered to be spiritual, as making contact with her spiritual being?

> *Caroline:*   When I'm in company with people it is as though I'm see-
> ing myself in a clearer light, as though the cloud has lifted
> and I see Christ transfigured on the mount, especially if
> they are what I call 'giving of themselves' types of people,
> open people, who are not afraid to expose their vulnera-
> bilities and inadequacies … It's the mountains, I suppose,
> that give me a more proportionate sense of my being in
> the universe, of knowing who I really am and of my place
> and purpose for being here.

I felt at one with Caroline as though we had connected with no boundaries of Self, and although our spiritual exchanges ceased some time ago now, I cannot look at mountains without recalling the closeness I shared with Caroline during our work together. When I meet interesting people with whom I share mutual vulnerabilities and deficiencies in spiritual therapy I still become mindful of what Caroline taught me in our sessions together.

What is Really Going on in Spiritual Counselling?

A series of largely unanswerable, rhetorical questions arise from viewing the healing relationship of counselling through a lens of seeing the transcendent, numinous 'Other' in the person of my client. I close this chapter with questions for your consideration:

- In asking *'What is really going on* in spiritual therapy', is it possible, or productive, to isolate spirituality specifically from other traits of human makeup?
- Is there evidence of *spiritual emergence* when young people become traumatised by loss, and if so do you think they receive insights from a transpersonal agent?
- If I am *being drawn* towards my client by powerful feelings of non-sexual love (or even sexual feelings of love), can I not regard such overwhelming attraction as the spiritual counterpart of the excitement experienced as of two lovers in warm embrace, or two newly-weds on their honeymoon?
- As I face my clients in continued spiritual work, and I trace within myself prevalent ulterior reasons for continuing therapy – which may have sexual inclinations, unmet needs to protect or parent my client, feelings of being needed and wanted by them, or of hindering them in any way from trusting their own experience – should I terminate therapy through fear of transgressing boundaries (if

only in my imagination), or should I view such impulses as the life-blood of my own humanity made evident through being in relationship?

- Whereas religion may have its social, emotional or behavioural elements, are there comparable associations attached to spirituality?
- Is it possible to identify a spiritual centredness that does not involve going out to the Other, or to become emotional, or to satisfy psychological needs, or is spirituality essentially non-social, non-emotional and non-psychological?
- Is speaking about the numinous, the Other, and the transpersonal a disguised manner of talking about God in secular and respectable postmodern language that is used to reach the atheist?
- And is the language of *presence, peak experience* and *connectedness* not a universal means of speaking about spiritual or religious experience?

The reasoning above of the healing process being the *activity* of spiritually-centred counselling, is no different to many other psychotherapeutic approaches, and other writers have coined their own terms, such as psychospiritual or spiritopsyche (West, 2000) work, to describe the particular process of healing and change of an otherworldly dimension. To see spiritual work as different only in name to other kindred styles of therapy is to assume that the spiritual cannot be separated from the psychological, emotional, cognitive, behavioural or social etc. (Benner, 1988; Gergen, 1999). It is to say that it cannot be recognised as an entity in its own right. This, of course, is a presupposition, and generally doesn't match people's reflections on *above* and *beyond* experience. If we cannot even be sure that there exists innate and universal cognitive and emotional categories within persons – when 'looking inward', after all, what are we 'looking at' – it is unlikely that we will ever 'locate' or 'identify' the spiritual as a distinctive category. But that doesn't prove there isn't such a thing as a *spiritual* dimension within the person, which a particular style of working can suitably address. These questions have occupied greater minds than mine over the centuries, and in the final analysis it seems to me that the label of *spirituality* is not nearly as important as the *activity* it is attempting to convey, but you may think otherwise.

Conclusion

In examining the healing process of spiritually-centred counselling, this chapter discussed again the psychological tension between the two realities of empirical, biological accounts of Self and transpersonal, mystical ones. Since research of factors for therapeutic change have offered no definitive conclusions in isolating the healing process from the person of therapist, the style and approach used, or the techniques and interventions employed, we looked at *spiritual emergence* in early Self through youngsters encountering loss. I asked whether healing occurs for young people through their belief-system to cope with the loss of a close family member. Adolescents are on a biological treadmill towards individuation and to aid the process they will instinctively seek to normalise their experience. Experimentally, by isolating the therapist, participants of the bereavement group session through their own *spiritual emerging resources* were able to accelerate the healing process through social discourse amidst the group relational dynamic.

The counselling relationship is crucial in light of research supporting its importance for healing. This chapter looked at the potential for the spiritual counselling relationship if transcendence was viewed through a lens of human relating. A case vignette illustrated the perspective and highlighted again the need to engage in internal dialogue as well as formal supervision. A series of rhetorical questions to help the practitioner reflect on the nature of therapeutic healing closed the chapter. In asking what is really going on in spiritually-oriented therapy, we are considering the special character of the counselling relationship, particularly in regard to the transpersonal dimension.

As a footnote to this chapter, and before moving on, it is important to recognise the growing relevance of recent studies in neuroscience to an emergent sense of Self. Various philosophers turn to the work of neuroscientists for evidence to support their particular hypotheses. Margaret Wilkinson (2006) gives an informative overview of research on neuroimaging techniques and mind mapping from a Jungian perspective, research which has relevance for therapy. Such study points to the plasticity of the brain during childhood and adolescence and the human reaction to trauma. However, these techniques are still in their infancy and have been conducted mainly on animals. Neuro-imaging consists of milliseconds and is not easily able to isolate genetic from environmental variables. I have not drawn from neuroscience for the reason that it is too early to speculate from such data just how a sense of Self is created within the brain. As Wilkinson frames the question, it is not clear how 'the various elements of experiences merge and then emerge to give us that moment by moment awareness out of which emerges a sense of self, a sense of what it is to be me?' (2006: 171).

7

The Spiritual Journey

If you understand, things are just as they are...
if you do not understand, things are just as they are
  The obstacle is the path

                                            Zen Proverbs

I have no difficulty about believing in God
  but great difficulty about the kind of God I believe in.

                                            C. S. Lewis

The spiritual journey as a metaphor for life is not new, but the implications of this are not always realised, particularly in regard to humanistic ideals. The aim in this chapter is to listen to the voices of religious and non-religious dialogues of Jung's scheme of individuation through a metaphor of life as a journey. An attractive feature of narrative therapy is the pose of a therapist who is fascinated to learn of the client's intra-psychic and social world through their personal stories in life. There are no universal maps or pre-programmed routes for travelling the client's journey, but an opportunity in spiritual therapy to engage with a companion on a road of spiritual transcendence.

The Buddhist strives as an individual for personal enlightenment, and a prominent feature of psychotherapy is to assist clients to gain insight into a particular emotional or psychological difficulty. Enlightenment and insight are similar discourses that occur in styles of counselling which aim to discover an inner, intuitive Self (analytical, person-centred psychology), or to fashion a preferred Self (socially constructed). Enlightenment, therefore, is a metaphor that has eclectic possibilities and pluralistic relevance.

The history of religion has a rich repository of journeying narratives to account for existential experience, but these narratives are parochial and culturally restricted. There is good linguistic evidence to suggest that religious narratives were composed through principles of aetiology (the idea that individual experience prompts a story), but through oral traditions these stories configure common human experience through repetition and ritual. Personal experience becomes the datum of authenticity, but in our secular age many religious stories have lost their relevance and impact. In this chapter, I draw on some of these narratives and demythologise them for application within therapy.

The journey archetype is first drawn on through an ancient Sumerian epic and through a number of beyond-death narratives. Then I examine well known discourses on the religious traditions of Judaeo-Christianity and Hinduism. There is a sound psychology in the journey narrative and this is then examined through the secular equivalents of rites of passage and initiation. Transitional moments in life, particularly for adolescents and mid-life clients, involve a balance of risk and security, and this is explored through presented casework.

The Archetypal Spiritual Journey

Immortality: The Epic of Gilgamesh

The common wish to leave our mark and deny our mortality has been a powerful incentive of the religious life. Religious devotion and organised cultic ceremony across cultures have often had one central aim – to achieve personal immortality. From the pharaohs of Egypt to the modern-day religious person, considerable investment has centred on the possibility of reaching divine status and of living perpetually within the realms of Paradise. The Sumerian story of Gilgamesh (2700 BCE) stands as an archetypal spiritual journey (see Figure 7.1). It is an epic written in cuneiform (wedge shaped characters) on clay tablets that closes in a quest to reach personal immortality (Heidel, 1951). Gilgamesh sets out on a perilous voyage to the mouth of all rivers at the end of the world (Keenan and Jackson, 1999). He journeyed to find Utnapishtim and his wife, the only mortals on whom the gods had granted eternal life after surviving the great flood (details of this epic are strikingly similar to those written later in the Genesis narrative of Noah. Plato also knew of an ancient flood).

Gilgamesh fails in his first test to stay awake for seven days to become immortal, and is granted an opportunity to become young again by eating a plant from the ocean bed. He ties a stone to his feet, sinks to the bottom and grabs the magic plant. But he distrusts its magical potency and wants to take it back home to try first on an old man. Alas, whilst asleep, the plant is snatched away and eaten by a snake, and so he is robbed of eternal life for lacking faith. Gilgamesh is forced to accept his mortal condition. In spite of the long arduous journey, he has 'gained absolutely nothing' but the *experience of the journey* and a greater appreciation of life.

Figure 7.1   The Epic of Gilgamesh discovered at Nineveh © The British Museum.

The epic of Gilgamesh is archetypal and is reflected in the secular world where individuals pay considerable money and attention to preserve their youth. Paradoxically, there is not nearly the same attention given to preparing for one's decease and extinction as, for example, there was for the pharaohs of Egypt, where furniture, jewellery, clothing, statues and sculptures, games and chariots were stored for use in the afterlife journey with Osiris (over 3500 artefacts were found in the relatively modest tomb of Tutankhamen). Heroic novels and clients in therapy recognise that *the journey is more meaningful than reaching the destination.*

Journey at Death

Satirist Will Self has asked what it might be like to die without any idea of the Transcendent through his novel *How the Dead Live* (2004). The

Tibetan *Book of the Dead*, from which his narrative draws, is a manual of instructions to be read out to the ill when dying. Tibetan Buddhism claims that when you die your psyche will dis-incorporate and this phenomenon will be terrifying as your passions, which were part of your nature, will come back to you in the form of a chimera play in which you were involved. You are advised not to be taken in, but to see it as a delusion, and that by doing so you will reach nirvana and escape rebirth. If you are fooled and taken in you will be reborn. John Hick, in his study of *Death and Eternal Life* (1976), draws on these Tibetan poems to argue a case for a series of trials to improve our characters beyond mortal existence.

The Qur'an and The New Testament take life beyond the grave as an incentive for the religious life, eastern writings stand against a back-cloth of the cycle of rebirth, but through the Jewish writings there is a curious development ranging from eternal destiny through one's descendents to personal immortality through physical resurrection. An individual might be raised from the underworld, or *Sheol*, and this later view underlies the Christian belief of Jesus' resurrection reflected in Paul's letter to Corinthians and the closing Gospel records. The Fourth Gospel has the incarnation of the Logos as the theological frame for the Jesus story as the Son of God becoming flesh before journeying home-ward to be with his Father – although no dependence has ever been established, there are echoes here of Gnosticism and Hellenistic mythol-ogy. The speculative enquiry into post-death experience is shadowed in religious narratives which emphasise through the journey metaphor that *life is a preparation for death and beyond*, but this teaching holds no credence for the atheist.

Religious Narratives of Journeying

The Exodus Narrative

The Hindu scripture, *Bhagavad gita* (Song of Lord Krishna), is an extensive poem debating the philosophies of going to war against members of one's family, but the Judeo-Christian scriptures are novel in that they are pre-sented as history. In the biblical programme, the history of Israel begins with the narrative of Abram (later renamed Abraham) being called from his native land, Ur (modern Iraq) to Canaan (modern Israel) in fulfilment of God's promise. Canaan was a territory of city states and of local cults and fertility worship of *Lord Baal*. Although no archaeological evidence supports his migration to Palestine, Abraham, nevertheless, is presented in late records as a nomadic shepherd who worshipped Yahweh, and as the patriarch of the Jewish and Arab populations.

Abraham was the notable figure of faith for Jews, Christians and Muslims. The descendents of Abraham find themselves in slavery, and the history of Israel narrative continues with the exodus of Abraham's descendants from Egypt to Canaan through the deliverer, Moses. The journey is an epic 40-year exodus in Sinai desert, and the programme closes with a series of conflicts and deliverances through successive saviours. The exodus had profound significance religiously and experientially as the foundation of Jewish identity.

The Christian proclamation spiritualises the exodus story as a *walk in life* through the Spirit of the risen Christ. The new-born convert enters a new community of faith after being initiated through the rite and ceremony of baptism, and the New Testament programme closes with a message of hope, which is interpreted for some as a current revitalised life in the Spirit within the Church, and for others as a long awaited new order in the second advent of Jesus to set up the kingdom of God.

The Qur'an regularly cites Abraham as a veritable religious servant and as an example for those who leave aside the cares of this world in response to the call of God. Every Muslim will attempt the journey to Mecca to visit the Kaaba at least once in their lifetime, and there can be no doubting the significance of this pilgrimage as a *preparatory experience in life for a future reality*.

Ibn:	The real climax, I would say, was when I went to Saudi Arabia for Hajj. There were round about three million people, other Muslims who were there. There is a grand mosque there.
Dennis:	The Kaaba?
Ibn:	The Kaaba, yes, yes. And that's when I felt there is that spiritual power there which I did not feel anywhere else. It sort of gripped me, and I realised that the reality is not this world, reality is not this life; this is simply a temporary life; it's going to end, and it's basically of very little value. The reality is still to come. And that's what I felt in my heart, my spirit, whatever you call it; that I was closer to God then than I have ever been.
Dennis:	And do you still have the memory of that that keeps you going through each day?
Ibn:	Yes, that memory will never go; it was an experience of a lifetime … This spiritual awareness feeling kept increasing through the years, but, like I said, the Hajj experience was the climax. That completed, I would say, completed my enlightenment.
Dennis:	And do you see that as a taster of the life to come?
Ibn:	Oh yes, yes, in a way I could feel the ultimate reality to come. I was thinking how this life is not so important. Reality is still to come; it's going to come. What's going to happen there I need to prepare for, and that means preparing for what is to come after death.
Dennis:	Have you become a changed person since Hajj?

Ibn: Yes, definitely, I am more peaceful, you know, I'm talking about myself, my inner-feeling. I feel more in peace than I have ever been.

Dennis: What was it about the celebration of Hajj that made it the pinnacle of your experience of God? Was it something mystical that just happens?

Ibn: There are so many people praying together, and, because there is a spirit in each person, when you have so many people together there is a spiritual power there. The second thing is that there is history involved. The Kaaba, I understand, was built by the prophet Abraham and his son is Ishmael, although some people, you know, I mean the non-Muslims, are not quite sure that's what happened. But, we feel, I feel, that something big happened there.

Dennis: At that holy place?

Ibn: Yes, an event took place there, and therefore it's a special place and the whole atmosphere is different. I have never felt the atmosphere like that anywhere else.

These very different traditions have religious journeying programmes that serve as preparations for salvation. Throughout the last two millennia, the devout have felt compelled to make pilgrimages to centres of religious interest – Benares, Sinai, Jerusalem, Galilee, Rome, Lourdes, Mecca, and the Golden Temple, Gurudwara. As such the journeying archetype is unconsciously repeated from the times our human ancestors visited sacred trees, mountains and pools – where it was believed the Spirit resided – to the present with religious pilgrimages.

Stories of monks and pilgrims undertaking dangerous journeys into the mountains and through the deserts proliferate in the traditions of most religions – Moses returns to Egypt, Jesus walks to Jerusalem, Mohammed enters Mecca, Anthony moves to the desert, and Gautama leaves the palace for the street, etc. – and have inspired the masses to take up vocations of religious witness. There appears to be evidence of an archetypal aspiration of the human spirit, since there are similar quests within secular domains also, as pointed out in Chapter 5.

The Psychology of the Journeying Metaphor

Life as a spiritual journey is a common metaphor within humanistic therapy (McLeod, 1993) and religious counselling (Leech, 1977; Lyall, 1995).

> *Tony:* That's quite interesting, because you mentioned a journey at the beginning of this session, and I thought that I was not conscious of a journey, of being on a journey, but it is possible that I could be conscious of the journey, looking back, where I wasn't aware of the journey when travelling through it. If that would be the case, I assume that the journey continues but I'm not aware of being on a journey – that sounded very intelligent [*Tony smiles*].

Tony said that life did not present itself as a journey until mental processing and evaluating patterns and significances emerged through the discourse. Sam's use of vocabulary in various discourses carries more than a hint that her life is viewed as a journey:

> *Sam:* It seems to me now … in the assessment that you come to at this point, you think, 'it's such a pattern; it's a series of hurdles that everybody has to get over and everybody goes through – many are the same hurdles, maybe in a different order …'
>
> *Dennis:* If you were freed from all your responsibilities, where do you think your life would be directed?
>
> *Sam:* I don't know the answer to that. I've been asking people for 15 months. I haven't got a clue. I went through a really bad patch in September because I've got no idea. Of the two people I worked with in teaching, one of them has died, and I had to go last year on supply and help a teacher to put notices up on the wall and mark her register because she was so ill. And I look at people who are very involved

in teaching, who are in their fifties, and a lot of them *look dreadful*. So, I think, 'I've lost the plot with that'. I can't do it any more ... I'd like in respect of the religious context to be able to go to church on Sunday morning. I'd love that.

Transpersonal psychologists view life as a journey and encourage their clients to do the same by choosing the preferred path (Sutich, 1996), and such interventions carry for the client optimistic possibilities of a meaningful Self (Gergen, 2001).

In the final analysis, it is a personal interpretation, since most people in counselling say they are living largely commonplace, uneventful lives. One striking and controversial feature of spiritually-centred counselling, which may fill those of a psychodynamic persuasion with disdain, is a tendency to prompt clients with leading questions for *seeing* meaning in meaningless living, and for *re-viewing* relatively monotonous lives in an entirely different manner – such as suggesting metaphors for new meaning, or seeing the divine through the human lens, as suggested in the previous chapter.

There is theoretical tension between cognitive, solution-focused and narrative styles and psychodynamic and humanistic approaches in respect of leading questioning and the spiritually-oriented counselling I am promoting finds kinship in the former group, with the caveat that the interventions are not meant to be intrusive or to enforce the counsellor's agenda upon the client, but to suggest fresh possibilities for thinking, feeling and being. That said, spiritual work is not meant to be theory driven but theory informed. As Gergen (2001) maintains, theories are like lenses for looking at one aspect of reality that will satisfy at least some of the population. Theories serve to construct the world in particular terms; there is no means of empirically testing between them because each 'test' would inevitably construct the field of relevant facts in its own terms. Social construction models enlarge the options of choice, and therapists are invited to make use of the entire range of therapeutic intelligibilities and to employ whatever might be serviceable in the immediate context:

> This may include all existing forms of therapeutic discourse ... We must be prepared to rapidly expand the arena of usable meanings. For example, there is strong support here for those wishing to include spiritual discourse within the therapeutic process. (Gergen, 2001: 99)

As highlighted in Chapter 5, in eastern religious traditions a wandering sadhu might become an accompanying holy tutor for a youth as a rite of passage. A young initiate thereby would view himself as of being on a spiritual journey of non-attachment, across the subcontinent and for a significant period of time. The most radical sadhus test themselves through physical endurance – holding arms aloft for long periods, or standing for twenty-four hours a day. One of the considered demises of the modern period resulting from the erosion of religion has been the elimination of cultural rites of passage for the young, but, as pointed out by Joko Beck

(1997), the popularity of eastern esoteric philosophy, and Zen particularly, in American culture at the moment should not infer the copycat adherence of foreign realities which have little significance in western culture.

Juveniles have little concept of life-span development, naturally, since they live too near to the process of imminent physical and psychological change, and so religion has facilitated this requirement through ceremonial rites, such as Bar Mitzvah for Jewish boys.

For many secular societies, there are few common rites of passage apart from earning particular privileges at certain ages or joining political or social groupings where common interests occur. Similar to the influential missionary movements of the past, which have resulted in mixed reviews in modern times, and the evangelical compulsion to spread the Gospel, as referenced in Sam's experience, there have been secular revolutions and movements led by charismatic figures attempting to change the world by promoting the humanistic values of liberty and freedom – from the French Revolution to European laws of human rights.

Secular Journey Metaphors

Pychotherapy and counselling conducted without an understanding of and in disregard to life-span development is likely to be ineffective for most models and schools of theory (Thomas, 1990). But quite apart from unresolved decisions to join or leave political or revolutionary movements, which clients wish to explore with their therapists, there are other questions raised in spiritually-in-tune therapy that require articulation. There can be tension for many clients who are drawn towards the numinous but who also experience a longing for deeper and more enriched social engagements. Again, this highlights a common theme of this book, which is the recognition of empirical and mystical forms of reality. This is not to regard such quests as mutually exclusive, as though the mystical or numinous orientation to life involves monastic solitude, or an escape to the desert following a Damascus vision, since spiritual therapy is increasingly requiring a transition from a fundamentally isolated and contained Self towards Other-dependency, from beliefs of the self-contained individual towards a range of relational alternative perspectives (Gergen, 2001).

Demythologised Journey Metaphors

Religiosity or Human Service?

In essence, the monotheistic faiths of Judaism, Christianity and Islam are relational religions, both in respect to the divine and to the human. The Fourth Gospel through a historical framework of the ministry of Jesus portrays a mythological figure of the divine Son of God (Bultmann, 1971) revealed to the world through a series of signs (Dodd, 1953; Brown, 1971). He welcomes all believers to live alongside the Father in fellowship with the Son. Naturally, the Gospel message has a restricted interest for only those within the Christian fellowship, but to embrace a wider pluralistic perspective such a myth requires demythologising.

One very powerful tradition preserved in the Gospels which has great potential for universalism is characterised by a saying of Jesus as the judge in the final assize who invites anonymous disciples into the kingdom upon the grounds that they inadvertently serve Christ through their charitable deeds for the poor and needy (Matt. 25: 31–40), and this was offered to Dave, a Methodist pastor, in session:

Dave: I struggle with this through my life journey; I cannot reconcile an exclusive view of my parishioners being saved with those of humanists I know, even atheists, who live blameless lives that put mine to shame, who are supposedly not saved because they reject the Gospel.

Dennis: Mm. Over-zealous Christian certainty is troublesome. There is an authentic parable of Jesus preserved in Matthew's Gospel that has universal implications. When dividing the chosen sheep from the rejected goats, Jesus is challenged on the criteria of selection. His reply is telling and suggests that many carry out his teaching unaware that they do. By feeding the hungry, clothing the naked and visiting those in prison, they are, says Jesus, doing these things to me. But when the rejected appeal, 'When did we see you hungry and naked or in prison, etc.,' Jesus replies, 'In so much as you've done it to one of these the least of my brothers you have done it to me.'

Dave: I've always interpreted that as directed to members of the Church?

Dennis: Well, that would be convenient, wouldn't it, but not in line with scholarly opinion. Another saying is a rebuke by Jesus to a disciple during a missionary tour for resisting a fellow exorcist who was not one of the twelve: 'Do not stop him,' says Jesus, 'whoever is not against us is for us' [Mark 9: 38–41]. Now this saying must be authentic because it challenges Christian orthodoxy. The Church would have had an invested interest not to include it.

The journey, therefore, is characterised by everyday deeds of self-giving to the needy, which may supersede a life of religious practice.

End Time or Realised Judgment?

One controversial tension in New Testament scholarship is whether Jesus' message of the kingdom of God is to be understood as occurring during his ministry, what theologians term 'realised eschatology', or whether it should be conceived of as a future event in time at the second coming of Jesus, a 'final eschatology' (eschatology meaning last, i.e. end of the age). Needless to say, there will be Christian fundamentalists and evangelical theologians who take the latter position (discussed in Lines, 1995b) and critical theologians and philosophers who opt for the former (Cupitt, 2001). The difference in essence is the great calling to account at the end of time, or an ongoing self-assessment through life, and both views are commonly articulated.

> *Dennis:* Was there ever a time when you were expected to go to the mosque but didn't want to go?
>
> *Ibn:* No, I never felt like that, never. I'd never felt that I was being forced to go … They never said you have to go. They told me that it's my responsibility, and it is entirely up to me but if you don't go God is watching you and you will be accountable.

Tony's views on the final judgment were presented in Chapter 5 as realised eschatology. This extract illustrates how such views were shaped through his reflections on authority.

> *Dennis:* You say you want to be loved and valued, not judged.
>
> *Tony:* It would depend on what you mean by judgment. Does it mean passing sentence? Different words have different meanings to different people. I think you probably don't mind a judgment if you sense that the judgment comes from a position of love; you're not demeaned or lowered by that judgment but generally uplifted. I hear lots of times the phrase constructive criticism. However, I think ninety-nine percent of the time this is not the case. When considering what line of work I wanted to pursue I considered the Police and Teaching. I saw both of those jobs, at whatever level, as being in a position of authority. My desire was to demonstrate what I call *friendly authority*, because I think it's so important that authority is seen to be basically loving. I have at times pondered why I felt this. I do know that this approach has underpinned my work in teaching. I think it is important that the kids feel that this person who's an authority over them likes them … I feel I am able to create that feeling amongst those I teach.
>
> *Dennis:* Is that how you see God, as an authority figure who loves?
>
> *Tony:* They say that God is often a reflection of a father-figure, and you put onto God what you experience as a child.
>
> *Dennis:* That only works if you have a positive picture of your dad.
>
> *Tony:* I would see my dad as quite strict, and I have often thought that this may colour my image of God. I would say that Dad was a strict disciplinarian and slow to give praise. I see his possible impact on me as a result of the

impact of somebody else on him. I'm not able to blame anybody for anything. I love my Dad and miss him today!

Drinking the Eternal Moment

In the first three Gospels there is a mythological account of Jesus climbing a mountain with his closest disciples, Peter, James and John, to pray. Upon awakening they witness Jesus transfigured and brilliantly white and radiant, and in conversation with two great prophets of old (Moses and Elijah) about his forthcoming journey to Jerusalem. Each of the disciples felt that it was marvellous to be there and they began building temporary dens to stay in the heavenly place. Some critics regard this narrative as a further resurrection account misplaced, but the story as it stands may be demythologised to describe the universal experience along life's journey of having had *peak experiences* of numinous awe.

I think we sometimes have to draw the attention of young people to appreciate the beauty in nature, and also to offer clients in therapy alternative *re-visioning* of descriptive accounts they may consider to be insignificant. Being sensitively aware of *living in the present* by realising *the power of now* (Tolle, 2001) is offered to clients in metaphors, such as 'drinking the moment', to highlight a heightened sense of *connectedness* with the natural world, with other people, or with personal experience, particularly where clients have become stuck upon life's journey. The following extract became a profitable exchange with Sam in helping her evaluate her current path of boredom.

> *Dennis:*   Some journeys of life are merely about getting through as though life is a series of mental staging posts, or hurdles, whatever metaphor you choose. We think, 'Well, I've got to get to that bit; I've got to get over that. I've got to do the child-rearing bit, then there's the career bit. I've got to get the mortgage paid, and I'm heading for retirement. Blimey, I've reached retirement, next it's the grave. So, there's a sense of seeing life not as 'drinking the moment', but as getting to the next stage …
>
> *Sam:*   I'm not very money orientated, or thing orientated. Money doesn't bother me. People just give me things, so I don't need to go and kill myself to buy them for myself from a shop because people just turn up at the door and say, 'Have this.' Somebody said to me yesterday, a farmer, 'You must miss the money badly.' *No* [*Sam laughs*], because I've never had any money … You know that story about Chicken Licken going into the forest and an acorn falls on his head and he freaks out and goes into an absolute fit because he thinks the sky has fallen on his head. We think

the sky is going to fall on our heads with trivial things and really the big menace we don't even see coming.

Dennis: Does death bother you?

Sam: It did a while ago [*a change to sombre mood*]. I thought about it quite a bit in terms of not feeling quite finished, and also being aware of the passage of time and moving from 50 to 70, and you've got 20 years left. Another year goes by and you've got 19 now, 51 that's 18 left, but other people I've spoken to don't take it seriously at all; not even think about it, don't let it impinge on them or their working lives, and a lot of people I know make themselves very ill in that last 10 years.

Dennis: Death can also be a state of mind?

Sam: I think it probably is. In *Brideshead Revisited*, Lord Marchmend has all these false ends and Charles Ryder says to the priest, 'He's got a great will to live.' And the priest said, 'That's very strange Mr Ryder, because it struck me that he has a great fear of death.' I hear people in their seventies say to me, 'Well, I've had a good life', as though they've come to an assessment and are minding now – the box is ticked.

Dennis: I went through a stage of being bothered about death myself. There were two phases; one was during hospitalisation after the accident when trying to envisage a life of disability, and it was difficult for me to mentally construct a future that would be meaningful, but once I realised that that wasn't a reality, the sky didn't fall on my head, I saw things differently. The other phase was about three years ago when I had accomplished all my tasks, and things seemed to be coming to an end. There was a sense of looking for a summary of my life, a completion, an end.

Sam: What did you decide?

Dennis: I didn't decide anything specifically. Physical symptoms occurred due to negativity in thought which had an impact on my health. I remember writing in *Coming through the Tunnel* about a patient who willed himself to death, and a secretary in school used to work on a casualty ward and she told of many patients willing themselves to death, time and again. If there is a truth in this, then the converse must also be true; that if you mentally see yourself as being immortal, not in the sense that you deny the reality of death, but if you accept death when it comes, and know that you have very little control over it, you can say to yourself, 'What's the point of worrying about it'. It's the anxiety about the state of death that is worse than the state itself. What does it mean, after all? There's a sense in which you can drink each moment, as it were, and live for the moment in positive thought and this brings health dividends.

Sam: You're very good at drinking moments.

Role of Spiritual Therapist

Applying the spiritual journey metaphor of life opens again the role of the spiritually-inclined therapist. The therapist serves like a sports coach tutoring his client in some respects and an accompanying sherpa in others. In the sense of experienced fitness coach and guide, the spiritual counsellor serves to suggest different ways of achieving tasks, or of tackling obstacles in life. In the vignettes presented above, my tentative interventions involved suggestive questioning in asking how life might be understood *if viewed* through the journey metaphor, asking what could be made from a sense of mission or vocation, or of a summary account of one's life in terms of meaningfulness.

Sharing differing interpretations over the religious maps of the journey have considerable relevance, and teasing out fuller meaning through Socratic questioning within the enthused model of the narrative therapist hungry to learn more of the client's narrative also carries the hallmark of the companion life-guide. Such an approach will appear 'pushy' and controlling for some therapists. But, as I have said repeatedly, spiritually-oriented counselling of the form I advocate requires the practitioner to audit every intervention and to acquire the continual skill of internal dialogue of underlying values.

You may have noticed my need for specific analysis over Ibn's Hajj experience, my slight intolerance of Christian exclusivity in collusion with David, and I felt uneasy when Ibn spoke in ambivalent terms regarding being brought up to worship freely and yet being told that 'God is watching' and that 'you will be accountable'. I was aware of countertransference in my intervention with Tony, where my experience of counselling so many youngsters with negative experiences of their fathers was overriding the context of his material, and my positive life-enhancing philosophy on life was purposely used to encourage Sam to rise against her angst and boredom from a personal observation of how infectious optimism can uplift the human spirit.

A sports coach will attune what the athlete wishes to become with the particular exercises that best suits her capabilities, attempting to reach high but not push too hard beyond the limit. The sherpa will encourage the mountaineer to stop for a short breather to experience the view, to *learn to see* the spiritual in the natural, to *drink the moment* and not let it pass them by with an excessive preoccupation to reach the top.

These allegories should not be overstretched, however, since such life-guides will be viewed as having expertise in their own craft, and real-life journeys are varied and idiosyncratic, and as suggested to Sam, there will be no expert and no fixed way. The therapist–client relationship of the new spiritual paradigm is of a form of enquirer-with-enquirer rather than guide-to-novice or teacher-to-pupil, of two fellow spiritual travellers becoming intuitive to the inner promptings of the Other.

Conclusion

This chapter has asked what life might look like when viewed as a spiritual journey. Inevitably the reasoning has been circular and therefore essentially tentative. I have commended a perspective in counselling and psychotherapy through a theoretical understanding of human development and growth as the process of individuation where all life is as a journey of experience, but an experience conducted temporarily alongside a fellow tourist through life's twists and turns. Like Rogers' concern, such a perspective is not to take a Pollyanna view of human existence, since, as existentialist therapists point out, human life is fraught with despair as well as good fortune. The vicissitudes of life are unpredictable and the common experience of many – religious and humanist – is that blessings, however construed (gifts of God, or merited rewards) are not universally viewed as fairly distributed. Divine providence, if such exists, appears for many as more capricious than just.

The metaphor of the developmental journey of enlightenment has been linked in this chapter with epic journeys of antiquity, and with religious festivals and pilgrimages. There is value in demythologising some religious journey motifs to utilise in therapy the meaning they contain. Unfamiliar journeys involve risk as well as adventure, commonly by having to meet challenges and overcome obstacles encountered along the way, and some typical obstacles will be discussed in the next chapter.

8

Obstacles along the Path

A man in the East was found sitting on his roof because a great tidal wave was sweeping through his village. The water was well up to the roof when along came a rescue team in a rowing boat. They shouted, 'Well, come on. Get into the boat.' But he said, 'No, no. God will save me.' This happened twice, and finally along came a helicopter, but still he said the same. Eventually, the water covered his head and he drowned. When he got to heaven, he complained with these words, 'God, why didn't you try to save me?' And God said, 'I did; I sent you two rowing boats and a helicopter.'

Joko Beck

Wake Lord! Why are you asleep?
Why do you forget our affliction and oppression?

Psalm 44: 23–24

For some middle-aged clients who have conformed to a religious ideology without question throughout most of their lives the final stages of flowering as a person at the terminus point of individuation can be fraught with fundamental doubt and general scepticism. This can occur just prior to dying in some cases. Faith in something or other has no longer the power or security it once had for them. This chapter will explore the ambivalence of religious faith and spiritual insecurity that commonly occurs in life.

Secular-minded humanists, agnostics and atheists are not free from doubting the realities which appeared to have offered them security in the past, for their world equally shifts and is in transition. This chapter gives audience to one such voice, for he serves to sound out the hidden doubts of many of us. We shall explore what can be salvaged from the faith paradigm and become enduring for the religious, spiritual and sceptic alike. I shall first address the interesting topic of the social relevance of religion for clients in terms of mental health, and then look at the larger subject of faith as an ideology or as an attitude to life.

By following the reasoning to this point, and after comparing the selected extracts with discourse material of your own, you may have formed the impression that I view individuation as linear, progressive and a one-way process of self-actualisation. I am not sure this is the case, for whilst many adolescents appear to follow a progressive Freudian path of spurning metaphysical aspects of religion and mystery with newly acquired skills in cognition and reasoning there are some who become religious converts and who never appear to question their faith; some intuit quite naïve beliefs in their late teens and early twenties. No two paths are the same, and no one path is without its crossroads and in some cases immense obstacles.

Faith and Mental Health

John articulates the secular-minded position of atheism.

> *Dennis:* Did going to university give you the intellectual apparatus to challenge conventional belief?
>
> *John:* Intellectually, I was doing that myself, and had done that several years before I was 18. I can remember meeting a priest at Teacher Training College .., and he couldn't get his head round the fact that I didn't believe, and his usual line of attack would be: but surely there must be some purpose in life. What's the purpose in life if there is no God, John? And off we'd go. But I'd got that feeling at 15. I couldn't see any rational reason for there being religion.

His scepticism over his place in a Welsh chapel occurred in his teens:

> *John:* It dawned on me in a fairly short period of time, by which I mean a couple of months or so, that this was a load of mumbo jumbo … And I felt trapped in a way, because mom was the Sunday School teacher and I was by now an assistant in the Sunday School teaching the little ones; and general dog's body. And I can remember many a time sitting and listening to people praying and thinking [*John chuckles*], 'This is silly, this is. Why are we doing all this?' And then getting up for the hymn and having a jolly good shout, sort of thing, and enjoying that, and then sitting down and being berated by a preacher, whose morals

> might have been questionable as far as I was concerned.
> No, that's not true, but I was suspicious of his ability to
> live up to the principles of what he was trying to get us to
> adhere to…

I can still remember my religious conversion at seventeen, along with some of my friends, and the compelling feeling of spiritual urgency and openness to numinous experience. The numinous became evident through *solitude* and *reflection*, through *group worship* and through *listening to the charismatic preacher*. Some young people in counselling will testify to conversions if asked to do so (Lines, 2002), and the unquestioned religious adherence to fundamentalist groups, such as Waco, illustrates the abuse of conversion dynamics with impressionable young people. Sam spoke of such compelling movements during her younger university days, and it is debatable whether she is right in reasoning that such large-scale missionary enterprises will not take place as much today, or even whether such will become subsumed by New Age spiritualities (Heelas and Woodhead, 2005). There is an irony in that religious faith, which has survived through the modern period, has now in our time, since and because of the Enlightenment, become the very cause of doubt and scepticism.

There are many ironies that face religious and non-religious people. As John made clear, he loved hymn singing but could not go along with the Christian message in verse:

> *John:*   I learnt tonic sol-fa in the church and that's an ironic part of my life; I really enjoyed hymn singing and church music in spite of being atheist … There were ways in which I could compromise myself, not compromise myself. I felt that it was OK to do certain things. A good example is hymn singing. I mean, some of the words were absolutely, and totally [*said laughingly*], against my principles, but even today I can still do that because I like the music so much.
> *Dennis:*   So you switch off cognitively to what the words mean?
> *John:*   Yes, when I sing hymns, yes, because I enjoyed the harmony and the music so much … So I can let pragmatism rule and put up with the words.

Similarly, I valued the Church as a place to bring the young, but could not live with the blind acceptance of scriptural inerrancy in light of biblical criticism. Ambivalence over religious and spiritual matters is regularly an issue for clients in spite of counsellors having reservations about exploring such topics (Thorne, 2002; West, 2000, 2004), both in regard to social factors and ideology.

There is a dilemma that many psychologists have recognised in that there is sound research that supports positive health with religious practice (Richards and Bergin, 1997). John Swinton (2001) has demonstrated clearly the correlation of intrinsic religious faith and spirituality with mental health. Oliver James (2004) says that religion has been a rather tricky problem for social scientists. The trouble is that in study after study, people who attend a place of worship once a week come out as less likely to suffer depression or unhappiness than those who do not. I could not fail but be impressed with Ibn's devout certainty over the truths of Islam, and with his unshakeable conviction that God was continually with him.

Dennis: What do you mean when you say that God is with you, I mean in practical terms?

Ibn: I understand that if we do certain things according to the will of God then he will be with us, you know, if we need him at any time he is more likely to help us.

Dennis: Have you ever questioned this? Have you ever gone through doubts or experiences in life where you have wondered whether God is *really there for you*?

Ibn: Some people may not believe this, but *I have never ever felt God has abandoned me*, you know; that God has left me. Even if there are difficult times, say, for example, money is short, health is not good, if things are not working out, then I feel it's not that God has left me but he could well be testing me. He could be testing me to see whether my faith is still strong and because of that my faith never weakens ... During my life whenever I have needed something somehow a situation develops that my need is met.

Dennis: Really?

Ibn: Yes.

Few books on religion fill the shelves of high street booksellers these days and there is no clear reason why religious practice equates with positive mental health. It could be because religious people were actually more than averagely screwed up before God came into their lives, says James (2004), or it could be that it is not religion that is doing the business for them but the fact that religious people are much more likely to be actively involved in their communities. The fact remains that religious ritual and its secular equivalents have a positive effect on physical performance and mental health (Butler, 2002). There is even evidence that *high expectation* of being healed (as in a Gospel Healing Services) releases chemicals in the brain (dopamine) that result in improved health and functioning (Kathy Sykes: BBC2 *Alternative Medicine*, 31 January 2006). Each of us has a powerful self-healing mechanism that healers have found a way to manipulate.

West (2000) and Swinton (2001) distinguish between healthy and unhealthy forms of religiosity and spirituality through Allport's (Allport and Ross, 1967) distinction between mature, intrinsic religion and imma-ture, extrinsic religion. The former as practised by those who internalise their faith and follow it fully, and the latter as practised by those who use religion for their own ends, turning to God without turning away from

Self. Richards and Bergin (1997: 78–112) present research that correlates religion with positive mental health, yet Vaughan (1991 – cited by West, 2000) warns against the hazards of what she calls 'spiritual addictions', where clients, for example, avoid facing problems in life by using spirituality as a 'magic solution'. Healthy spirituality (Vaughan, 1991, cited by West, 2000) supports personal freedom, autonomy, self-esteem and social responsibility. It does not deny for clients their humanity or the need to suppress or deny their emotions.

Faith as Ideology

Turning now to Christian faith as a lived ideology, Charles Ryder reflects in the screenplay adaptation of *Brideshead Revisited* (Waugh, 1951) an ambiguous upper-class religious outlook:

> A view implicit in my education was that the basic narrative of Christianity had long been exposed as a myth, and that opinion was now divided as to whether its ethical teaching was of present value; a division in which the main weight went against it. Religion was a hobby which some people professed and others did not. At the best it was slightly ornamental; at the worst it was the province of complexes and inhibitions; patch words of the decade, and of the intolerance, hypocrisy and sheer stupidity attributed to it for centuries. No one had ever suggested to me that these quaint observances expressed a coherent philosophical system, and intransigent historical claims. Nor, had they done so, would I have been much interested. (Waugh, 1951 – Granada Television, 1981)

Waugh (1951) presents the intriguing and often debated relationship between religion and morality (begun by Kant) through dialogue with Charles and Sebastian, and as articulated by John:

Dennis: Would you go along with those philosophers of religion who claim that you cannot have a morality without a Lawgiver – some Being who is moral *per se*?

John: As though there is an absolute set of morals out there? I'm slightly uncomfortable with that as a conclusion. No, I think you could have a set of morals without tablets of stone, or anything like that, being handed down.

Dennis: I suppose what we don't know is that since our morals are culturally developed, and since religion has shaped our culture to some extent … it's hard to isolate morality from a Christian context.

John: But, if you go to a culture which is almost pre-Christian in many ways, and I'm thinking now of Ghana, of course [John spent two years in Ghana with the VSO] … It's my experience that they still have a lot in common about what was right and what was wrong, in treating a fellow human being. And so, I think that we as a species have sets of values which are common across us all regardless of what religion was holding sway. At the moment, yes, in this country, Christianity has laid down lots of patterns of religious behaviour which wash over into the general culture, but Christianity has only been going for two thousand years hasn't it.

Dennis: So, are you saying that human beings are moral *per se*?

John No, not at all. I think that most human beings recognise moral behaviour, and know what is right and wrong in various aspects of behaviour, and whilst most of us fall down in doing the right thing, too often we know that we've fallen down and are not doing the right thing ... Whatever culture you look at you'll find that people are the same whatever their religion. There's a wide range of interpretations within any one religion, but basically wherever you go you'll find people think it is not right to hit another person, that you shouldn't presume to touch a woman where you shouldn't touch a woman, and all these rules, cultural or whatever you want to call them, are part of people's behaviour that are sometimes broken. There are bad people who break these rules in all cultures and religions and there are good people who stick to them well...

Spiritually-centred counselling at best allows religious, anti-religious and spiritual opinion and ambiguity to be aired and explored, in a non-threatening and mutual-learning style of discourse. There are no right and wrong answers, since *perceptions are all there are*. Each perspective is a valid discourse, and the therapist, as Gergen (2001) maintains, is invited to use whatever makes sense, including the broad range of spiritual and philosophical discourses. Holloway (2004: 12, 132–71) is mystified with the meaninglessness of life but in regard to universal morality argues for *playing life by ear*, similar to a good jazz player.

Discourses on Faith and Evidence

The question of waning faith will have become for many clients a large stumbling block to spiritual growth and individuation. Biblical faith can be translated into personal trust in God, but since the Enlightenment, with Descartes' *Cognito ergo sum*, I think therefore I am, there has developed a conception of religious faith as holding particular ecclesiastical propositions against empirical evidence. *Faith* and *evidence* have become an antithetical means of measuring reality rather than different modes of discourse. Descartes was trying to find some form of knowledge that it was impossible to doubt. We can doubt the existence of the outside world, or that other people are there, because such knowledge can be illusionary – I could be dreaming, or be misled by another power. The only thing I can know for sure, said Descartes, is that I exist. At the centre of everything, there is Self doing the thinking, Self doing the doubting. And, as we saw in Chapter 1, David Hume was not even sure of his own sense of Self, let alone God.

As Hick (1990) illustrates, following Kant (*Critique of Pure Reason*, 1781), we see the world through already formed mental concepts, or templates, or schemas. If we believe the world is full of witches and demons, then when a black cat is seen, or when an unexplainable illness is suffered quite unfortuitously, then causality is understood within a worldview inhabited by demons and witches. The evidence of phenomena will confirm the belief to be correct. If the whole world is viewed within a Christian framework, where God is the divine architect having complete control over everything that happens, then the Christian hypothesis is confirmed (even if evil and ill-fortune cannot be explained) because no credible evidence to dispute it emerges from experienced phenomena. Inevitably, Naturalism is confirmed for those who view the world through a lens of naturalism. This is why beliefs become so fixed and rigid for many people, and why *evidence* is circular and self-reinforcing.

The philosopher, Antony Flew (Flew and Macintyre, 1955), has asked the fundamental question about the experience of difference. In the area of religious thinking, the challenge can be stated like this: if I believe God exists how would the world be different from one in which God did not exist? What would be the appreciable difference if my belief was wrong? Can I ever know if my belief is not mistaken? As Hick (1990) has said, to say that faith in itself is *evidence* is not sufficient, because a strong belief that witches exist would not make any appreciable difference if the belief was proved wrong. Are we therefore left with Pascal's argument that God might exist only on the basis of probabilities? It is curious that Flew, at 80 and as a long-time sceptic of religious belief, has recently announced that he has switched viewpoints. After examining all the data, he has concluded that the *evidence* now points to the existence of a higher power. Curiously, many physicists (Einstein, Heisenberg, Bohr) have held mystical beliefs (Wilber, 1984, 2001b). My argument at this point is not about belief-content, however, but about belief-formation in mental processing.

According to infant brain research and Kantian philosophy, we are indoctrinated so all-pervasively from an early age. The rules and theories we perceive as *self-evident* have become hard-wired into our brains through subtle manoeuvres of approval by powerful authorities. We fail to recognise that the beliefs about the world and about ourselves, which we carry around with us like sacred relics, are tentative and possibly wrong. We are completely convinced that our beliefs are true, because these concepts are literally part of ourselves. Our hard-wired brains give a spin for every phenomenon of the senses without question (Darling, 1996), but one prominent scientist (Damasio, 2003) argues that Darwinian evolution requires humans to 'live prudently and to care for one another' (Holloway, 2004: 28). But this reality has no objective status other than our perceptive awareness – *nothing is real, there are only perceptions.*

The modern obsession with our egos is nothing more than artefacts of brain developed for survival. According to the causal-materialist discourse, we are the dreams of carbon machines of electro-chemical activity, and our emotions, thoughts and sensations are bound together by that fragile thing called memory. This was how John viewed the world as a physicist.

John:	I read this book recently about Turing machines and it underlined for me that we are basically a bunch of atoms that behave in the way they do because of the forces between positive and negative charges and so on. And that's all that we are. And I had thought that ever since 15, or whatever, but I happened to read this book that talked about self-awareness. I don't know what religious people would say about the difference between human beings and animals, but they would talk about the spirit wouldn't they, probably …
Dennis:	They would talk about consciousness.
John:	Yes, and self-awareness, and consciousness, then, yes. The simplest machine, in computer terms, is a light switch because it can be either on or off; it has two states. If you put a lot of those on-off states together you get computers, and we know that computers can do quite a lot of things nowadays. And if you look inside our brain, you'll find on-off switches as well throughout our bodies. And so we are just more sophisticated computers, which at some stage have found switches which enable them to know, and be aware of, and be conscious of, other switches that are doing things in the system. And there are simple examples of that, for instance, thermostatic control of a heating system that knows that it's got too hot and it switches off. And that's a very simple form of self-awareness, and that's an argument which is developed in that book.
Dennis:	It doesn't know in the sense that it's conscious of itself knowing, does it? In a sense, surely, it operates mechanically by use of a bi-metallic strip?
John:	Yes, but it depends what you mean by conscious.
Dennis:	But you and I know something, and we know that we know something, which is a bit different from something which fulfils certain laws of mechanics or chemistry, isn't it?
John:	Is it … ? [*John laughs and I laugh as though in stale-mate*] To know that you know, I can see what you mean, but how do you know that what we're doing is not a much more sophisticated arrangements of bi-metallic strips?

John gives an account of 'scientific reductionism'. His interpretation of
the origin of religion centres on naturalism, which curiously, upon his
own reflection, touches on what he refers to as the common experience of
awe and wonder experienced upon a mountain, but which I might for-
mulate as a numinous experience.

John:	I think that religion has come from man's dependence on nature. We need to have a summer again otherwise we'll have no crops and we'll starve. We need to appease the gods because they send lightning and set our crops on fire, so that all those things come from superstitious beliefs in nature. And to me that's a *powerful argument* against any form of religion, because you go to any part of the world, you can use this both ways, and you'll find superstitious beliefs which developed people will poo poo, and think, well there're no gods in that lump of stone whatever.
Dennis:	I see what you're saying, but I'm not sure any of us can fully free ourselves from superstition. There are unconscious parts of our being which we still retain, as in your case, 'fallen angels'. It may be more ingrained within us than we like to think is the case. The sun will rise on the other side of the mountain and pleasantly surprise us, but then as a scientist you know its orbit follows certain laws.
John:	Yes, I know that *now*, but if I had been born two thousand years ago I wouldn't have known it then. I'm looking at it from that point of view. That's how religion started.
Dennis:	But is there a part of our nature which is receptive to more abstract notions of nature, as in your case music? Why should you just like hymn music? Why not see taste, music, art, as something which fulfils certain mechanical laws?
John:	Why not? Why not? I mean this frustrates me a little because people are almost trying to find arguments and it's often the awe and wonder when you stand on top of a mountain and think, *'God somebody must have created this'* and those arguments sometimes annoy me because they are held by people who have a religious belief, and they are looking for arguments to …
Dennis:	Support it.
John:	Support it, yes, and convince others, perhaps. That irks me a little. That's coming round to the question on the other side of the case. To answer your question about spiritual-ity, as well as the physical events around people in more primitive times, there were also occasions when they had perhaps gone on top of a mountain, and looked at the view, or, oh, I don't know, something wonderful happened and they will have that moment when they reflect within themselves and think, 'Something must exist which has

	made this happen.' And the awe and wonder feeling starts. I think most people have had moments like that.
Dennis:	Have you?
John:	Yes... I can remember one in particular on top of a mountain, and it was a view, but because I've had that I rationalise it the other way, you see, and I use that as evidence that anyone who has anything happen, which they would call a religious experience, is just having a bit of awe and wonder that I've had as well and they're interpreting it differently. So you can interpret it according to your own prejudices.
Dennis:	The school of humanistic psychology talks about peak experiences, which are transitory, and very common. Most people have peak experiences.
John:	Yes.
Dennis:	They feel a heightened awareness of something ...

I would be surprised if anyone reading this discourse would not find themselves siding with one point of view, and this will indicate where along the continuum they may be currently sitting. The opposite pole was represented by Ibn earlier. Here is a further extract of his views on the spiritual.

Ibn:	I believe that reality is spiritual. If I could give you an example, I would take the atom bomb. The atom bomb is energy and energy is created from material. Because of that, we know that there is energy in material. Material can be changed into energy, and energy can be changed into material, and this is how I believe the whole universe came about – the Big Bang, and so on. It was created from energy. For another example, electricity, we see an electric wire, there is a generator on one side but you can't see electricity passing through the cable.
Dennis:	No, we see its effects.
Ibn:	Yes we see its effect, we feel it if we touch it. Spirit is energy ... In Christianity we say, 'God is love'. Although I would say it should be, 'God is loving'. What is love? When you love another person, that person, say, might be in London, you still have that feeling of love existing between two people. So, what is that love?
Dennis:	Yes, it's like a bridge, isn't it?
Ibn:	Yes, so what is that love? It's that spiritual connection. It's not bodily connection. If one is in London and another in Birmingham, then that is spiritual connection.
Dennis:	I see what you are saying.
Ibn:	Now that is spiritual connection and because the source of our spirit is God, there has to be that relationship, that love between our spirit and its source. And that is the connection between man and God. God is loving, and we are supposed to love God as well. Six years before I went to Saudi Arabia for Hajj I saw a place in my dream. I saw my

father there. Out of the blue he was coming towards me smiling and he said, 'I was thinking of you. You may be late but you've managed to get here.' And for six years I kept thinking, now where is that place, because I haven't even seen a picture of that place. And when I went there I saw the exact place where it was flat and a ramp coming down and there I saw my father and I thought, *'This is the place* I saw in my dream'. Now it could only have been my spirit that was taken there, the place was shown to me, and perhaps even my father's spirit interacted with my spirit.

There is a sense in which both John's and Ibn's positions are correct, in that they represent two realities of human experience. I am sure a physicist would pick fault in Ibn's physics, and a philosopher would point out the common practice that people begin with a faith and then attempt to rationalise it later, as Aquinas did, rather than the other way around. There again, John's discourse operates within a closed belief-system; he chooses to interpret his mountain top experience non-mystically and views consciousness within materialistic constructs. In Wilber's (2001a: 93) scheme, interpretations of direct and immediate spiritual experience need to be checked against all four quadrants of reality. Personal evaluations of higher consciousness which account for phenomena as solely or predominantly from brain states (theta brain wave states, massive endorphin, hemisphere synchronisation) are mistaken if they disregard the possibility of an interior transpersonal state of consciousness – archetypal form, inner-voice, transcendental awareness, etc. Equally, Ibn's personal interpretation ignores the behavioural, social and psychological quadrants of Spirit manifestation.

These two conversations took place without any emotional feelings of personal threat, since each of the parties felt fairly secure to debate openly and dispassionately. They were largely cerebral exchanges, but they are accounts by which lives are lived. This may not always be the case, however, because religious beliefs, as John recognises, can evoke strong feelings. One reason for such strength of feeling over religious and spiritual attitudes is that they are held to be founded on the *sure ground* of absolute inerrancy of sacred scripture (see Appendix). There is hardly a debate in Anglicanism or Catholicism – gay priesthood, women in the Church, birth control, euthanasia, etc. – that will not draw upon scriptural endorsement to carry the argument. Similarly, within Islam at this time feelings are running high in terms of internal dialogue of Muslim factions (Manji, 2004) and on the world political stage where east meets west. From articles of faith, the argument moves on to explore how Self is understood since different perceptions may hinder spiritual healing.

Rival Discourses on Self

John's discourse above underlies the tenets of reductionism, but is this how we experience incoming data? Clearly, modern physics has revealed beyond reasonable doubt that atoms consist almost entirely of empty space. And even the supposedly tangible nuggets of matter inside atoms (quarks and electrons) give no sign of extension. But matter *is experienced* as solid material not empty space. In a similar way, it is absurd in the light of what we experience to be told that the Self has no real existence. On one level, at least, we are just as entitled to regard Self as an entity in its own right as we are to credit an independent existence to anything, from germs to galaxies. The existence of the soul appears to lie beyond the realm of scientific inquiry, but this is not true of the Self.

Anatomical research and psychology will probe the Self in many different ways and, as a result, will hope to learn more about what it means to have a Self – and to lose it. We are left with two realities, therefore, one where Self receives information through selection before organisation in order to survive, and the other how Self experiences phenomenon that is perceived as reality. Social discourse in reflective conversation, as in therapy, will reflect these two realities.

Secondly, Descartes' certainty has become the great trap for the modern period by locating certainty within the individual (Gergen, 1999), and philosophers have found it impossible to discover a bridge that links one's own personal reality with that of another (Wilber, 2001a). Gergen (1999: 50–8) amplifies the fragile foundations of modern science and the erroneous public confidence in its certainties. Philosophically, the concept of knowledge where the mind functions as a *mirror to nature* has never been established, linguistically, since Wittgenstein. The scientist has failed to recognise the 'language game' in which his methodology is embroiled. From a social construction perspective, what constitutes *fact* as opposed to *opinion* obscures the notion that a particular researcher works within a *paradigm* (Kuhn, 1962) designed to silence objectors, create a 'high priesthood' of *expertise* (by mystifying information that is unintelligible to the masses), and to establish its own power hierarchy as the ultimate authority in the quest for *the truth*.

But, 'scientific revolution is essentially the shift from one paradigm to another' (Gergen, 1999: 54). Gergen (1999: 91–4) shows how the 'certainty' of empirical research is based upon a 'network of interlocking assumptions' of the individual knower, the promise of objective truth and the progress through research. Regarding dispassionate research, scientists typically have an investment in particular outcomes and a preference for numbers over words in data analysis. Statistics create an illusion of greater accuracy in silencing objections. Cause and effect methodologies are socially constructed – there is often an a priori commitment of selection of antecedents rather than a quest to discover the world as it is. Constructionists do not aim to invalidate empirical research but to expose – as in all claims to *the truth* – the inherent values and intelligibilities lying behind traditional science and its particular location in culture. Gergen's call is to abandon the prefix *is true* for a perspective that values its relationship to other social realities.

We are left stranded within Self and the solitary prison of an 'I' locked within the individual. Poets and writers have spoken of this condition as alienation, speaking of a yearning to find a sense of reality that connects us back with each other and the world in which we live. When two lovers embrace, or when a baby is being fed by her mother, these are not two realities desperately trying to infer the reality of the other. No, they are in relationship, and their individual reality is fused within the reality of the Other. The primary reality is not two autonomous Selves struggling to find each Other. 'Relationship exists prior to private selfhood. *Relationship*, our fundamental *connectedness*; these come first' (Frazer, 2005). Like Henry Moore's 'Mother and Child' we are all carved from a single piece of stone, or for the theist, God is the love that binds us all together (Frazer, 2005). Whilst 'experience', say, of compassion, of being in love, or of envy, may be reduced to neuron activity and hormonal activity, and thereby be a misnomer, a product of folklore inseparable from cultural linguistics (Gergen, 1999), I cannot see that some 'feelings' related to those terms are not universally a reality of private possession. How else can the artistry of Michelangelo, the language of Shakespeare and the lyrics of the Beatles find such universal appeal if they each in their own way did not touch some human experience within our makeup that corresponds with common, culturally unified emotions.

Ravinder: I've lost my faith after leaving India and moving to Birmingham. My parents would never stand for this, not attending the Temple and mixing with non-Sikhs. And when I moved in with Peter, God you'd think I'd personally insulted them and deliberately gone out of my way to offend them.

Dennis: Perhaps you've grown up and begun to make decisions on your own authority.

Ravinder: Yes, I know that, but why do I feel so damn guilty about everything I do?

Dennis: It's a funny thing, guilt. There seems to be different layers of guilt. Personal guilt for having not reached the standards we set ourselves. Guilt stemming from others for having made conscious decisions to live by our own dictates rather than those of our parents, religious teachers, or whatever. And guilt arising from avoided opportunities for having not responded to another person's need.

Ravinder: You're trying to make me feel better by implying I should not be held accountable to my parents' value system.

Dennis: I don't think I have any power to control the way you feel; I can only describe the way I see things and what I have learnt from my own experience and inner reflections.

Ravinder: It's as though I'm divided up with horses pulling me apart like Hercules. There's my Rational Self which tells me it's insane to feel guilty over something I have no shame for. Then there's my Adult Self that says I should grow up and not worry ... Then there's my Inner-Child Self that says, 'Sod off. I'll do as I please; I'm not a little girl anymore.' There's my Altruistic Self that tells me not to be selfish by ignoring the wishes of my parents ... And then there's my Sensitive Self that reproves me for being so hard-hearted ... But then there's my Accountable Self that says, 'Ravinder, this is your life. Be happy, you're not actually injuring any third party, so live your life.'

Dennis: And underlying this divided Self there is an attempt to live in harmony with mind, heart and spirit – *just You*. Maybe God can see beyond all such division?

Ravinder: Yea, just me. Maybe he can. Maybe he does.

Dennis: Where does it feel right: being with Pete and not attending the Temple, or complying with your parents' wishes and being the Obedient Self?

Ravinder: When I'm with Pete it feels that we are one and that we belong together. I feel *connected* with him and disconnected with mom and dad.

The Obstacle of Human Suffering

The pupil dilates in darkness and in the end finds light, just as the soul dilates in misfortune and in the end finds God. (Hugo, 1980: 382)

Religious Discourses on Suffering

C. S. Lewis (1940) said that the problem of pain is atheism's most potent weapon against Christian faith, and Jung in his *Answer to Job* (1954) found archetypal foundations in his biblical commentary on innocent suffering. For Jung, the story of Job postulates God as a morally evolving personality. The problem of pain and unjust human suffering has entertained the minds of religious and secular philosophers through the ages. The earthquake in Lisbon in 1755 took the lives of 70,000 people, and prompted Rousseau and Voltaire to correspond with each other on the nature of innocent suffering. The problem was that some of the casualties were worshipping in church at the time and had been brought up to believe that earthquakes were acts of divine punishment. In January 2006, 345 Muslim pilgrims were crushed to death in a stampede during the Hajj stone-throwing ritual in Saudi Arabia, and when returning home 800 sojourners were drowned as an Egyptian ferry sank in the Red Sea. Clearly, natural tragedy is no respecter of persons. Various interpretations still serve for people today as a range of dialogues through which sense is made of human frailty, or through which trials of faith are explored.

The Tsunami tidal disaster in the Indian Ocean took over 150,000 lives and provoked again that well-rehearsed dialogue on human suffering. Whilst the bombing of the trade towers might be put down to human evil, the Tsunami flood throughout Sri Lanka, Indonesia and Thailand was an event of natural cataclysm – for some, an 'act of God'. What sense do various peoples make of disasters of apocalyptic proportions? For those most affected by the disaster, the indigenous Hindu populations, the geological shifting of tectonic plates that created havoc was *karma*, the law of cause and effect, the second law of thermodynamics which states that for every action there is a reaction. Although Hindus believe in a spiritual order above the natural order, and in a personal manifestation of God, these two orders are quite separate and it is not felt that natural disaster has any bearing, or any consequence, on the spiritual realm. *The Hindu aims to reach absolute love, but salvation involves escaping the material world through reincarnation.*

For Buddhists, all is suffering and transience. We live in a universe which is largely disinterested in human concern, and as such the Tsunami tidal wave has no more or less significance than being symptomatic of the human condition. *Buddhism aims to respond to suffering with compassion and generosity, but with wisdom.* Existential therapeutic approaches have evolved from these discourses, in seeing natural as well as human tragedy as being the givens of life on planet earth.

Such explanations are not as convenient for the Abrahamic traditions. For Jews, who have suffered much in history, the question to ask is not why the suffering but *what can I do about it*, or as Jonathan Sacks (2005) wrote on the Tsunami disaster:

> Unlike the ancients who held the gods accountable for human tragedy, the God of monotheistic faith has set life within a non-discriminate range of happenings out of which hope can become born. Natural disasters are the physical conditions of life on planet earth, with all the implications of capricious dealings of fate or fortune: freedom, pleasure, achievement, virtue, creativity, vulnerability and love. The religious question is, therefore, not: 'Why did this happen?' but, 'What then shall we do?'

Judaism challenges God for allowing suffering but will see it as an opportunity to bring out what is noble in the human spirit.

Christianity promotes a personal, benevolent God who cares for his children, and this is not easy to square with natural adversity. Various explanations, such as God creates a universe of fixed laws where such calamities will occur in due course, and that it is a matter of chance whether an individual is struck or spared, do not fully get round the problem of a universe where God's activities appear capricious (Goulder and Hick, 1983). Christians believe that God has entered into the world of suffering – the Incarnation, the Cross – and can be 'touched' by human suffering, but Christian teaching endorses followers to pray ardently to be released from suffering (threat of cancer, escape from earthquake, etc.) under an assumption that God *can if he chooses* alter natural laws. Some fundamentalist Christian groups apply this teaching to such epidemics as

AIDS, and contend that 'God is teaching us that our mores on sexual behaviour are wrong', other Christians view disaster as Christian opportunity – the organisational abilities of religious groups still can exert influence in the world compared to contemporary human spirituality (Holloway, 2004: 50). *The answer for Christians is to view God in human suffering, and to hope for the New Age where death and suffering are transformed.*

The position for Islam is to view trials in life as a test, as Ibn outlined. For the Muslims of Indonesia, God is all powerful and ever merciful, but everything happens according to his will. Although natural tragedies confound us at times, we have to be encouraged to see the bigger picture in an assurance that all will be well for those who keep to his word. God causes the disaster (rather than the conditions where it will occur) to 'test the individual' in some way, and while there may be a clash between his benevolent 'nature' and his questionable 'activity', our place is to submit to Allah's will. *The answer for Muslims is to get on with your life and try and improve yourself and the world where you can in preparation for future life in Paradise.*

Humanistic Discourse on Suffering

Humanists have a point when they say that monotheists cannot have it both ways – a benevolent God has little credibility in the face of non-discriminating natural disasters. Geologists have said that the only way the earth can replenish itself and avoid becoming infertile is through the geological upheaval of Teutonic plates rubbing against each other. The earth would otherwise become smooth with erosion, and with water become a swamp, supporting only simple forms of life. To maintain a habitable earth and keep the equilibrium of the planet there must be a movable crust and material replacement to avoid decay and stagnation. Meteorologists tell us that rapid changes of air temperature are essential for life. The hurricane in New Orleans was necessary to have heat exchange from one part of the continent to the other to support life. In other words, natural disasters are built into the fabric of the universe. Ours is the only possible world that can sustain life, but, as a by-product, such a system is not always going to be kind to individuals at the cutting edge, and many will die in occasional earthquakes, tsunamis and hurricanes – *time and chance happen to all people.* Life, death and regeneration are part of the human condition, and are reflected in religious discourses like Lord Shiva, the Creator and Destroyer, and a saying of Jesus: 'Unless a grain of wheat falls into the earth and dies, it remains alone; but if it dies, it bears much fruit' (John 12: 24).

Dostoevsky (*The Brothers Karamazov*) raised the question in 1881: if God could not create a world without some degree of suffering, then why bother in the first place? Clayton's (1998) reply was that he imagined the divine poised over the button weeping, yet feeling that it was better to have us than be in eternal emptiness. We would probably not have pushed the button, but when he pushed it there is a hint that creation is something we don't understand. But why couldn't God step in occasionally and intervene to prevent a catastrophe? Moral philosophers have reasoned that if this did happen human beings could not make the connection between an action and its consequence, and as such it is difficult to imagine how we could be moral and become responsible for our actions. There cannot be human goodness without human tragedy.

Some judge that God can be seen active in addressing disaster through saints like Mother Teresa, or in saving people through human agency, as in the quote from Joko Beck which opened the chapter. A similar story is presented by Wilber (2001a: 289) from the tradition of Vedanta Hinduism to stress that Brahman can be found in everything and that all is one in Him. A man tests this out by standing in the path of a striding elephant. In spite of shouts to get out of the way by the elephant's rider, he stands sure in the belief that if Brahman was one with him the elephant should do him no harm. When being flattened he was asked by the sage why he chose not to listen to Brahman speaking through the rider. The Big Question of suffering may be answered for some through the human-divine lens (Buddha leaving the palace, Christ on the Cross), or by viewing *human suffering as an opportunity for giving*.

The tidal wave of Asia brought universal generosity in donations for humanitarian relief (one billion pounds in the UK during the first week), and on other occasions, as articulated with Sam, human tragedy often prompts international sympathy that reminds us of our human *connectivity*.

The Big Question Why

I call aloud, but there is no justice. (Job 19:7)

The book of Job reads like a play that addresses the question of why God allows good people to suffer (Kushner, 2002). Although suffering Job remains faithful to God, he does not remain silent: *what have I done to you, you tireless Watcher of humanity?* Towards the end of the book there is a curious turn. Job repents and acknowledges God as being righteous, but then God's reply is, *'No, actually, you're right; the others are wrong'*. This remarkable series of discourses does not answer the human plight so much as reflect it, and the Qur'an, which draws on many Jewish stories, significantly edits out of the narrative of Job any hint of questioning God's justice. Allah is not to be interrogated. He is Most-Merciful, and although He hears Job's prayer and removes his affliction, there is no calling to question His justice (21: 83; 38: 41). It seems to me that the original story captures an existential drama that later rewriting has tended to disguise (Appendix).

Counsellors and psychotherapists will have occasion to listen to clients who are struggling with matters of faith and justice, and who may have suffered 'unfairly at the hand of God', or malevolent forces. Therapists may refrain from comment, but the spiritually-in-tune counsellor will enter these dialogues collaboratively with experiences of his own, which will not only be valid but also of benefit in reshaping the cognitive grasp of the Big Question 'Why'. It is not a case of foisting his own unresolved tensions upon his clients, or abusing their right for unqualified attention for something deserved and for which they have paid, but more a case of a different understanding of therapeutic *presence*, a case that for one to grow both will grow.

> *Simon:*   Why did God have to take her? Why did she have to die? All our married lives we've given to the Church and to his service. Every night she'd prayed to be free of cancer; everything was given to those worse off than us. Ask anyone, they'll tell you. There's no justice in this universe and as for God, and that bloody Church, I'm finished! [*Simon breaks down for a few minutes*] … and now I've lost her; now she's gone; now life is over [*Simon sobs a while longer, then rubs his eyes with open palms. I reach forward and touch his knee*] … Sorry …
>
> *Dennis:*   It's OK. I don't know what to say.
>
> *Simon:*   No, there's nothing anyone can say. She's gone, and that's it.
>
> *Dennis:*   What will you do?
>
> *Simon:*   Thanks for staying with me, for being here. I don't know; I just don't know.

I felt powerless through Simon's sadness. He didn't know what to do, and neither did I. As counsellor, I could *feel* his sadness, but I couldn't take it away. I could not replace his loss, fill the gap, or relieve the pain, I could only *be there*; I could only *travel with him* into the cold darkness of his cave of despair; I could only *bridge* his separation with human *connectivity*. For those religiously in-tune with divine providence, any gesture of sympathy is a sign of God's care for suffering made evident through a human being, but for the humanist, who is equally concerned but who cannot see God's invisible hand through human kindness, sympathy is a token of the human spirit feeling *connected* to human suffering.

Faith as Trust in Life

I have found on occasions clients in therapy whose discourse indicates for me that they live on a spiritual plane of being open to the numinous. They are not always members of religious communities, but what is common amongst them is their sheer optimism for the future, their implicit trust in human potential and their intuitive openness to directives in life which prompt their courses of action. They rarely pray formally but live within a mystical communion with life as though in constant prayer. They are not psychotic or devoid of reasoning, far from it, but see the reasoning course as being limited if applied as the only discourse on life. They are one with the *Spirit of life* and they live as though permanently in love with nature, deriving from the cosmos greater depth and expanding consciousness (Wilber, 2001a). They are not hedonists but are self-sacrificial and it seems to me that they are to be found at the empirical as well as the mystical position of the empirical–mystical continuum. Their faith is not in God necessarily, or in creed, or in ideology, or in the scriptures, but in something which encompasses all these and yet is above them all: 'A genuine spiritual Self does manifest its own reality', says Wilber (2001a: 289).

It is from such clients that I learn most since they have moved on from a faith in something to a trust in all the *connected* elements of the universe. It is impossible to represent this sense of spirituality in mere prose – because the feeling of their perceptions and insights is more than the words of transcript dialogue can relate.

Counselling on Religious Doubt

Throughout this book, I have spoken of two discourses of realism that will emerge in spiritually-centred counselling and that I think reflect common experience. The first is the traditional religious view of modernism, which corresponds with a mystical sense of an innate Self under a possible influence of a higher power. Such a notion of Self may equate with the religious doctrine of the soul (whether or not it is conceived to be immortal) and an external spiritual agency.

The second is the postmodern view whereby Self, and conceptions of reality, are socially constructed, a perspective that has rendered the task of finding an objective reality 'within' or 'out there' meaningless if not impossible. We have no way of knowing whether God and the soul exist as identifiable entities, but they are certainly meaningful constructs if understood as poetic metaphors. Paradoxically, there was more confidence in scientific means of measuring the human psyche in the modern period than in our postmodern times, and our sense of reality appears to be moving towards the Buddhist view of all being an illusion – *there is no such thing as reality, perceptions are all there are.*

It goes without saying, therefore, that the aim in therapy for the first discourse is to assist clients to understand and relate to their inner-world through deep forms of psychotherapy which address issues of personal being, whereas for the second the aim is to assist in creating a preferred Self, or a Self which might better suit the current living situation. I have also said that most of us, clients and counsellors alike, fit somewhere along a continuum of two poles, from empirical–materialistic to mystical–intuitive, with very few taking up positions at any one extreme.

Life brings change, the world doesn't stand still, and all too regularly clients in therapy are sharing frustrations about their altered worlds. When people want things to be other than the way they are, their beliefs will affect the way they feel about the way matters 'should be' – the cognitive revolution has taught us that. Where clients lie on the belief, or reality, spectrum will not be fixed but is likely to move in any one direction, and the therapist will need to handle inconsistencies, contradictions and ambiguities when aiming to explore Self and to assist in healing by overcoming cognitive obstacles along the path of individuation.

All counselling is tailored to supporting those who perceive they cannot get through, but when therapy moves towards the spiritual dimension there are opened up new possibilities of insight and healing of a transpersonal potential to transcend Self. Therapeutic treatments have well practised means for responding to loss and suffering, but the spiritual counsellor places trust in life and human potential following a lead from person-centred therapy. Trust is reapplied in spiritually-oriented therapy as the dynamic security which replaces the divine subject of faith with secular equivalents, and as such the paradoxical nature of faith as *certainty within the uncertain* becomes fitting for pluralistic realities.

Conclusion

This chapter has addressed the phenomenon of religious doubt. When societies became less homogenous through education, industrialisation and the breakdown of taboo, there occurred the possibility for breadth in interpreting human experience. The Enlightenment endorsed a critical spirit and gave doubt and scepticism a platform of philosophical legitimacy. Agnosticism, and more particularly atheism, became a social discourse arising from scientific studies of evolution and astronomy and the validity of religious faith was under question. The result of this questioning, as far as psychology and psychotherapy is concerned, led to the notion of a divided Self, to naturalist accounts of religion, and to sociological, empirical interpretations of phenomenon. Obstacles along the path occur for all clients, whether they view themselves as religious or not, since analytical science has created a *fractured Self* within the fractured society. All is not lost however for the holistic revolution is on its way.

We have seen in this chapter how the process of individuation is not plain sailing. Life presents toil and strife and a range of experiences which existentialists understand as living within a thrown condition. Personal suffering has frequently been an obstacle to faith for many clients, and religious narratives have provided dialogues for addressing this existential dilemma. For the religious person, faith can be an impetus, or a stumbling block, for a smooth passage through life. A significant strain in biblical theology is an interpretation of faith as trust, as opposed to an acceptance of propositions, as it became with the rise of modern science in the eighteenth and nineteenth centuries. Faith is not restricted to those who view themselves as religious, however, for spiritually-minded clients may begin to view life optimistically and learn to trust in the human spirit in all its various manifestations.

To this point, case material has illustrated few novel techniques and interventions that might not occur in other approaches of counselling and psychotherapy, but religious and transpersonal therapists have developed more imaginative and less verbal interventions than I have demonstrated so far in this book. To this topic we now turn.

9

Religious and Spiritual Techniques in Therapy

When I meet a man, I am not concerned about his opinions. I am concerned about the man.

I have not the right to want to change another if I am not open to be changed by him as far as it is legitimate.

I knew nothing of books when I came forth from the womb of my mother, and I shall die without books, with another human hand in my own. I do, indeed, close my door at times and surrender myself to a book, but only because I can open the door again and see a human being looking at me.

Martin Buber (http://courses.washingtom.edu/spcmu/buber/)

Throughout this book, I have presented extracts of client material primarily with adolescents and middle-aged clients, and in nearly every case the interventions and techniques employed have not been entirely novel. The differences between spiritual and non-spiritual therapy are more a style of questioning and alignment than of distinctive intervention. The type of discourse, for example, is controversial for some established approaches in that there is an endorsement of the counsellor sharing of Self and of personal information. There is also a predisposition towards Self-transcendence, and towards focusing therapy through a lens of viewing the spiritual through the natural in an attempt to integrate the two discourses of mystical and empirical reality. My intention throughout is to encourage therapists from a broad range of approaches to be enterprising by engaging with their clients on spiritual issues as they emerge in session.

This book would not be complete, however, if techniques and interventions, as regularly occur in religious and pastoral counselling, or in transpersonal therapy, or in body psychotherapy, were not covered. As these are briefly introduced it will become apparent that some will remain entirely inappropriate for the secular counsellor, or the psychotherapist who is not proficient in or committed to such approaches. For example, some of the techniques applied in body psychotherapy require skills training and appropriate supervision. Before more novel interventions are applied in spiritually-centred work, there will be a need for self-scrutiny and reflection on what underlying theory informs practice, a judgment on the appropriateness of matching technique with desired outcome, and recognition of the client's dominant mode of functioning – I offer exercises designed to assess this.

First, the techniques commonly occurring in religious and pastoral counselling are covered before examining those used in transpersonal therapy. I will show how religious techniques can be adapted for secular spiritual therapy. Consistent with person-centred theory, I will argue that it is the counselling relationship that is regarded as the substantial means of healing rather than sophisticated techniques. Spiritual development and growth are the mystical product of an extra dimension of human relating which is regarded by some as the transpersonal dimension, by others as a sense of mystical *presence,* others still as *relational depth,* or by therapists like me as a numinous phenomenon of *human-divine relating.*

Techniques in Religious and Pastoral Psychotherapy

Lambert's research (1992) highlights the importance of therapeutic factors outside the counselling room that contribute towards a successful outcome. Extra-therapeutic factors, such as personal and environmental resources and fortuitous events, represent the largest contributory factor in successful outcome (40 per cent), followed by the counselling relationship (30 per cent), expectancy of positive change (15 per cent) and specific techniques (15 per cent). Such research places the factor of particular technique and intervention as significantly low in respect of successful outcome and personal healing, and I consider spiritually-centred counselling to be no exception. Certainly, techniques are a less contributory factor than client expectations and the counselling relationship (Steering Committee, 2002; Mearns and Cooper, 2005: 160). Counsellors have a professional role to motivate their clients to be optimistic about positive outcome, but one significant environmental factor for the spiritually-inclined therapist will be the numinous or transpersonal dimension as personally experienced. But how on earth do we measure this? Whilst not elevating technique too highly, let us look at the broad range of interventions available for the spiritual counsellor.

The comprehensive study of Richards and Bergin (1997) presents a range of religious techniques and interventions which are 'advocated by most of the world religious traditions', and these are prayer, scripture reading, forgiveness and meditation – which is popular in transpersonal therapy. Furthermore, the authors illustrate how these techniques can be applied innovatively in detailed case examples (1997: 259–306).

Prayer

The inward or vocal communication of prayer is common to eastern traditions – Hinduism, Mahayana Buddhism, Religious Taoism and Shintoism – and western monotheistic religions – Judaism, Christianity and Islam – through a variety of forms, including petition, intercession, confession, thanksgiving, lamentation and adoration. It is the first four forms of prayer, however, that most commonly occur in session or which are encouraged outside therapy by counsellors (supposing they believe in the efficacy of prayer).

Research on the effectiveness of prayer for physical and psychological health remains inconclusive (Richards and Bergin 1997: 202–3). Swinton (2001: 87–8) presents evidence in support of the efficacy of prayer through the paradigm of quantum physics and the work of Larry Dossey (1993). However, the Duke University Medical Centre studied 700 patients and concluded that prayer proved no aid to heart patients. The report said that music, image and touch therapy appeared to reduce patients' distress, whilst those who were prayed for within Christian, Muslim, Jewish and Buddhist groups were as likely to have a setback in hospital, be re-admitted, or die within six months as those not prayed for (*The Lancet*, 15 July). The British Heart Foundation in reply said that although prayer cannot improve the clinical outcome for patients undergoing heart procedures, positive emotional states are beneficial to heart care, and that patients being aware that others are thinking about them undoubtedly results in optimism and positive outcome (BBC News, 15 July 2005).

Some young people in counselling speak of regularly praying to a spiritual *presence* even though they have not been tutored in their environment to do so, as though prayer is archetypal, an innate response to anxiety. And this was John McCarthy's experience in 1986 when kidnapped in Beirut (McCarthy and Morrell, 1994: 98). The psychological benefits of collective prayer were evident for Ibn:

> *Ibn:*   When I come out of the mosque I would feel sort of light, and in peace and quite content, and a kind of happiness would go through my whole system, mind and body. I would feel *this is good* … The first moment that I felt good was when I had a first glimpse of the Kaaba … And about three million people were there that day, together, and the only thing that was on their mind was praying to God. Nothing else; there was no other intention, or interest, or anything like that, except to pray to our Creator. And it felt so overwhelming, so incredible.

Reading Scripture

Reading scripture has regularly been viewed as appropriate in religious counselling, both for spiritual edification and as a source of teaching on how to live. Religious texts have a rich store of spiritual and moral wisdom, though not all religious writings are claimed to be revelations from God or the gods. Some writings are judged to be divine revelation whilst others are regarded as commentaries, or reflections, on the sacred text. The Torah, for example, is God's revelation to Moses for Jews, but the Talmud is a huge collection of traditions which explain the Torah. Given the broad diversity of holy writ, and in light of postmodern consciousness, as outlined earlier, it is hardly surprising that such authorities for meaning are not credible in our pluralistic age (Appendix).

Counselling research on practitioners reading from scripture in session, as presented by Richards and Bergin (1997), seems to indicate that quoting from the Bible and other sacred texts is a common practice, at least in the USA. Challenging dysfunctional beliefs through scriptural exegesis has proved successful for cognitive therapists (1997: 210), but, as the authors point out, there is always the risk of offending some clients, or encouraging others in diversionary tactics which become a resistance to facing the central problems that need addressing in counselling.

Forgiveness

Sin, guilt and pardon have religious connotations when applied to a higher Being from whom forgiveness is desired and repentance required. Two core conditions of the therapeutic relationship are empathy and the non-judgmental stance of holding the client in positive self-regard, and these will not sit comfortably if clients feel deeply a need to appease a higher authority which through transference may be projected on to the counsellor. If repentance is the prelude to forgiveness, there may occur in therapy an unhelpful pressure to express remorse when what might be needed is a cathartic expression of anger.

Naturally, the means and rituals of seeking forgiveness and demonstrating repentance will vary considerably with different religious traditions, and some requirements of forgiveness are more exacting than others. For example, Christian believers are required to 'forgive enemies' and to 'resist not evil', whereas in Jewish tradition it is not desirable to 'forgive people who do not acknowledge the injury, or even worse, rationalise their injurious behaviour as having been deserved' (Lovinger, 1990: 177). Whilst forgiveness for Christians restores a devotee's relationship with God (Lines, 1995b; Schucman and Thetford, 1996), from a psychological perspective encouraging forgiveness fosters positive changes in affective well-being, physical and mental health, restoration of personal power, and reconciliation between offender and offended (Richards and Bergin, 1997: 212). Forgiveness involves *Self-forgiveness*, which, according to Boorstein (1996: 415) can lead to a more compassionate view of others.

Richards and Bergin (1997: 213) summarise the research evidence and psychotherapeutic practice of the relationship between forgiveness and psychological healing, but how forgiveness is endorsed in therapy is not entirely clear (Casework on forgiveness is illustrated in Richards and Bergin, 1997: 275–86). The obvious harbouring of nagging feelings of hatred is detrimental to a peaceful state of mind, and to helping clients move on, but, as the authors stress, there are necessary stages of affirmation that must occur before premature forgiveness is encouraged.

The final religious interventions Richards and Bergin (1997) discuss are the place of worship and ritual, fellowship and service and moral instruction, but these confuse the role, it seems to me, between the therapist and the priest, minister, rabbi or imam.

Transpersonal Techniques in Psychotherapy

Those clients suffering such dilemmas as 'narcissistic character pathology' or an excessive dread of mortality have been shown to be receptive to transpersonal psychotherapy in combination with psychoanalysis and cognitive behavioural techniques (Boorstein, 1996). Other clients have been counselled with spiritual approaches exclusively; for example by recommending *A Course in Miracles* for creating a peace of mind through the practice of forgiveness (Schucman and Thetford, 1996), or by self-talk meditative trance (saying 'May I be happy? May I be peaceful?'). The most common spiritual techniques applied in transpersonal therapy, as covered by Boorstein (1996), are mindfulness, meditation and various forms of yoga.

Mindfulness

Mindfulness is attempting to 'be here now', and as a form of psychotherapy has been applied for neurotic, anxious and depressed clients. Mindfulness as founded in Buddhist practice is directed towards the goal of enlightenment; it is not about changing but 'noticing' and 'accepting' (i.e. chronic stress and pain) experiences that appear impossible to shut off. Mindfulness has been likened to 'learning to sit by the bank of the river of your emotions and letting them flow, coming and going, without getting caught up in them or in the occasional torrent' (Pointon, 2005: 5).

The first technique of mindfulness needing to be mastered is breathing observation and the naming of interruptions like remembering, worrying, hearing, image work and fantasising through what Deatherage (1996) terms *the watcher self*, and as articulated by Treya Wilber in *Grace and Grit* (Wilber, 2001b). Deatherage commends mindfulness as a means of avoiding energy spent in the not-too-comfortable present. Mindfulness is a form of meditation that aids a client to explore their inner-world, and as such differs from meditation on external transcendence, as practised by Christian or Jewish mystics (Hoffman, 1996). Mindfulness-based Cognitive Therapy has been developed and widely applied in the treatment of depression (Pointon, 2005).

Meditation

Contemplation and meditation as practised in all religions, particularly in the East (*vipassans* or insight, mindfulness, transcendental reflection, Zen, visualisation and devotional meditation), has been utilised in counselling and psychotherapy, largely as behavioural and cognitive-behavioural techniques with biofeedback within programmes of desensitisation and relaxation (Goleman, 1996). The eastern emphasis on meditation is different to that of the West, in that it involves the shutting down of mental activity. Most forms of meditation require a passive attitude of release and surrender of control, mental isolation from distracting environmental interference and noise, refocusing or repetition of thoughts in combination with muscular relaxation.

Meditation is a spiritual practice for the soul to venture inward and find ultimately the supreme identity with the Godhead (Wilber, 2001b: 76). Ultimate superconscious states for Wilber (2001a: 198–217) – where the Spirit actively unfolds in evolution to recognise itself – are through meditation as elaborated through two schools of eastern enlightenment. The *Causal Unmanifest* state is likened to a deep dreamless sleep as the Self becomes 'drenched in the fullness of Being'. Through exercises of observing Self – by separating what we do from what we are – the individual enters a state of 'pure emptiness' and all object–subject realities disappear within a 'vast expanse of freedom'.

But the *Causal* is not the end state; it must give way to the *Non-dual* state, which is best understood through the Zen koan, 'What is the sound of one hand clapping?' The subject and object have become one: the mountain and the phenomenon of the mountain in mind are a single entity – you simply are the Cosmos. For Wilber (2001a: 209), the state is not something you can *bring about*; it is uncontrived; it is 'effortless effort'; it is a case of recognising what has been there all the time and which just needs *pointing out*. He does, however, commend practice by seeking out a qualified teacher (2000: 136–8).

Hinayana meditation aims for individual enlightenment, but Mahayana meditation goes a step further in stressing the enlightenment of all beings, in a practice known as *tonglen*, which means taking and sending. The individual during meditation visualises someone they know who is suffering an illness or loss, and they breathe in through the nostrils and into the heart all the suffering imagined as dark black smoke. By holding breathing, the suffering is contained and through exhaling all peace, freedom, health, goodness and virtue are sent out to that person in the form of healing, liberating light (Wilber, 2001b: 247–51).

Physiologically, meditation evokes a relaxed response, trains and strengthens awareness, centres and focuses Self, halts constant verbal thinking and relaxes the body-mind. It calms the central nervous system, relieves stress, bolsters self-esteem, reduces anxiety and alleviates depression. Given the empirical evidence in support of such meditative states for producing significant healing of body and mind, it comes as a surprise to Richards and Bergin (1997: 206) that such techniques are not utilised more commonly in psychotherapy.

Contemplation on spiritual images and mantras has been effective in the treatment of reactive depression, anxiety, panic attacks, adjustment disorders, PTSD, hypertension, cardiovascular problems, cancer and weakened autoimmune systems (1997: 206), as well as less-severe psychotic disorders. Jung (1964) used mandalas (Sanskrit word meaning 'circle') in contemplative analysis to help clients to centre and express the journeying Self. Mandalas are of many traditional designs and patterns (see Figure 9.1), and can be created by the individual; they may incorporate astrological symbols, but often have a centre and symmetry. The mandala represents the mid-point, the central path towards individuation.

Figure 9.1   Mandala of Samvara, Tibet, 1534 © 2004 Photo Scala, Florence, The Newark Museum

Addressing Physical
Symptoms Holistically

Holistic approaches are becoming popular in meeting clients' needs, where there is less emphasis upon objectified knowledge and more stress upon self-knowledge of human interconnected mind–body–spirit relationships (Edwards, 1992) – the seeing of wholes rather than isolated parts (Elkins, 1998: 103–20). Studies in psychoneuroimmunology (how the brain affects the body's immune cells and how the immune system is affected by emotions, feelings and behaviour) emphasises the wholeness of the person and the interconnected nature of emotions, experiences and somatic processes (Swinton, 2001). Keane and Cope (1996) illustrate the integration of yoga and psychotherapy and of mind, body and spirit, and the linking of one's spirit or life force to the yogic goals of aligning the person's vibration energies with those of the universe. With those clients finding difficulty in vocalising feelings and thoughts, the yogic approach, which begins with bodily feelings, can frequently be an excellent way to release those blocked emotional feelings, particularly with concentration and mindfulness practice.

Somatic Techniques

A fuller holistic treatment of mental health and spiritual well-being through body psychotherapy has been published by Linda Hartley (2004). Hartley gives an extensive account of somatic psychology, as the science that challenges the Cartesian duality of mind and matter that has preoccupied the postmodern thinking and outlook since the Enlightenment. By reintegrating the separated processes of psyche, soma (body) and spirit, she has rediscovered the lost wisdoms of body–mind interrelatedness.

Hartley is an established practitioner of Body–Mind Centring and a senior registered dance movement therapist. In following her detailed casework, the reader is confronted by aspects of psychotherapy that traditional approaches discourage, such as touch and physical contact – an area where, apart from Brian Thorne, mainstream therapists view as confusing therapeutic boundaries and as jeopardising the transference relationship. Hartley reminds us of the long relationship between dance and spirituality, and the phenomenon for some of seeing an aura about the person (as experienced also by West, 2000), but she also demonstrates techniques of cellular touching, firm holding, dance, art therapy and image work, together with Jungian dream analysis. Take, for example, the extensive case of Arlene, over a two-year period of body psychotherapy (Hartley, 2004: 224–45). Arlene was a client of 29 years who suffered ME from a spinal injury after falling from a hot air balloon. She felt unable to work and had no wish to live in her body. She was shocked to learn that her father had incestuous relationships. This affected her 'relationship with her own spirituality'. Her mother never really wanted her, and her marriage was on the brink of failure.

During therapy, Hartley conducts body awareness exploration by placing her hands lightly over her body, in what is termed 'cellular touch' (on one occasion around the fatty tissues surrounding the womb), to take her awareness through the tissue layers. When she felt tightness in her solar plexus, like a clenched fist, as she said, Hartley held her open hand over the area till she felt released enough to experience her womanhood. Scapulae massage was given to help her feel released from the restricted flow of feeling in her arms, which led in the next session to a dance with her arms flowing freely and strongly. Body awareness was accompanied by psychotherapy through relating body with mind with spirit, in order to enter a dialogue with her 'wise inner figure', and to find her centre by pushing her therapist away. At times, body focusing and active imagination with images were linked with drawing therapy to represent her anger, and image work and role-play to come to terms with her adversarial sister-in-law. Arlene engaged in body-focused work, and Hartley held her head firmly in one session as though in a cradle. Her throat, chest and root chakra became a focus for therapy at times and dream analysis was a regular feature.

She was encouraged to stay with her pain, 'in a more fluid and organic way', rather than avoid it. The transpersonal element of therapy was Arlene's inability to embody Self, and to connect with her spirit world. The close of therapy was indicated when Arlene had come to love her body, when she had become integrated more fully with her shadow and inner critic, and when she had accepted the responsibility of facing the world without the assistance of her therapist.

Chakras

The chakras are vortices, or wheels of energy, lying along the front of the body in front of the spine. Chakras are believed to be channels of energy that flow into and out of the core of the person. According to eastern spiritual anatomy, energy from the universal source will flow into the core of the individual if not obstructed: 'Physiological and psychological health depend upon a natural and unimpeded rhythm of energy flowing into and out from the core' (Hartley, 2004: 44). Seven chakras are usually identified as shown in Figure 9.2.

Any disturbance in the chakra zones indicates a related psychological dysfunction and poor health due to low energy flow. It is important to recognise that authorities are not in full agreement on the number and

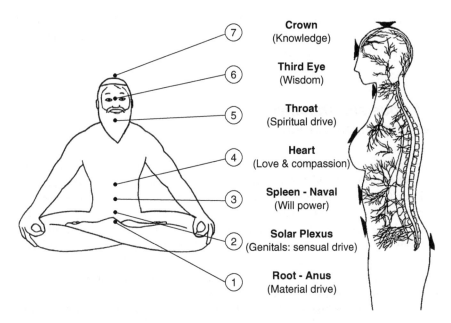

Figure 9.2   The seven common chakras

relationship of chakras, but, in general, like Chinese acupuncture, there is agreement, following Leadbeater's (1927) work, that the roots of the chakras are located at specific points along the spine and in the brain and are related to nerve plexes and endocrine glands lying close to them (Figure 9.2).

Body–mind psychotherapy views a direct relationship between various chakras and emotional and mental issues, and the therapist trained in body psychotherapy will work on these physical zones through active imagining, meditation and cellular touch (Hartley, 2004).

According to the new paradigm, physical symptoms may be understood metaphysically as emotional blockages carrying metaphorical messages. Thus, a stammer or panic attack resulting in a speech impediment might be treated not with drugs or behavioural remedies but by attending to the throat chakra which has influence on restricted self-expression (Nelson, 1996: 316–8). By focusing upon the body's energy centres (chakras) on three basic levels – pelvis, chest/heart, and throat/head (Kelly, 1996: 54–63) – through breathing, relaxation and imaging exercises with the aids of music, candles and mantras, the client dissociates with the stresses of the day's preoccupations in order to move onto the highest level.

Level four is particularly relevant in spiritually-centred counselling, and is located in the spine just between the eyebrows. It is called the 'third eye', or the 'inner guru', of insight. This chakra is believed to be the store of inner wisdom, and focusing upon this centre helps the client in decision-making and, ultimately, in healing.

Religious and Transpersonal Techniques Reapplied

Customarily, clients will be directed to religious leaders if their difficulties are related to the need for spiritual redirection and guidance, but recent authors (West 2000, 2004; Thorne 2002) have called for such issues in religion and spirituality to be addressed with more confidence in secular-spiritual therapy. Spiritual redirection by re-referral to religious authorities may be easier to carry out in the US than in countries like the UK, where religious adherence is less common (Lines, 2002), but even in the States, as Richards and Bergin (1997) point out, research into the practice and benefits of referral to the client's priest, minister, pastor, bishop, rabbi, guru, etc. is inconclusive. Therapists are cautioned by these authors not to rush into re-referral without checking out whether this is in the best interests of the client.

Richards and Bergin (1997) have reservations about praying alongside the client in session for fear of confusing the boundaries. Reading sacred scripture has its secular equivalents in therapy where clients are directed to consult self-help books, novels and autobiographies which have something to teach about coping with the vicissitudes of daily living. In addition, whether clients are committed to a faith or not, the scriptures of most religious traditions contain wealthy narratives of moral and spiritual lessons that are appropriate and suitable for clients in therapy, as I have shown – I regularly draw on biblical stories in counselling, such as *the writing on the wall* to King Belshazzar, the *still small voice* to Elijah, and many of the parables of Jesus.

Religious pilgrimages, such as Hajj, visits to Lourdes, the Vatican and the Holy Land, have great significance for religious people, but secular retreats which focus on nature, art and music therapy have proved popular in modern times and these often have New Age spirituality lying at their heart (Soskin, 1997). Clients are encouraged to consider attending Buddhist (*Vipasanna*) retreats (Boorstein, 1996: 183–93) rather than expecting meditative worship to occur in session.

Meditation as a route of self-exploration is becoming increasingly popular in the West for controlling physiological conditions (such as high blood pressure), for bringing about healing, and for gaining a sense of self-actualisation and self-responsibility (Kelly, 1996). Meditation has been recognised as a significant way of transcending self-centredness and of opening the way to a larger experience of being human. Gerald

May (1996) uses meditation, biofeedback, rediscovering one's religious roots, and mysticism to help clients along their pilgrimage journey by 'just sitting there for a while, letting things come and go'. Meditating along the journey allows the client to begin to see life *as-it-is*. May (1996) argues that people sometimes just experience things, which leaves the world much the same but inwardly they have changed to see things quite differently. We don't fully know the nature of such experiences that make people change inwardly but we know of its reality – it is just a *happening*: 'If I can blink my eyes and see what's there, and quit thinking about it, then there may be some space for healing to occur' (1996: 35). This intuitive experience is what I have described formerly as *drinking the moment*. To see life *as-it-is* requires the sacrifice, at least temporarily, of both one's self-importance and one's preconceptions and prejudices.

For Bloomfield (1996), enlightenment through transcendental meditation is not achieved through seeing visions in a cave, retreats to the desert, or withdrawal from work, family and friends forever; rather, it is achieved through practical exercises that enhance and increase *connectedness* with the external environment. It gives deep-rooted happiness, a sense of personal freedom, rest and spontaneity.

Butler (2002) draws attention to the importance of ritual in daily living, after observing how successful athletes remain on top of their game by developing particular idiosyncratic rituals. Tennis players serve as an example in that particular set rituals are performed in the brief pauses (15–20 seconds) between points. During the momentary ritual phase, the heart-rate drops as much as fifteen to twenty beats between points (Schwartz and Loehr, 2002 – cited in Butler, 2002). Winning competitors also display a confident posture (conscious or otherwise) of what she terms 'the matador walk' that telegraphs to the opponent *no big deal* when a point is lost. Her point is not to advocate religious ritual as an end in itself, but to encourage the allocation of time for set rituals during each day. Islam upholds this principle by having set times for prayer which interrupt business schedules or manual labour, and no doubt there is much wisdom in this prescription.

Spiritual therapists might benefit their clients by helping them design rituals and daily rhythms for physical renewal: perhaps a walk in the park during lunch, a mid-morning yoga break, a short cycle ride, electing to work a day a week at home, or whatever seems appropriate. Time is set aside for regular rituals and rhythms for higher quality relating to one's inner being or the environment. Through games and activities, individuals can rediscover the values that bind people together and that heighten our *connectivity* to the sentient world around us. Couples might be encouraged to ritualistically set aside time for communicating with each other and to recognise that missing ingredient of *spiritual connectedness*.

What is Your Dominant Spiritual Self?

Presented below are five exercises I have used in therapy and on counselling course training to help clients refine their dominant sense of spiritual being.

Exercise 1: Defining the Spiritual

This book has presented different perspectives of religion and spirituality. Try and define religion for yourself in a sentence or two, and then attempt to define spirituality. Compare your definition of spirituality with those listed by course delegates:

Spirituality is:

- Seeking God within
- 'In touch-ness' with the Divine
- An awareness of more than physical (or mental) concepts
- The ability to be or the experience of being at peace with ourselves and the world around us
- The connectedness of being at one with the Soul and thus to all that is
- The communication with and to all life forces that accesses oneness and truth
  It is the essence and core of all things:

    the authentic person
    the vibrant soul
    the thing through which all things are possible

- A heightened awareness of consciousness and of the oneness of being
- An acceptance in the universal nature of existence and our own role in its continuity

Exercise 2: My formative influences

Many of our beliefs and assumptions do not come into play consciously day to day, but are a complex formation of what we have internalised and experienced. This exercise encourages you to reflect and examine the primary influences and beliefs of your upbringing and development (see Table 9.1).

    A   Place a tick in whatever cell applies to you (where applicable)
    B   Consider what you've ticked and reflect on the implications of your response.

Exercise 3: Recognising Spiritual Needs

This exercise identifies more clearly your spiritual needs and how they relate to your psychological, emotional, social and aesthetic needs.

Table 9.1 Assessing formative infulences

What I currently think	Response									
	Yes	No	Don't Know	Mother	Father	Family member	Friend	An extraordinary event	Book or TV programme	Teacher or leader	Idea emerged intuitively
Do I believe in God?										
Was I brought up in a religious household?										
Are my family members religious in any way?										
Did I go to a place of worship when younger?										
Did I read religious material?										
Did I watch religious programmes?										
Have I become ambivalent about religion?										
Am I an atheist?										
Am I agnostic?										
Have I *strong* views on belief, atheism or agnosticism?										
Could I argue for God's existence convincingly?										
Has my moral outlook been influenced by one factor?										
Three beliefs I hold *strongly* that are radically opposed to those of my parents?	1 2 3									
Three elements of religion I find repulsive?	1 2 3									

Copy Table 9.2 and tick whichever applies. Then reflect on what you have ticked as that dominant need of your Self, and consider whether you are primarily an emotional, social or aesthetic type of person. How are these needs being met at the moment?

Table 9.2   Assessing the nature of spiritual needs

Psychological needs	That was me once	This is me now	I think this will apply in future	Dominant need of my Self
I need to be valued				
I need to be recognised as my own person				
I need to keep working and be efficient				
I need to be alone and engage in pleasure				
I need to resolve conflicts of childhood				
I need to address a symptom of irritation				
I need to satisfy ambitious drives				
I need to broaden my outlook and become better educated				
I need to examine more critically my prejudices and social attitudes				
I need to understand why I feel guilty about being happy and putting myself first				
I need meaning in my life				
I need to let my children go and move on				
I need a child or partner, I cannot be alone				

Emotional needs				
I need to be loved				
I need to love another				
I need to get over a loss that holds me back				
I need to be listened to and respected				
I need to develop self-belief				
I need to express my sexual feelings and overcome hang-ups				
I need more space to be me				
I need to voice my anger and thrash out an issue that is causing grief				
I need more passion and intimacy				

Social needs				
I need to change my job				
I need to join a club or small group of people having my interests				
I need to get out of this rut of social isolation				
I need to get away from a family member				
I need to emigrate				
I need to change my circle of friends				

Table 9.2 (Continued)

Social needs (Continued)	That was me once	This is me now	I think this will apply in future	Dominant need of my Self
I need to settle in a stable relationship				
I need to repair a long overdue argument that is causing hurt for someone I really love				
I need to let my children go, and recognise that my life is not ended because my parenting role has ended				

Asethetic needs

I need to be alone to reflect				
I need to create something of lasting value				
I need to discover a latent talent				
I need to find a medium to express who I am				
I need to find an audience to recognise my skills				
I need to recognise who I am				
I need to reach my potential				
I need to discover in what way I am unique				

Exercise 4: Life Events which Shape our Being

It goes without saying that life events shape our identities and outlooks on life, but it is not always clear where spirituality has an affect. This exercise aims to identify the distinctive elements of emotional and spiritual aspects of Self. Compose a life events diagram as shown in Figure 9.3

Draw a horizontal line to represent your date of birth to the present time, and bisect this line with a series of vertical lines of varied lengths that denote significant events in your life in which you have been emotionally

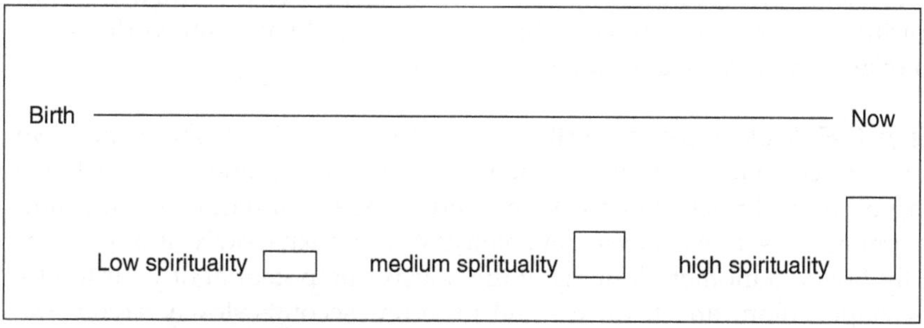

Figure 9.3   Life events diagram

affected. Draw the lengths of these bisecting lines to represent the charge or potency of each emotional state at this particular life event. This exercise cannot be rushed, because the more we reflect over the series of events that have occurred in our lives the more it will be difficult to ascertain how much of our emotional resources were drawn upon at that moment, particularly over events which occurred long ago. You will note, that my life events diagram shown in Figure 9.4 illustrates periods of emotional highs as well as lows.

Upon your life events diagram identify those stages in your life that have been the most emotionally significant, and at each stage draw boxes and rectangles in coloured pencil to denote those occasions when you have felt the most spiritual. When first conducting this exercise, I drew many boxes and rectangles below the life events line. The more I thought about this, however, the more I wondered whether we can ever be spiritually negative. It seems more appropriate to judge ourselves as being absent or devoid of spiritual thoughts and feelings, to be or to feel mundane and commonplace, rather than to judge ourselves as being spiritually in a negative mode. Take some time over this exercise, and try to ascertain whether your spiritual highs and absences correspond with your emotional highs and lows. For example, taking a look at my life events diagram there was an occasion in my life, shortly after a spinal injury accident, when I contemplated suicide. I was low and yet I did not feel compelled to deny that God existed just because I had suffered. I am not too sure how much I prayed, in a conventional form of prayer, that is, as opposed to meditating (or, more likely, wrestling with doubts), but I did feel driven to fight on with my rehabilitation and to discover somewhere an impetus to fight against the easy option of rolling over and giving up.

Look at your life events diagram and reflect on similar periods in your experience whereby you may have felt spiritually high and yet emotionally low, or vice versa.

Exercise 5: Making Contact with Your Environment

This range of exercises is designed to broaden awareness of how you wish to connect with your environment – physically, socially, aesthetically and spiritually. Some of us have inclinations to be in the natural world, some to relate with others, and others to be alone.

Step 1 Reflective Eating   Fritze Perls (Perls et al., 1972) shows how we can connect with our environment through the manner in which we approach mealtimes. Prepare a meal and change your regular eating habit to a more reflective exercise. Sit comfortably and eat slowly and thoughtfully. Spend a moment looking at the nourishing potential of your food – its shape, colour and texture – and for a few seconds slowly savour the sweet smells. Take a portion at a time and relish the taste, chewing each

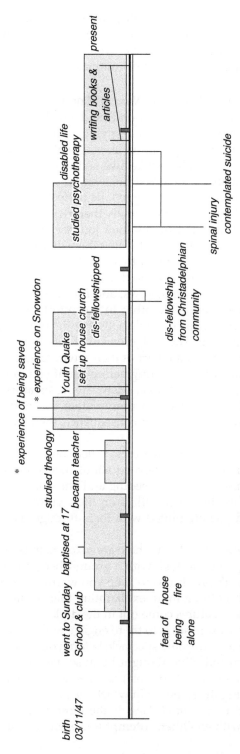

Figure 9.4   Life events diagram of D. Lines (03.11.1947–) in 10 year periods

piece, slowly and purposefully, with a desire to extract every ounce of nourishment. Avoid swallowing quickly and think of the energy and goodness this is adding to your state of well-being. Practise reflective eating routine regularly until it becomes routine.

Step 2. Making Contact with the Natural World   Some of us by nature relate well to countryside sights, sounds and smells, and to being in the open air, and become animated when spying a rare bird, seeing a stag in the Highlands, or in spotting salmon leaping waterfalls, or just being in the mountains, for such sights evoke awe and wonder.

Go into a garden and lie amongst the long grass, turning your head to the side, or if you prefer sit cross-legged. Be perfectly still and observe all the creatures crawling close to you. Study their rich and varied forms, and pick one or two in turn and follow their journeying and sense of busyness. Consider from your restricted vision the patterns of these creatures' diverse existences, the fact that they by right share the same planet as you.

Set out early one morning close to dawn for a secluded woodland, or a garden rich in foliage and hedgerows, and find yourself a very comfortable position and sit very still, either in a comfortable chair or upon a ground sheet, for as long as possible. Observe the birds and creatures as they emerge around you. The hedgerows will soon burst into life if you remain still, as though you are part of their environment. You will notice more of the natural world appearing before you if you can be still and sit downwind than if you are active. Many living creatures, particularly birds, have developed instincts of preservation by being ultra-cautious and wary of human beings, and in consequence, the more you move the less you will see.

As you watch these living creatures, reflect on their senses of being, how they communicate, how they go about their daily business, their play, their courtship ritual, their feeding and parenting, viewing the natural world in all its diversity. Reflect on life's virility through nature's dance and be glad you are united with them through the common spirit of life.

Select an area where you know there are foxes, rabbits or badgers. Plan a night vigil and go out at dusk with a groundsheet, an infrared camera and torches, and with provisions to keep you warm and comfortable and keep still. There is nothing more exhilarating than seeing very shy, and possibly quite rare, creatures come out in the dark.

The point of these exercises is to try to engage with living creatures, not merely to observe the awesome spectacle before you for its own sake, but to try to engage in reflective thought because they, like yourself, are a unique species of intricacy and of priceless worth, sharing the same planet and breathing the same air in which we are all privileged to live.

This final exercise of *connectedness* is the most challenging because it involves relating with an Other. Attempt this exercise with someone you know only casually, a person you customarily have invested little of yourself in the past. Ask yourself what form of converse you have previously had with this person, whether it has been merely a transactional relationship. Try and approach that person within a renewed mindset. Keep the importance of their unique personhood and being in the forefront of your mind as you engage in conversation. Let this be a communion of *being* with *being*, of mind with mind. Through this engagement, predetermine not to obtain anything specific from them, but rather consider what that person can teach you, how she can enrich your existence, and through eye contact and genuine interest keep within the forefront of your mind the question of how this relationship in which you are privileged to engage can change who you are.

Now select a day when you have time and no demands and move into a busy area. See yourself like a camera panning those around you and *notice* a particular person who may be struggling with something and, putting aside any embarrassment, approach them and offer your assistance – at all costs, avoid patronising them. If they are happy to receive your help, reflect on how it has made you feel and what you may have learnt about your spiritual nature.

Mystical Relating

Gergen's (2001) pluralistic views on meaning through dialogue were examined earlier in which he, along with other constructionists, are arguing for a relational psychology through the linguistic import of language, but the most articulate expression of relational depth is provided by a mystical Jewish philosopher by the name of Martin Buber. His venerated work, *I and Thou*, was published in 1955, but his influence upon social attitudes, education, psychology, philosophy and religion has been immense.

Buber sets out to describe two fundamentally different kinds of relations, and these are termed *I-it* relation and *I-Thou* relation. *I-it* relations are the everyday communications of common discourse which human beings enter with each other and towards things of the resourceful environment, and which may be understood as functionally determined. Most of our dialogue is an *I-it* relation, comprised of unequal partners who view the encounter at a distance and who engage in a utilitarian dialogue for personal advantage. These are transactional relations and although they are necessary and part of our objective experience of the world, they are not enriching but are forged into the chains of causality. They are what David Mearns refers to as a sophisticated range of social skills where individuals 'project self images' at the presentational level (Mearns and Cooper, 2005: 59).

I-Thou relations are substantially different in that they are characterised by seeing the world and one's fellow human being from the motive of self-learning. Such relationships are founded upon mutuality, openness and directness – they are genuine dialogues. In everyday encounters most communications are shallow and functional, but on occasions something magical occurs between two parties, an experience whereby each is giving and not using:

> If I face a human being as my *Thou*, and say the primary word *I-Thou* to him, he is not a thing among things. (Buber, 1958: 21, 38)

When we enter into the eternal *Thou* relation with our innermost and whole being, such inter-human meetings are a reflection of the human meeting with God. Buber had not the slightest doubt that such a meeting was possible, even though details of the nature of the relations were not spelt out in clear and coherent terms. In fact this is one of the great problems when reading Buber; he writes in mystical poetic language rather than a form which is deductive and analytical. Needless to say, we really get when entering the mind of Buber a feeling of resonance with an intuitive outlook of *relational interconnectedness*. The mystical philosophy of Buber (1958) is a form of *seeing* the individual as a very special person in relationship, which, naturally, is the ideal underlying all counselling relationships. When Buber's biographer first met him he said, 'This man who I had felt so close to seemed so really Other to me. He was much shorter than I could have imagined him. His eyes were the most striking part about him – gentle yet penetrating. And he said to me, '"Do not think I am mostly interested in you because you have written a book on me. I am more concerned about you as a person."'

Brian Thorne (2002) has explored the mystical power of person-centred therapy through drawing more pointedly to Carl Rogers' writings in the latter part of his life – West (2004) also singles out Rogers' latter mystical writing. Thorne relates to a mystical *presence* through the 'flow or experiencing' within him, which, he stresses, is somewhat out of kilter with current evidenced-based therapeutic outcomes. John Rowan (2005) describes the experience as *linking* and Mearns and Cooper (2005) speak of working at *relational depth* for those special moments where the boundaries of individual Self for counsellor and client disappear and where therapeutic change is most potent. Working at this level requires an engagement of mutual receptivity and self-expression where therapists cultivate the skill of 'holistic listening' which 'breathes in' the client (Cooper, 2005). Many philosophers, psychotherapists and phenomenologists have attempted to describe this in-depth mode of relating that occurs during brief periods of 'mutual intersubjectivity' (Jordan, 1991). Gergen (1999: 138) writes on *the idea of the relational Self* as a way of conceptualising ourselves and transforming western culture – we are on the brink of 'a second Enlightenment'. Along with the holistic revolution, then, it would appear that the relational discourse is becoming the most meaningful source of healing in modern times.

Connectedness

Thorne draws attention to Carl Rogers' belief in a sense of *connectedness* –
even entertaining a continuous identity beyond death. *Connecting* occurs
when creating the conditions of healing through being fully human, by
practising the core conditions, and by a deeper awareness of 'spirituality',
'mystical experience' and the 'transcendental' sense of *presence* in therapy
(Rogers, 1980).

The case of Jim was presented above to stress the importance in spiritually-
centred counselling of self-disclosure. As counsellors and psychotherapists engage with different clients, it would be unrealistic to assume that
they could bond with every client in the same way. Every so often, however, all counsellors, I suspect, meet a client for whom they are particularly fond and would wish to engage with on deeper levels, and it is in
such cases that they need to address their own strong feelings and motivations through supervision to ascertain that it is the client's best interests
and not their own that warrants continued work.

I felt a powerful bond with Jim at the point of asking him to assist me
after school, and I felt incredible warmth towards him, a *glow within* and
an impulse to rise from my wheelchair and hug him, should this have
been physically possible (or ethically appropriate). My disposition
towards Jim was at risk of shifting from one of professional engagement
(help him to stop fighting) towards one of a caring parent (longing to raise
him), rationalised as a compulsion to provide a more suitable role model
to emulate than those within his immediate family. If I had projected,
or worse still, stated my inner desire, however, I would have violated
a boundary of confusing for him the needs of his situation with my
personal feelings of fondness. The feeling was obviously one of sacrificial
love, and of *longing to be always there*. I could not alter what I felt, but I
could check temptation by keeping clear in my mind what therapy could
offer him and what his needs were.

There was a sense of *mystical connectedness* that was palpable, and
where our personal boundaries, at least for my part, had temporarily vanished into a sense of one-ness or psychological union. Although the word
is inadequate, I felt *loving towards him*, but not in love with him, and in
every session time just flew by.

Therapeutic *connectedness* must be more than a loving feeling of fondness. Our growing attachment within the therapeutic encounter has to
present an opportunity for change to occur. Through engaging in spiritually-
centred counselling the will was borne for Jim to allow that part of his
altruistic nature to flower and be brought to the surface of his awareness
through the practical means of giving assistance to his Other – whether
myself or his neighbours – and by ceasing to fight by continuing to care.

Joko Beck (1997) presents a rationale of *life as Spirit*, similar, I think, to
the mysticism of de Chardin and Freud's *libido*. In one chapter she writes:

'Life doesn't care about your relationship. It is looking for channels for its power so it can function maximally' (1997: 90–91). It is an illusion to think that relationships will work, she says. I expect there is partial truth in this if it is an observation of current western familial relations. On a positive note, she says that the only thing that works is to support *all life*, which may, but not necessarily, include personal relationships. The problem is that nobody really wants to support *all life*; we want to draw from an individual relationship. Love expects nothing but we play games with our relationships.

She then relates a true story of a wife whose husband had been in Japan during the war. He had fathered a couple of children from an affair with a Japanese woman, but on his return he kept this from her till just before he died. At first she was very upset, but then she dealt with his disloyalty by promising her husband before he died that she would take care of them. She went to Japan, found the woman and brought her family back to the States. Making a home for them, she taught them English and assisted in finding them work. That's what love is, and it is very rare indeed. *Active love* is perhaps the best description of human and divine relating, whether in counselling or in any other social partnerships.

If the counselling relationship is viewed as a transpersonal experience – in spite of a difference in background, intelligence, life-experience and inclination – the potential for healing and growth becomes exponential. If children and adults have biological predispositions to be drawn to one another (Lines, 2006), this powerful chemistry of attraction prompts mutual loyalty and a longing of *connectedness* as each party instinctively projects feelings of want and wantedness in the encounter. For adults in therapy, the dynamics will be just as potent. Naturally, unethical standards, sexual impropriety and misunderstanding must be avoided, but *without love we cannot feel*, and *without feeling we cannot be genuine or congruent*, and *without congruence and genuineness there will be no quality counselling relationship of depth to bring about healing*. What marks the spiritual therapeutic relationship from the traditional person-centred one is the nature of a *mystical* union of two searching souls, who each respond to the Other in the interests of promoting mutual spiritual growth.

I find it impossible to imagine how a style of what I call spiritually-centred counselling, which is essentially a *peak experience* of *connectedness*, can begin to flourish without sharing something of *my being* with my *client's being*. I suspect all counsellors will claim that during their work with clients, where the therapy has become intensive and deep, *peak experiences* have occurred and a genuine sense of *connectedness* has taken place through their own styles and approaches but might never regard their therapeutic relationship as in any sense mystical. They may never use language to describe what they personally feel as a *presence*, or as a transpersonal dimension, or a numinous phenomenon, but would nevertheless share with me the recognition that some therapeutic relationships are very, very special. I contend that, if you have not already done so, you may consider the benefits of giving your clients, where appropriate, a little of *your being* through exposing a little vulnerability at times and a little more of your experiences as they relate to the particular therapeutic discourse.

I have offered a lens through which spiritual therapy might be viewed, which is to *see the divine through the natural*, that in approaching my client sitting before me I may see through her the splendour of divinity; that I may afford her all the zeal that inspired great works of religious art; that I may treasure this human being with all the passion of a Muslim celebrating Hajj; and that I may go out of my way to heal my client as Christ did the leper in Galilee – that through my client's face I may behold the face of God. This, in essence, is what Buber (1958) advocated, the bonding of *being* with *being*, and this insight stands above all techniques and interventions. It is not a case of *seeing* my client in reverential awe as she sits before me as God, but as perceiving her as my fellow companion on the journey within a *mystical* attachment. Whatever language we use is unimportant in relation to the quality of relational experience the language is attempting to convey. This form of spiritual counselling relationship recognises the worth and unique-ness of each party, client and counsellor alike.

Conclusion

This chapter has covered a broad range of spiritually-oriented techniques used in religious and transpersonal counselling, and has suggested how some of these interventions may be applied in secular therapy with a spir-itual emphasis. A major stress of counselling research for bringing about healing has fallen on the particular nature of the therapeutic relationship, and I have attempted to articulate this special, *mystical* level of relating through the insights of Martin Buber. My intention of illustrating more reserved and less-ambitious techniques and interventions throughout this book is to encourage you my reader from your own school of thought to take on this promising work of mutual growth. For this reason, I ask you through those special relationships that feel as though love has grown between practitioner and client to view the quality of that relating as a *mystical communion* of divine-human relating if that has meaning for you, or of becoming *one with life* if it doesn't.

10

Closure in Spiritual Counselling

As a man casts off his worn-out clothes and takes on other new ones, so does the embodied self cast off its worn out bodies and enters other new ones (Bhagavad Gita: 400–22)

Many of those who sleep in the dust of the earth will awake, some to everlasting life, and some to the reproach of eternal abhorrence (Daniel 12: 2)

The kingdom of God comes not with observation: Neither shall they say, 'Lo here! or, lo there!' for, behold, the kingdom of God is within you (Luke 17: 20–21)

'Men of Galilee, why do you stand looking into heaven? This Jesus, who was taken up from you into heaven, will come in the same way as you saw him go into heaven' (Acts 1:11)

Jesus said: If you bring forth what is within you, what you bring forth will save you … the kingdom is within you (Gnostic Gospel of Thomas 3(3))

They shall be adorned with bracelets of gold and wear green robes of fine silk and rich brocade. They shall be reclining in these upon raised couches. How excellent the reward! And how beautiful the resting place! We shall soon cast into Fire all those who deny all Our Messengers. As often as their skins are burnt up We shall replace them with other skins that they may taste punishment (Qur'an 4: 56; 18: 31)

Endings in counselling are seldom clear-cut and are rarely predictable, unless they are pre-programmed at the contract setting stage, but how can termination be planned in a style of counselling that by definition is open-ended and without closure? This final chapter will consider this matter. Apart from task specific, time limited therapy, where closure occurs naturally with meeting the specified goal, ending sessions in most forms of counselling and psychotherapy have presented issues for both client and therapist alike. Solution-focused approaches ask clients to specify what they feel they need to have achieved to signal the close of therapy. A similar question may be asked towards the closing sessions in spiritually-oriented counselling to signal the recommencement of the work initially undertaken before diversion to spiritual issues took place.

In this closing chapter, I trace the religious theme of hope and salvation through the Judaeo-Christian and Islamic traditions, and through the Indian perspective of the transmigration of the soul. These discourses, though meaningful for some, have lost relevance for many in the secular world. Theologians and philosophers of religion have come up with new spiritual discourses, however, which might better fit the existentialist outlook, and whether you view yourself as a counsellor or psychotherapist I hope you will become more confident in addressing spiritual issues as clients raise them in therapy after being briefed as to where theological discourse is moving in current times.

If salvation and enlightenment are the ultimate goals of religion, how can such states, which can at best be realised in part or at worst be verified beyond mortal life, have comparable meaning with regard to the termination of a spiritual mode of counselling? A demythologised perspective of hope is articulated in this chapter to promote healing as the common currency of both religion and psychotherapy.

Religious Discourses of Salvation

A woman once approached the Buddha and begged him to raise her dead son to life. He instructed her to go through the villages collecting as much mustard seed as she could find, but only from those houses in which no one had ever died. There was not one home where death had not left its mark. So, although she returned to the Buddha having no mustard seed, she had a richer understanding of the universality of death (Elkins, 1998). This Buddhist legend illustrates the sobering fact that we all shall die one day, but the prospect for many religious people of the world is that death is not the end but the beginning of life in a new sphere of existence. Counselling and psychotherapy may offer amelioration from stress, insight into inner conflict and the psychodynamics of intra- and inter-personal relations, or a practical solution to a pressing problem, but it certainly cannot offer salvation; that is the domain of religion. Psychotherapy is not so pretentious as to comment on a journey towards salvation, but one emphasis of being saved centres not on metaphysics but on heightened perspective, and here therapy competes very well.

Jewish Hope in Physical Resurrection

There is no systematic teaching on the nature of life beyond death found in the Torah and the Prophets, but a series of ideas that develop as the nation of Israel had moved into different historical situations. In the early period, 'eternity' was thought to be the continuation of the nobleman's progeny; thus, Abraham, the father of the Hebrew tribe, was promised: 'I will make your descendants countless as the dust of the earth … Look up into the sky, and count the stars if you can. So many shall your descendants be' (Genesis 13: 16; 15: 5). The belief of corporate-tribal identity continuing through the patriarch's offspring rendered any notion of individual survival meaningless. There was little prospect of life beyond death for the early Hebrews. The grave was *Sheol*, a vast underground pit, or dark subterranean world, where the dead *shades* exist, from which no one returns: 'As clouds break up and disperse, so he that goes down to *Sheol* never comes back' (Job 10: 20–22; 7: 9).

There were other texts that spoke of God's power and supremacy over death, and this opened the way for the post-exilic prophets to conceive of an after-life (Isaiah 26: 19). A religious sense of individuality occurred for the Jews around the sixth century, during the exile of Judah's prominent persons to Babylon, with the great prophets, notably, Jeremiah, in what has become known as the 'axial period' of revelation (BCE 800–200 ACE). The Israelite nation went through a bleak period of martyrdom later on, and a further insight was born from national crisis. It was inconceivable that death would mark the end for those faithful Jews having died unjustly. Surely, as Daniel imagined, Yahweh's life-giving Spirit could raise the dead from sleep? In these later writings, the Jewish hope was of a physical resurrection of the corpse by God's Spirit. Belief in a physically revived or animated body as the post-mortem state continued through the two centuries leading up to the Christian era, although beliefs in a non-material soul began to circulate from Zoroastrian and Greek sources.

Christian Hope of Life Eternal and the Kingdom of God

Two general post-death conceptions comprise Christian belief. One is centred on the Greek influence of an immortal soul, which might enter heaven or hell, and the other on the second coming (*parousia*) of Christ to establish the kingdom of God.

The Immortal Soul   The early Greek conception of an after-life is found in the Iliad and the Odyssey, and it centres upon the psyche or soul, *the body's shadow-image or the feebler double of the man* (Hick, 1976). At death, the spirit goes down into the murky underworld of twilight unconsciousness, Hades, there to exist in a bloodless doublet, in a miserable state of helplessness. The first systematic beliefs in an optimistic destiny of the immortal soul have been traced to the cults of Dionysus and Orpheus, where souls were imagined as being separate and distinct from the body and where they were believed to begin their long journey of reunification with the divine. Plato believed in an immortal soul in Hades (*Discourse to*

Phaedo, 106: 14), and similar beliefs are still held by western mainstream Christians and peoples of Australia, Polynesia, Africa and South America (Hick, 1976). Beliefs in ancestral spirits which might threaten the living and be in need of placation continue to survive amongst some communities and Australian Aborigines believe in spirits living in a Dreamtime World.

Christian Resurrection   Every converted Christian *was a saint:* sainthood was not a state reserved till after death (Wright, 2003). When Christians die 'in their faith', they live not as a resurrected being, or as a disembodied soul in heaven, but in some undisclosed form in an intermediary state 'with Christ'. The New Testament is surprisingly light on detail, but the writings of Paul and John appear to hint that the state, which is referred to as *being asleep*, is a conscious existence that is better than mortal life but not as good as the life to come at the general resurrection. In the resurrection we receive a similar 'material form' of body but of different composition. The Jewish belief was in physical resurrection through regeneration by the Spirit, and Christianity retained and developed this belief by making it Christianised. In some way, the believer is raised to a new form of life, not as a disembodied spirit but as a changed person – a person having a physical body *animated* by God's Spirit.

Heaven or Hell   There is no biblical teaching to endorse the general conception that we have an immortal soul that may enter heaven at death. Jesus, according to one evangelist, guarantees the 'thief on the cross' some inheritance of life beyond his death not by going to heaven on the day but by *entering paradise* (Luke 24: 43). Paradise is not explained; it is assumed the reader is conversant with what is meant. Wright (2003) thinks that heaven stands as a synonym for a different order of existence, or sphere of reality. In spite of modern New Testament scholarship, there is no shifting the Church from its traditional belief-system of good souls entering heaven at death or wicked ones departing to the fiery torments of hell.

According to the Gospels, hell was Gehenna, a valley on the southwest slopes of Jerusalem. In Gehenna, a continual fire burnt the city's rubbish and meat that was thrown over the wall. Hell became a rich metaphor of oblivion (nothing escapes the fire and the maggots!), and when Jesus used the metaphor he spoke of hell in terms of the plight of the city of Jerusalem rather than of the destiny of human souls. Modern scholarship (Wright, 2003) has concluded that there is no New Testament basis for the medieval conception of the Devil's underworld, or a location of eternal torment, as portrayed by Dante, the Italian poet of the fourteenth century, or as depicted by artists like Hieronymus Bosch (see Figure 10.1).

Purgatory   The doctrine of purgatory (a non-biblical term) arose in the sixth century from Gregory the Great as a means of explaining why the prayers of worshipping Christians were to be offered 'on behalf of the

Figure 10.1 Hieronymus Bosch's graphic images of heaven and hell (sketched by Jean Barley)

dead'. Thomas Aquinas developed the teaching and then purgatory was adopted as official Roman Catholic doctrine at the Council of Lyons in 1274. Purgatory is not official Anglican teaching, however, since the reformers from Martin Luther onwards denounced the flagrant abuse that arose from this teaching, notably through the 'sale of indulgencies'. There was believed to be a need to promote human justice in daily experience, and since human ill-fortune and prosperity were experienced as quite capricious and arbitrary there was felt the need for punishment, or purging (cleansing to become holy) beyond the individual's death. Purging resulted in the saints moving on to heaven and the wicked being sent for endless torment in the flames of hell (Wright, 2003).

The Second Coming and the Kingdom of God   Beliefs about the Second Advent of Jesus, the Messiah, to set up God's kingdom are held primarily by fundamentalist sects and denominations, and the evangelical wing of the mainline Church. The basis of such a belief is that it conforms to the expectations of the first-century Christian community and sayings as reported in the New Testament. Some groups interpret the kingdom belief in material terms as though Jesus comes in person to establish a religious-political kingdom on earth, and others translate the teaching as though an unspecified spiritual kingdom is the intended meaning.

Most linguistic authorities agree that Jesus spoke and taught in Galilean Aramaic, and inform us that the expression, the kingdom of God, meant 'the reign of God', or 'the kingly rule of God' (Perrin, 1963: 23–8).

Matthew's preferred title, the kingdom of heaven is a literary convention of this evangelist, for heaven in Matthew is a circumlocution for God, not an ethereal place above the clouds. There is a saying in a context of exorcism that provides a clue as to how the kingdom was first understood by the Galilean villagers: 'If it is by the finger of God that I drive out the devils, then be sure the kingdom of God has already come upon you' (Luke 11: 20). This enigmatic saying of Jesus (similar to the Gnostic Gospel of Thomas saying that opened the chapter) asserts that the kingdom *had come* and that *now* the disciple must live within it. The kingdom therefore is a heightened perspective of living in the Spirit.

Islamic Hope of Entry to Paradise

In Islam, the same scheme of salvation by entry into paradise or hell is carried over but with more graphic imagery. The motivation for conversion and response is through fear and reward, and this does not alter from the first to the last verse of the Qur'an; in fact the stressing of fear of hell fire for forsaking Allah, and the prize for observing imperatives of the Qur'an, become more pronounced in the closing chapters than early on. The Qur'an records examples of existence in paradise or hell as collated below.

For those forsaking Allah the future is bleak indeed:

> *We have prepared for the unjust a fire whose enclosure will surround them. If they cry for water, they shall be helped with water (boiling) like molten lead, which will scald their faces. How dreadful the drink and how dismal is a resting place (18: 29) ...*
>
> *Every time they seek to escape from there in anguish they will be hurled back into it. Keep on suffering the torment of burning (22: 22) ...*
>
> *When the shackles and the chains are round their necks they shall be dragged into boiling water, then they shall be burnt in the Fire (40: 71) ...*
>
> *On that Day We will ask Gehenna, 'Are you filled up?' It will go on saying, 'Are there anymore?' (50: 30) ...*
>
> *And string them with a chain the length of which is seventy cubits (69: 32) ...Dry, bitter and thorny herbage shall be their only food (88: 6).*

But for the chosen ones who keep to the teachings of the Prophet, as outlined in the Qur'an, a blissful future awaits them in Paradise:

> *We shall pair them with pure ones having beautiful large eyes. They will order therein every fruit, and will be safe and secure' (44: 54) ...*
>
> *Therein are streams of water unstaling, and streams of milk the taste and flavour of which does not change, and streams of juice extracted from grapes, a delight to the drinkers, and streams of clarified honey, and they will have in it all kinds of fruit, and protection from their Lord (47: 15) ...*
>
> *They will experience therein neither excessive heat of the sun nor intense cold (76: 13)*

Paradise is pictured as a garden of eternity with running streams, where the faithful are served by maidens.

Escaping the Cycle of Rebirth and Reaching Nirvana

Hinduism and Buddhism have no equivalent concepts of going to heaven or of being raised physically from the dead, but have long traditions of escaping the cycle of rebirth for the former and of reaching nirvana, or of extinguishing desire, for the latter. In eastern thought, the idea of a period of consciousness occurring at birth and concluding at death is unthinkable. The central belief of reincarnation involves the soul in transmigration; its conscious-self (bearing character-memory) passes from one body to another under the principle of *karma* and rebirth.

Hindu teaching resolves the moral dilemma of universal inequality, in that promotion or demotion of each respective reincarnation is determined by the individual's moral and spiritual conduct in past life. There is also a different emphasis of thought in Hinduism, as compared with Buddhism, regarding the nature of human beings and their ultimate blissful state. Hinduism is an optimistic faith whilst Buddhism tends to be pessimistic.

Theravada Buddhism is largely atheistic, but even so there is the belief that human beings are under illusion of *maya*; they are in need of enlightenment because they experience *dukkha*, a sense of being unsatisfactory and misaligned with the Ultimate Reality.

Instructions from the Tibetan *Book of the Dead* (*Bardo Thodol*, 800 ACE) are read to the dead to describe what happens to the soul 49 days after decease, before the new body is ready for entering. In this limbo-state, the mind is believed to create its own illusions within the process of continual purging. These illusionary experiences are shaped within the subconscious mind from the images and beliefs of the person's cultural upbringing. In a sense, we create our own gods and devils, heavens and hells, from our own subconscious libraries (Hick, 1976). A documented perspective of this belief with its paranormal dimensions can be found in the death of Treya (Wilber, 2001b).

Religious Discourses and Pluralism

It would be out of place in a book on spiritual counselling, which has endorsed the merits of various discourses of reality, to present a critique of those salvation beliefs presented above. It goes without saying that such beliefs are held passionately by those adherents of the particular faith, but the fact remains that such teachings are largely metaphysical, future-oriented and beyond empirical enquiry – they are unfalsifiable. As such, we have to acknowledge that in light of the Enlightenment they have become untenable and unconvincing for many secular folk, and the denial in seeing the problem has largely contributed to the decline and disinterest in religion in modern times. Before closing at this point, it is worth saying that some philosophers, theologians and social commentators have attempted to reformulate faith, and I am thinking primarily of Christian faith, to meet the needs of pluralistic requirements and secular spirituality.

Don Cupitt, in *Reforming Christianity* (2001) begins with the premise that there is not literally a God out there. There is no life after death. The end of our life is simply the end of our life. There is no ready-made cosmic order, no moral order, and there is not even a ready-made Self, or ready-made meaning to life. We are given, says Cupitt, the temporal flow of life and the disorderly tumult of sense experience, together with language to describe the stream of experience and feelings. His new vision is to shed what he terms 'Church Christianity' for *Kingdom Christianity*, and to engage in solar living in action. In the better world – the kingdom of heaven, or the communist society – religion no longer exists as a separate institution and sphere of life because its task in that role has been completed. Instead, he says:

- All life becomes a sacred continuum. God is scattered into everyone ...
- All value in life becomes intrinsic ... there is no further reality beyond the here and now
- Ethics become purely humanitarian... all life becomes a flow of exchange, called in religious language 'communion', and in modern language 'communication'
- Human culture becomes fully globalised. The misunderstandings caused by language differences and the conflict caused by ethnic differences disappears. (Cupitt, 2001: 103).

Cupitt's reformulation certainly confirms the humanistic spirit and the ideals of pluralism, though I suspect many religious folk would find his critique too radical.

The recent wake-up call for Muslims presented by Irshad Manji (2004) is a invitation for honesty and assessment of the Qur'an and of Islamic political violations of human rights occurring among countries like Saudi Arabia. Manji, painstakingly and with great courage, calls on Muslims, particularly reflective peoples of the western world, to question the grounds for the Qur'an to be 'the final manifesto of God's will' (2004: 42), and to embrace *ijtihad*, an unpublicised teaching of Islam that advocates tolerance, openness and civil relations with Jews and Christians alike (2004: 177–207).

We are left inevitably with divided opinion and different accounts of religious and spiritual experience, and these will be reflected in the rich discourses of clients in therapy. Hick (2001), in customary pluralistic style, draws attention from metaphysics towards human behaviour:

> If we define salvation as an actual human change, a gradual trans-
> formation from natural self-centredness (with all the human ills that
> flow from this) to a radically new orientation centred in God and
> manifested in the fruit of the spirit, then it seems clear that salvation
> is taking place within all of the world religions – and taking place,
> so far as we can tell, to more or less the same extent. (Hick, 2001: 127)

Thorne (2002) sees a way of uniting the world religions through person-
centred values which bear the fruits of harmonious reconciliation, particularly
through the teaching of empathy. Whilst religious doctrines separate peoples,
similar practices of reflective meditation and prayer are common across most
of the religions of the world. Wilber (1998), whom Thorne draws on, reasons
that all religions should apply the 'deep science' of testing and evaluate their
contemplative elements. However, whereas many belief-systems are open to
rigorous scrutiny, *direct spiritual experiences* and *peak experiences* of awe and
wonder are less available – they are essentially subjective with only the resul-
tant state being open to external observation (Lines, 1995b). For Wilber, we
must avoid *repression*, since religious worldviews – from archaic, magic,
mythic and rational to existential – are merely evolving maps that were
shaped through changing survival conditions of communities (foraging, hor-
ticultural, agrarian, industrial, informational: Wilber, 2001a: 52–62). The
human survival needs of hope, faith, purpose, a search for meaning, and a
need for forgiveness, are the evidence of our spirituality (Swinton, 2001).

We could close this discussion at this point by concluding that each
party is left within their own convictions, that life is a rich tapestry of various thoughts and opinions, and that each discourse is valid for the person concerned within the constraints of pre-formed schemas. After all, *we
are all like other people*, we are like *some other people* and we are like *no other
people* (Swinton, 2001). Having said that, I would like to inform the therapist who wishes to engage in spiritually-centred counselling that we are
not left at the point of advocating patience and tolerance, but that indeed
we can move forward. It remains in this final chapter to look for common
discourse that can resonate with the religious, secular and spiritual mind
alike, to serve, as it were, a synthesis of divergent accounting of reality.

Hope Re-visualised

Hope re-visualised embodies the reformulated thinking of those outlined
above, and can be summarised as follows:

- Religion and psychotherapy, faith and spirituality, empiricism and mysticism,
  are all centrally involved in healing.
- On occasion, we have to learn to surrender the ego, to let go of cognitive control and to let the Spirit speak more eloquently.
- Transcending Self and negating Self are not competing alternatives; the route
  to the former is through the latter.

- A difficult external situation is often the springboard for spiritual growth and for transcending Self.
- Meaning in life begins to show new possibilities when we turn to face the Other and choose to connect with the Spirit in life which pervades all existence.

I close this book with a brief commentary on these five eternal principles of spirituality for your reflection.

Healing

Healing becomes common currency in the differing enterprises of spirituality, religion and psychotherapy. The spiritual counsellor is not a minister of salvation or a curer of souls, neither is he a medical practitioner, or a faith healer of the traditional kind, but he is a companion upon life's journey who endeavours by his *presence* and by his skilfully tuned spiritual *intuition* to restore his client's healthy functioning and state of well-being. Perfect health, like total analysis, like salvation, is never completely reached, and so, like the brief psychotherapist who views the work as regularly transitional and in need of revisiting, the spiritual mode within the overall work will become complete when the client has experienced a degree of healing.

The new vision I have stressed is looking at spiritual work through a lens which translates the divine in human terms. Spiritually-centred counselling is never finished but involves creating different perspectives to suit the particular stage of the journey. For clients like Sinita healing *might* mean finding that inner source to become Self, for empiricists like John it *may* involve re-viewing his experience of awe and wonder as emanating from non-causal, mystical sources, for devoutly religious people like Ibn it *could* centre on some empirical testing of faith-experience, and for reflective people like Sam *a possible need* of redirection towards practical alternatives to staying home alone. Closing spiritually-centred discourses will be indicated when all have become lifted to a heightened plane of consciousness through an experience of seeing the world differently and through a re-visualised hope for a future. We know that healing and well-being are positively correlated with knowing Self, with having a spiritual outlook and orientation, with having reasoned through those empirical features of the numinous, and with having meaning and purpose in one's life. To achieve psycho-spiritual healing is as much the province of religion as of counselling and psychotherapy.

Surrendering Ego

The Buddhist's aim in reaching pure nirvana is to experience the *dissolving* of ego, for the Christian to be saved it involves *knowing only* Christ crucified and *living love*, and for the Muslim to be accepted it requires one to *submit* to Allah and to *tithe* personal wealth. Thorne (2002) speaks of a mystical feeling of powerlessness to change things, where he just dwells in the relationship and claims that without expectation new possibilities emerge. The task is 'to cultivate a willingness to *let go into powerlessness* as a positive response to difficulty and confusion and wait patiently for the invisible world to reveal its resources whether through thoughts or feelings or the intervention of unexpected external forces' (2002: 44 – my italics).

A Sufi story tells of a great teacher who tells his son he can no longer teach him what he needs to know. He sends him to a wise but illiterate farmer. The young man was not happy to be humbled but nevertheless did as ordered. He approached the farm and met a peasant on horseback whereupon he came near and bowed. The farmer looked at him and said, 'Not enough!' The young man bowed to the farmer's knees. He said again, 'Not enough!' Then he bowed to the horse's knees, but again the teacher said, 'Not enough!' This time he bowed to the horse's feet, touching the hooves. The peasant teacher then said to him, 'You can go back now. You have had your training' (Joko Beck, 1997).

The lesson is to *know Self through exposing vulnerability*, and David Mearns (Mearns and Cooper, 2005) demonstrates the paradoxical healing power through exposing vulnerability before his clients, Dominic and Rick. Entering counselling and psychotherapy requires the risk of exposing Self to the therapist, but when Self is surrendered by both client and therapist together, there will appear a further *presence* of transpersonal dimensions – *it is allowing the Spirit to speak through surrendered egos.*

Transcending Self

Giving up one's life for God is a repeated theme in the history of religion. When the great religious faiths became humanised, then the face of God became the helpless child, the infirm pensioner or the AIDS-stricken victim of Africa. The humanistic requirement of transcending Self does not involve taking up religious orders, but turning towards the Other (Lynch, 2002). Self-transcendence, for Wilber (2001a: 21), is linked with the directional move of evolution and 'appears to be built into the very fabric of the Kosmos itself'. The *means* of transcending Self through eastern meditation, as articulated by Wilber, leaves me feeling lost in absolute subjectivism and an anticipated feeling that such states might become tedious and boring. Again, transcending Self through cessation of desire becomes meaningless to me since 'who I am' is integral to my personality. For me, transcending Self does not involve the abolition of personality but the heightening of humanity. Wilber (2001a: 208) recalls a Zen Master who once said, 'When I heard the sound of the bell ringing, there was no I, and no bell, just the ringing.' I am content with dissolving subject and object in forms of transcendental meditation, so long as *I* can still *hear* the bell ringing.

A wealthy eastern ruler rehearsed his life story: 'You know when we're young we become idealistic and wish to change the world. Then when we discover it cannot be done, we decide to get married and have children and then try to change them. But when we fail in that also, we realise there is nothing we can change but ourselves' (*The Himalayas*, BBC, 2005). This echoes an old Chinese proverb:

If there be righteousness in the heart, there will be beauty in the character.
If there is beauty in the character, there will be harmony in the home.
If there is harmony in the home, there will be order in the nation.
When there is order in each nation, there will be peace in the world.

Buddha said, 'Be a lamp unto yourself', Jesus said, 'Let a man deny himself and take up his cross and follow me,' and Boorstein (1996) commends the forgiving nature. One common problem arising in cognitive-behavioural counselling is where clients wish that everyone else but themselves should change; that their well-being can only be secured when everybody else acts differently. The spiritually-in-tune counsellor, like his cognitive counterpart, has reached a terminus point when a client discovers that personal happiness is what occurs *within* not without.

When Self is put second it is thereby transcended. West (2004: 39) speaks of a mystical force compelling him to move into action against his volition: 'Soul or spirit nudges me and I either listen or the nudges get louder and louder'. I can certainly relate to this phenomenon, but what I cannot be sure about is whether this is universally experienced. What I am sure about is that when clients *change within* there is a healing payback in terms of better social functioning.

Growth through Misfortune

'The mournful fact is that life is indifferent to our fate; it is programmed to care for the species, never for the individual; and, without death, life as we know it would be unsupportable'. (Holloway, 2004: 194)

A man was being chased by a tiger and in his desperation he dived over a cliff and grabbed a vine. As the tiger was pawing away above him, he looked down below and saw another tiger at the bottom of the cliff. To top it all, two mice were gnawing away at the vine. At that moment he spotted a delicious strawberry and holding the vine with one hand he picked the strawberry and ate it. It truly was delicious! What happened was tragedy. (Joko Beck, 1997: 112)

The point is that when faced with a dilemma we can either waste our last moment of life or we can appreciate it. Life is opportunity. As counsellors we are philosophers hoping to change the world through our interactions with clients. My philosophy is to *drink the moment*, not in spite of misfortune but because of it.

'It is just such an exceptionally difficult external situation which gives man the opportunity to grow spiritually beyond himself,' wrote Frankl (1959: 80). Frankl gives anecdotal evidence of the psychological mechanisms that function to endure hardship and tribulation by visualising a future beyond suffering. He records how the death rate increased in the camp between Christmas and New Year's Day in 1945 because of unrealised hope for many that they might be home for Christmas. Another inmate prophesied that he would be liberated on a certain day, but died immediately after it didn't happen. Citing Nietzsche – 'He who has a why to live for can bear with almost any how' – his daily experience was that when folk give up on life mortality sets in (1959: 141), which is a common experience in trauma wards and what I found personally at Oswestry (Lines, 1995a). The pursuit of happiness, or Freud's 'pleasure principle', is not enough, human beings need a *reason* to be happy, and so, argues Frankl, '*No meaning* is the existential vacuum of the twentieth century to which suicide victims fall prey'.

In one touching narrative, Frankl speaks of a dying woman who said that she had been spoilt in life and had not taken her spiritual accomplishments seriously. She pointed through the window of the hut and said, 'This tree here is the only friend I have in my loneliness.' Through that window she could see just one branch of a chestnut tree carrying two blossoms: 'I often talk to this tree,' she said to me. Anxiously I asked her if the tree replied and she said that it did: 'It said to me, "I am here – I am here – I am life, eternal life"' (Frankl, 1959: 78). The spiritually-centred counsellor will not dismiss his client's expressed narrative of misfortune, neither will he invalidate it by not allowing it sufficient airing, but he will help her see that healing and recovery are not in spite of hardship but because of it.

Connectedness

A common feature of the humanised world religions is the perspective of service to one's God requiring service to one's fellow, but might I push this a step further in seeing the two as being synonymous? We often feel as though things should be better than they are, but in thinking so we miss opportunities for Self transcendence through service to others. There is not a day goes by where need does not hit us western people in the face – *if our eyes remain open* – and I consider that the great impoverishment of the poor is that because of their insufficiency they are denied the opportunity to give.

Throughout this book, I have suggested a numinous presence with nature, the cosmos and with the Other, and it is principally *human contact* and *connectivity* that lies at the base of all effective counselling and psychotherapy, not least spiritually-centred therapy, in my opinion. In Calcutta there appeared a Mother Teresa to touch the hand of the dying, in Africa Bob Geldof touches consciousness for the hungry, and in the Gospels Jesus touches a leper to bring him life. Whether physical or psychological, the hand reaching forward to touch is the contact point for giver as for given in the moment of *therapeutic connectedness*. Whether the therapist touches his client's hand, embraces his body compassionately, dances with his being, strokes his skin with cellular touch, invites his physical support for a disabled condition, or makes only psychological connection, the healing nature of two individuals coming together under lies not only our common humanity but the holistic–relational paradigm of the newly emerging world.

Appendix: Scripture as Revised Discourse

An enormous gulf exists between the conclusions drawn by a consensus of biblical scholars and fundamentalist Christians regarding the origins of scriptural texts. A strong case can be made for viewing the developing nature of biblical writings as satisfying natural religious interests which change over time. One inference of viewing the Bible as the authoritative word of God is that human error is avoided by the superintendence of the Holy Spirit, but such a proposition carries unexamined presuppositions and confusion.

We begin by asking what the Bible is. In so doing, we make no assumptions about the influence of the Spirit, or the numinous, or even the Church during the canonising of the Bible, but simply look at the writings as they are in the light of scholarship (Beckford, 2004).

When Jews and Christians revere the holy writings they do so as though the Torah or the New Testament arrived in completed form – *handed down by God* – in one magical process, whereas both are compilations of documents brought together that have undergone writing, rewriting, revision and alteration to suit a particular audience by a particular person or group. In addition, there is evidence that *those who are the most powerful have the final say of what constitutes the final version of history* (Carr, 1987).

The religious writings that are sacred for Judaism are the Torah and the Prophets. The Torah contains the first five books of the Old Testament that are purported to have been written by Moses. This presents a problem in that one book describes the death and burial of the writer. In addition, these books have similar stories of the same events as though two versions have been preserved and placed alongside one another or interwoven. There are two creation stories, two flood stories and two calls of Moses. A German scholar (Julius Welhausen) identified four different sources within the Torah, which suggests that Moses could not have been the author. These sources are known as J, E, P and D, and stand for a tradition which knows God as Yahweh (J), another which knows him as Elohim (E), another which is a priestly source (P) and a fourth known as Deutero (D). The call of Moses in J illustrates the interests of this Israelite community in portraying the Lord as *dealing with man directly*, whereas the same stories covered in E reflect a community which believed that God must be approached through intermediaries (angels and dreams), hence Moses is called through the medium of a burning bush.

Sometime during the seventh century BC, there was felt a need to bring these traditions represented by anonymous writers (or schools) together by two influential kings, Hezekiah and Josiah. Psalm 78 is interesting in that it illustrates how editors wished to preserve different traditions without the need to do away with alternative accounts. It stands as a mosaic of the sources in one hymn. It is as though each sector of the Israelite community viewed these traditions as authentic dialogues that expressed their life concerns and relationships with God; that all traditions were equally valid and equally true in these terms; that all represents the word of God. The early Bible then was the product, not of Moses, but of editorial combinations of different descriptions of the same histories which served the social and religious purpose of holding the community together.

The next point to make is in regard to what we today call political spin. It appears that when Old Testament accounts of historical events are compared with archaeological records there is evidence that each party has selected and slanted what took place to achieve political advantage. The court recorders of the times of Hezekiah were of the school of D, and so endorsed strict monotheism but with a keen interest now in projecting Jerusalem as the centre of Israelite cult. During this time, some early history was rewritten, but it was when the Assyrian armies attacked Hezekiah at Jerusalem that we take up the story.

According to the biblical account, God brought about the victory and saved the day by means of a mysterious event by an angel, but an inscription of the same episode has Hezekiah paying heavy tribute to buy off the Assyrian general. Hezekiah's scribes have a vested interest in having God delivering the victory, and the court scribes in Lachish would not wish to humiliate the king by having an embarrassing record in the palace. So whose record is accurate and whose is spin?

Josiah was the next monarch and he is presented as a religious reformer, but in 609 BC he was slain at Meggido by Neco, an Egyptian Pharaoh. This event threatened the religious outlook of the Bible to this point but also brought about a new vision of God's hand in history. It was a tragic blow for writers of the Bible. The result was political decline, but the new writing was to install hope through a coming Messiah like King David of old. During the exile of 560 BC, a final rewrite of the Old Testament turned persecution around with a new insight on the meaning of sufferings and liberation. The book of Isaiah was added to by an anonymous writer, who reviewed the past and put a spin on history after asking, why the persecution? The writer, known as second Isaiah, reinterpreted the exile by declaring the captivity of Judah to serve a universal purpose: the deported Israelites were a sign amongst the nations that the suffering of one is for the benefit of all. These occasions of spin brought the Bible towards the inter-testament period.

The third point is the effect of canonising the Bible as a means of arresting the process of rewriting history. In 1947 the Dead Sea scrolls were discovered. These documents never found their way into the Old Testament, even though they represented a group (Essenes) who had a genuine identity in religious history and an authentic relationship with the Jewish God. This was because the canon was fixed at 100 BCE. Amongst this collection was the Thanksgiving Scroll, written by a hard-liner who describes himself in vision as being divine and as a suffering servant – just as Jesus was presented in the New Testament.

The New Testament is believed to be a record of eyewitness detail, but scholarship has rendered this view improbable. Christianity continues the process of revision of the Bible with the view that Jesus was the Messiah. The most dynamic evangelist of the early Christian period was Paul, a Pharisee who formerly persecuted the faith as a *wayward Jewish sect*. Paul sees a vision of the risen Jesus and is converted to become the missionary to the non-Jews. Paul had never met Jesus personally, and although he wrote fourteen letters, it never occurred to him, or to anyone else of the immediate followers, to write an account of Jesus. The tradition was passed on orally and through the liturgy.

The Gospels are alleged to be records of genuine eyewitness accounts of historical events, but this is not the case, reasoned David Straus in 1835 (Schweitzer, 1936). They are late compositions of people removed from the setting. It never seemed to have occurred to Christians before the sixties, thirty odd years after the crucifixion, to have a documented life of Jesus. While Paul was in prison in Rome awaiting persecution, two years after leaving Ephesus, there began large scale persecution of Christians. After Paul's death, Emperor Nero martyred Christians to serve as a scapegoat for the fire of Rome. Deep in a catacomb there is evidence of secret Christian burial and martyrdom.

According to some scholars, it is this situation and in this setting that prompted Mark to compose the first Gospel. There is no internal evidence that Mark knew Jesus personally and, curiously, the original version records no actual resurrection appearance (Lüuddemann, 1995). The central purpose of this document may be to give encouragement to martyrs facing tribulation by highlighting Jesus' execution. For this community, in order to make sense of their persecution, they were to look up to Jesus, the first martyr. And so *Mark served as moral exhortation.*

Matthew, writing from Antioch, felt Mark had not done justice to Jesus' Jewish roots as being grounded in the habits and laws of Judaism, and therefore steered his account accordingly. He copied much of Mark, but supplanted his overall impression by Judaising the record with additions to redress this deficit. And so *Matthew served as Jewish propaganda.*

Luke was an educated writer somewhere in Greece, and he *plagiarises previous records to demonstrate that the new movement was not a religious backwater.* The Gospel and history of the Church (Acts) documents how Christianity became a world religion through a scheme of the advance of the Jesus movement to the early Christian Church from Jerusalem to Rome – here again was well-crafted propaganda to show the Jesus brotherhood as being highly respectable and ideologically commendable for all noble citizens.

John felt the preceding versions of Jesus were lacking and not quite correct. Feeling inspired by the Spirit, he sees it as legitimate to compose original speeches and narratives that in essence portray Jesus' divinity. John meditated seriously on the events and rejigged the ministry to present what others had not fully grasped.

The Gospels, like the sources of the Torah, are products of communities attempting to express elements of their faith that describe their relationship with God. Two hundred years after the death of Jesus there were dozens of Gospels. Inevitably, the question would soon arise of what was scripture. Papyrus, used for the first documents, was replaced by animal skins and this meant that many documents could be arranged in large volumes. But other accounts – such as the Gospel of Truth, the Gospel of Philip, the Gospel of Thomas and the Gospel of Mary Magdalene – were suppressed as the New Testament canon arrested the process of revision and rewriting. Books like the Apocalypse contain forecasts of the future, but even these writings can be shown to be coherent deductions made by interpreting past scriptures with the way political factors were bearing upon those whose interests were reflected by the author (Goulder, 1994).

Many scholars point to the all-too-human forces guiding the selection of 'inspired writings' from heresy. Features in other portrayals of Jesus did not fit the *accepted version*, and some things were said that other people did not want to hear – Gnostic teaching, Jesus' relationship with Mary Magdalene, and sayings which indicated that women were as fit to hold office as men. History is always written by the winners, and chauvinism lies at the heart of the Bible. Those who fixed the canon were guided, they said, by the Holy Spirit, but might also be judged to have been directed by male prejudice and issues of power and control.

Church councils and religious writing were all controlled by men. The last verses of the Book of Revelation threatens that if any man adds or takes away anything written in this book their names would be taken from the book of life. We might say that the Spirit operates today in allowing us to see through Bible history as a long drawn-out process of bigotry, bias and prejudice, and to respond accordingly.

A good example of how biblical narratives become open to multiple interpretations is the book of Job. The narrative reads like a play whereby Job receives misfortune in losing his prosperity and family, and then finally his comfort through insufferable boils. Yahweh has allowed Satan to have his way and put Job's trust under trial. The body of the text is a series of speeches given by three comforters, Job and Yahweh. The general point of the dialogue is where the comforters take the 'traditional religious line' of promoting God's justice through the maxim that God humbles the proud and exalts the contrite. Job contests this point, and claims, not least from his own experience, that the wicked do not suffer but prosper. The theology of these discourses has become an enlightened commentary on innocent human suffering, and Jewish rabbis over time, particularly in the camps of the Holocaust, were confident in putting God on trial to account for their existential dilemma from the lead of Job's audacity.

The power of Job's rhetoric was slightly watered down during an unknown period (600–300 BCE) when an editor sandwiched the speeches between an introduction and an epilogue, which can stand alone, and which makes the point that all turns out fine in the end. The Qur'an, under a general theology that Allah is All-wise (His ways are beyond comprehension and his Justice is righteous), omits every reference to questioning God's judgment.

Jung, in *Answer to Job* (1954) develops a complex theology which strikes at the heart of God's justice. Jung claims he is a (transpersonal) psychologist not a theologian, but nevertheless he illustrates a scholarly mastery of biblical passages, particularly in seeing the central import of Job's anguish. Jung distinguishes between two kinds of facts: physical (historical, empirical) facts and psychic facts – his commentary is on the latter. Whilst his whole scheme will appear surreal and fantastical for many, his main point is intriguing. His claim is that through his suffering servant, Job, God has become conscious of himself. Being Almighty, God has no contender (even Satan is subject to him) and is detached from his omniscience and unaware that his morality is less than that of Job's. In calling to question God's justice, Job awakens Yahweh to a higher morality than he had shown during his non-reflective past – 'the Creator needs conscious man'. From regular analysis where he observed in his patients that individuation involves recognising one's dark side, Jung postulates that the book of Job is the story of a faithful moral being revealing for Yahweh the polar opposites within his own nature. Although such an exegesis is radical and irreverent for religionists, there is no doubt in my judgment that his commentary in parts does justice to the import of the text of Job.

Thus, the book of Job may be interpreted as an old religious tale of a suffering servant receiving good fortune in the end by God (early source), a wisdom tract on God's injustice (edited speeches), a commentary on human ill-fortune (Jewish rabbinical discourse), an illustration of God's unswerving justice (the Qur'an), or the archetypal conflict of the divided psych becoming evident in God's own being (Jung).

References

Beckford, R. (2004) Channel 4 on Christmas Day, 2004.
Carr, E. H. (1987) *What is History?* Harmondsworth, Middlesex: Pelican Books.
Goulder, M. (1994) *A Tale of Two Missions*. London: SCM Press Ltd.
Jung, C. G. (1954) *Answer to Job*. London: Routledge.
Lüuddemann, G. (1995) *What Really Happened to Jesus?* London: SCM Press Ltd.
Schweitzer, A. (1936) *The Quest of the Historical Jesus*. London: A & C Black Ltd.

References

Allport, G. W. and Ross, J. M. (1967) 'Personal religious orientation and prejudice', *Journal of Personality and Social Psychology*, 5: 432–43.

Anderson, H. (1997) *Conversation, Language and Possibilities: A Postmodern Approach to Psychotherapy*. New York: Basic Books.

Anderson, H. and Goolishian, H. (1988) 'Human systems as linguistic systems: evolving ideas about the implications for theory and practice', *Family Process*, 27: 371–93.

BACP (2002) *Ethical Framework for Good Practice in Counselling and Psychotherapy*. Rugby: British Association of Counselling and Psychotherapy.

Bandura, A. (1977) *Social Learning Theory*. Englewood Cliffs, NJ: Prentice-Hall.

Beck, A. T. (1976) *Cognitive Therapy and the Emotional Disorders*. Harmondsworth: Penguin.

Bellah, R. N. (1973) *Emile Durkheim: On Morality and Society, Selected Writings*. Chicago: The University of Chicago Press.

Benner, D. G. (1988) *Psychotherapy and the Spiritual Quest*. Michigan: Baker.

Bergin, A. E. and Garfield, S. L. (eds) (1994) *Handbook of Psychotherapy and Behaviour Change*, 4th edn. New York: Wiley.

Bevan, T., Fellner, E. and Ujlaki, S. (Producers); Henderson, J. (Director) and Fusco, J. (Writer) (1995) *Loch Ness* [Motion Picture]. United Kingdom: A Working Title Production in association with Stephen Ujlaki Productions.

Biddulph, S. (1998) *Raising Boys*. London: Thorsons.

Bloomfield, H. H. (1996) 'Transcendental meditation as an adjunct to therapy', in S. Boorstein (ed.), *Transpersonal Psychotherapy*, 2nd edn. Albany, NY: State University of New York.

Bonhoeffer, D. (1970) *Letters and Papers from Prison* (ed. E. Bethge). London: SCM Press Ltd.

Boorstein, S. (ed.) (1996) *Transpersonal Psychotherapy*, 2nd edn. Albany, NY: State University of New York.

Bray, P. (2004) Spiritual Emergency, *CIE (BACPJ)*, Autumn: 16–19.

Brierley, P. (2000) *Religious Trends, No. 2: 1999/2000*. London: Christian Research.

Brookes, C. E. (1996) 'A Jungian view of transpersonal events in psychotherapy', in S. Boorstein (ed.), *Transpersonal Psychotherapy*, 2nd edn. Albany, NY: State University of New York.

Brown, R. (1971) *The Fourth Gospel*. London: Geoffrey Chapman.

Bruce, S. (1995) 'The truth about religion today in Britain', *Journal for the Scientific Study of Religion*, 34(4): 417–30.

Buber, M. (1958) *I and Thou*. Edinburgh: T. and T. Clarke Ltd.

Bultmann, R. (1952) *The Theology of the New Testament*. London: SCM Press Ltd.

Bultmann, R. (1953) *Kerygma and Myth*. London: SPCK.

Bultmann, R. (1971) *The Gospel of John*. Oxford: Blackwell Publishing.

Butler, K. (2002) 'Living on purpose: the seeker, the tennis coach, and the next wave of therapeutic practice', *Psychotherapy Networker:* www.psychotherapy networker.com

Clark, J. (1967) 'Toward a theory and practice of religious experiences', in J. F. T. Bugental (ed.), *Challenges of Humanistic Psychology*. New York: McGraw-Hill.

Clayton, P. (1998) *God and Contemporary Science*. Grand Rapids, MI: Eerdmans.

Cooper, M. (2005) 'Working at relational depth', *CPJ*, 16(8): 16–20.

Crawford, M. and Rossiter, G. (1996) 'Spirituality development of adolescents: an Australian perspective', in R. Best (ed.), *Education, Spirituality and the Whole Child*. London: Cassell.

Cupitt, D. (1980) *Taking Leave of God*. London: SCM Press Ltd.

Cupitt, D. (2001) *Reforming Christianity*. Santa Rosa, CA: Polebridge Press.

Damasio, A. (2003) *Looking for Spinoza*. London: Heinemann.

Darling, D. J. (1996) *Zen Physics: The Science of Death, the Logic of Reincarnation*. New York: Harper Collins.

Deatherage, O. G. (1996) 'Mindfulness meditation as psychotherapy', in S. Boorstein (ed.), *Transpersonal Psychotherapy*, 2nd edn. Albany, NY: State University of New York.

De Chardin, P. T. (1955) *The Phenomenon of Man* (ET 1975). New York: Harper & Row.

De Chardin, P. T. (1957) *Le Milieu Divin*. Paris: Éditions du Seuil.

Diamond, J. (2000) *Narrative Means to Sober Ends*. New York: Guilford.

Dodd, C. H. (1953) *The Interpretation of the Fourth Gospel*. Cambridge: Cambridge University Press.

Dossey, L. (1993) *Healing Words: The Power of Prayer and the Practice of Medicine*. San Francisco: Harper.

Dryden, W. (ed.) (1984) *Individual Therapy in Britain*. London: Harper & Rowe.

Dryden, W. (1991) *A Dialogue with Albert Ellis*. Buckingham: OUP.

Durkheim, E. (1933) *The Division of Labour in Society* (1972). New York: The Free Press.

Edwards, G. (1992) 'Does psychotherapy need a soul?', in W. Dryden and C. Feltham (eds), *Psychotherapy and its Discontents*. London: OUP.

Eliade, M. (1961) *The Sacred and the Profane*. New York: Harper and Row.

Elkins, D. N. (1998) *Beyond Religion: A Personal Programme for Building a Spiritual Life Outside the Walls of Traditional Religion*. Wheaton, IL: Quest Books.

Elkins, D. N., Hedstrom, L. J., Hughes, L. L., Leaf, J. A. and Saunders, C. (1988) 'Toward a humanistic-phenomenological spirituality: definition, description, and measurement', *Journal of Humanistic Psychology*, 28(4): 5–18.

Ellenberger, H. (1970) *The Discovery of the Unconscious*. New York: Basic Books.

Ellis, A. (1962) *Reason and Emotion in Psychotherapy*. New York: Lyall Stuart.

Ellis, A. (1989) 'The history of cognition in psychotherapy', in A. Freeman et al. (eds), *Comprehensive Handbook of Cognitive Therapy*. New York: Plenum Press.

Epston, D., White, M. and Murray, K. (1992) 'A proposal for a re-authoring therapy: Rose's revisioning of her life and a commentary', in S. McNamee and K. J. Gergen (eds.), *Therapy as Social Construction*. London: Sage.

Erikson, E. H. (1963) *Childhood and Society*. Harmondsworth: Penguin (rev. edn 1965. London: Hogarth Press, Vintage).

Erikson, E. H. (1968) *Identity: Youth and Crisis*. New York: Norton.

Flew, A. and Macintyre, A. (eds) (1955) *New Essays in Philosophical Theology*. London: SCM Press Ltd.

Frankl, V. E. (1959) *Man's Search for Meaning* (2004). London: Rider.

Frazer, G. (2005) Thought for the Day, BBC Radio 4, 5 March.

Freud, S. (1899) *The Interpretation of Dreams*. London: Pelican Freudian Library (PFL 1990, Vol. 14).

Freud, S. (2003 [1920]) *Beyond the Pleasure Principle: And Other Writings*. London: Penguin.

Freud, S. (1927) 'The Future of an Illusion', in *The Complete Psychological Works of Sigmund Freud* (trans. James Strachey). London: The Hogarth Press Ltd.

Freud, S. (1933) *New Introductory Lectures on Psychoanalysis* (trans. James Strachey (1991)). London: Penguin.

Gergen, J. K. (1999) *An Invitation to Social Construction.* London: Sage.

Gergen, J. K. (2001) *Social Construction in Context.* London: Sage.

Glaser, B. G. and Strauss, A. L. (1967) *The Discovery of Grounded Theory: Strategies for Qualitative Research.* Chicago: Aldine.

Goleman, D. (1996) 'Meditation and consciousness: an Asian approach to mental health', in S. Boorstein (ed.), *Transpersonal Psychotherapy*, 2nd edn. Albany, NY: State University of New York.

Goulder, M. and Hick, J. (1983) *Why Believe in God.* London: SCM Press Ltd.

Greeley, A. M. (1975) *The Sociology of the Paranormal: a Renaissance.* Beverly Hills, CA: Sage.

Grof, S. (1985) *Beyond the Brain.* New York: State University of New York.

Grof, S. (1996) 'Theoretical and empirical foundations of transpersonal psychology', in S. Boorstein (ed.), *Transpersonal Psychotherapy*, 2nd edn. Albany, NY: State University of New York.

Grof, S. (1998) *The Cosmic Game Explorations of the Frontiers of Human Consciousness.* Albany, NY: State University of New York Press.

Grof, S. and Grof, C. (eds) (1989) *Spiritual Emergency: When Personal Transformation Becomes a Crisis.* New York: GP Putnams.

Grof, S. and Grof, C. (1990) *The Stormy Search for Self: A Guide to Personal Growth through Transformational Crisis.* Los Angeles: J.P. Tarcher Inc.

Halmos, P. (1965) *The Faith of the Counsellors.* London: Constable.

Hartley, L. (2004) *Somatic Psychology: Body, Mind and Meaning.* London: Wurr Publishers Ltd.

Hay, D. (1979) 'Religious experiences among a group of post graduate students – a qualitative study', *Journal for the Scientific Study of Religion*, 18(2): 164–82.

Hay, D. (1982) *Exploring Inner Space: Scientists and Religious Experience.* Harmondsworth, Middlesex: Penguin.

Hay, D. and Hunt, K. (2000) *Understanding the Spirituality of People Who Don't go to Church.* Centre for the Study of Human Relations, Nottingham University.

Hay, D. and Morisy, A. (1978) 'Reports of ecstatic, paranormal, or religious experiences in Great Britain and the United States – a comparison of trends', *Journal for the Scientific Study of Religion*, 17(3): 255–68.

Heelas, P. and Woodhead, L. (2005) *The Spiritual Revolution: Why Religion is Giving Way to Spirituality.* Oxford: Blackwell Publishing.

Heidel, A. (1951) *The Babylonian Genesis* (2nd edn). London: The University of Chicago Press.

Heron, J. (1998) *Feeling and Personhood.* London: Sage.

Hick, J. (1976) *Death and Eternal Life.* London: Collins and Sons Ltd.

Hick, J. (ed.) (1977) *The Myth of God Incarnate.* London: SCM Press Ltd.

Hick, J. (1990) *Philosophy of Religion.* Upper Saddle River, NJ: Prentice Hall.

Hick, J. (ed.) (2001) *Dialogues in the Philosophy of Religion.* Hampshire: Palgrave and MacMillan.

Hoffman, E. (1996) 'An introduction to kabbalistic psychotherapy', in S. Boorstein (ed.), *Transpersonal Psychotherapy*, 2nd edn. Albany, NY: State University of New York.

Hollingdale, R. J. (1969) 'Introduction', in F. Nietzsche (1883) *Thus Spake Zarathustra.* London: Penguin Books.

Holloway, R. (2004) *Looking in the Distance: the Human Search for Meaning*. Edinburgh: Canongate.

Howard, A. (2000) *Philosophy for Counselling and Psychotherapy: Pythagoras to Postmodernism*. London: Macmillan Press Ltd.

Hugo, V. (1980) *Les Miserables* (1862). Harmondsworth: Penguin.

Jacobs, M. (1993) *Living Illusions: a Psychology of Belief*. London: SPCK.

James, O. (2004) 'The Psychologist', *The Observer Magazine: Question Time*, August: 40–1.

James, W. (1961) *The Varieties of Religious Experience* (1902). London: Fount/Collins.

Joko Beck, C. (1997) *Everyday Zen*. London: Thorsons.

Jordan, J. V. (1991) 'The development in women's sense of self', in J. V. Jordan, A. G. Kaplan, J. B. Miller, I. P. Stiver and J. L. Surrey (eds), *Women's Growth in Connection: Writings from the Stone Centre*. New York: Guildford Press.

Jung, C. G. (1913) 'Transformations and Symbols of Libido', in *The Collected Works of C. G. Jung*. London: Routledge and Kegan Paul.

Jung, C. G. (1933) *Modern Man in Search of a Soul*. London: Routledge and Kegan Paul.

Jung, C. G. (1952) 'The Shadow', in *The Collected Works of C. G. Jung*. London: Routledge and Kegan Paul.

Jung, C. G. (1954) *Answer to Job*. London: Routledge Classics.

Jung, C. G. (1978 [1964]) *Man and his Symbols*. London: Picador.

Jung, C. G. (1969) *The Archetypes and the Collective Unconsciousness*. (trans. R. F. C. Hull). London: Routledge.

Kagan, N. (1990) 'IPR – a validated model for the 1990s and beyond', *Counselling Psychologist*, 18: 436–40.

Kant, I. (1781) *Critique of Pure Reason* (trans. N. Kemp Smith). London: Macmillan and Company Ltd.

Keane, W. M. and Cope, S. (1996) 'When the therapist is a yogi: integrating yoga and psychotherapy', in S. Boorstein (ed.), *Transpersonal Psychotherapy*. 2nd edn. Albany, NY: State University of New York Press.

Keenan, J. G. and Jackson, D. P. (1999) *The Epic of Gilgamesh*. Wauconda, IL: Bolchazy-Carducci Publishers.

Kelly, G. F. (1996) 'Using meditative techniques in psychotherapy', *Journal of Humanistic Psychology*, 36(3): 49–66.

Kirkland, J. P. (1996) 'Helping to restore spiritual values in abused children: a role for pastoral carers in education', in R. Best (ed.), *Education, Spirituality and the Whole Child*. London: Cassell.

Kirschenbaum, H. and Henderson, V. (eds) (1990) *The Carl Rogers Reader*. London: Constable.

Kübler-Ross, E. (1982) *On Death and Dying*. London: Tavistock.

Kuhn, T. (1996 [1962]) *The Structure of Scientific Revolutions*. Chicago: Chicago University Press.

Kushner, H. S. (2002) *When Bad Things Happen to Good People*. London: Pan Books.

Lambert, J. L. (1992) 'Implications of outcome research for psychotherapy integration', in J. C. Norcross and M. R. G. Goldfried (eds), *Handbook of Psychotherapy Integration*. New York: Basic Books.

Lannert, J. L. (1991) 'Resistance and countertransference issues with spiritual and religious clients', *Journal of Humanistic Psychology* 31(4): 68–76.

Lao Tzu (1997) *Tao Te Ching*. Hertfordshire: Wordsworth Editions Ltd.

Lazarus, A. A. (1981) *The Practice of Multimodal Therapy*. New York: McGraw-Hill.

Leadbeater, C. W. (1927) *The Chakras*. Wheaton, IL: The Theosophical Publishing House.

Leech, K. (1977) *Soul Friend*. London: Sheldon.

Lewis, C. S. (1940) *The Problem of Pain*. London: Fontana Books.

Lines, D. (1995a) *Coming Through the Tunnel*. Birmingham, UK: D. Lines: dennis@schoolcounselling.co.uk

Lines, D. (1995b) *Christianity is Larger than Fundamentalism*. Durham: Pentland Press Ltd.

Lines, D. (1996) *Early Secondary Pupils' Experiences of Name-calling Behaviour through a Discourse Analysis of Differing Counselling Interviews*, unpublished dissertation, Westhill College, Selly Oak, Birmingham.

Lines, D. (1999a) 'Secondary pupils' experiences of name-calling behaviour', *Pastoral Care in Education*, 17(1): 23–31.

Lines, D. (1999b) 'Bereavement group therapy in school: the role of a belief in a post-death existence within adolescent development for the acceptance process of loss', *Journal of Children's Spirituality*, 4(2): 141–54.

Lines, D. (2000) *Counselling Approaches for Young People in Secondary School: From Traditional Approaches to Eclectic and Integrative Counselling*. Birmingham, UK: D. Lines: dennis@schoolcounselling.co.uk.

Lines, D. (2001) 'An approach with name-calling and verbal taunting', *Pastoral Care in Education*, 19(1): 3–9.

Lines, D. (2002) 'Counselling in the new spiritual paradigm', *Journal of Humanistic Psychology*, 42(3): 102–23.

Lines, D. (2006) *Brief Counselling in Schools: Working with Young People from 11–18* (2nd edn). London: Sage.

Lovinger, R. J. (1990) *Religion and Counselling: the Psychological Impact of Religious Belief*. New York: Continuum.

Lukoff, D., Francis, L. and Turner, R. (1998) 'From spiritual emergency to spiritual problem: the transpersonal roots of the new *DSM-IV* category', *Journal of Humanistic Psychology*, 38(2): 21–50.

Luxmoore, N. (2000) *Listening to Young People in School, Youth Work and Counselling*. London: Jessica Kingsley Publishers.

Lyall, D. (1995) *Counselling in the Pastoral and Spiritual Context*. Buckingham: OUP.

Lynch, G. (2002) *Pastoral Care and Counselling*. London: Sage.

Manji, I. (2004) *The Trouble with Islam Today: a Wake-up Call for Honesty and Change*. Edinburgh: Mainstream Publishing Company.

Masson, D. (1988) *Against Therapy*. London: Harper Collins.

May, G. (1996) 'A pilgrimage of healing', in S. Boorstein (ed.), *Transpersonal Psychotherapy*, 2nd edn. Albany, NY: State University of New York Press.

McCarthy, J. and Morrell, J. (1994) *Some other Rainbow*. London: Corgi Books.

McGregor, E. and Boorman, C. (2004) *Long Way Round: Chasing Shadows Across the World*. London: Time Warner Books.

McGuiness, J. (1998) *Counselling in Schools: New Perspectives*. London: Cassell.

McLeod, J. (1993) *Introduction to Counselling*. Buckingham: OUP.

McLeod, J. (2003) *Introduction to Counselling* (3rd edn). Buckingham: OUP.

McNamee, S. and Gergen, J. (1992) *Therapy as Social Construction*. London: Sage.

McNeil, J. T. (1951) *The History of the Cure of Souls*. New York: Harper and Row.

Mearns, D. and Cooper, M. (2005) *Working at Relational Depth in Counselling and Psychotherapy*. London: Sage.

Mott-Thornton, K. (1996) 'Experience, critical realism and the schooling of spirituality', in R. Best (ed.), *Education, Spirituality and the Whole Child*. London: Cassell.

Nelson, J. E. (1996) 'Madness or transcendence? Looking to the Ancient East for a modern transpersonal diagnostic system', in S. Boorstein (ed.), *Transpersonal Psychotherapy*, 2nd edn. Albany, NY: State University of New York Press.

Nelson-Jones, R. (1996) *Effective Thinking Skills*. London: Cassell.

Nietzsche, F. (1969 [1883–5]) *Thus Spake Zarathustra* (trans. R. J. Hollingdale). London: Penguin Books.

Noonan, E. (1983) *Counselling Young People*. London: Routledge.

Otto, R. (1958) *The Idea of the Holy* (trans. J. W. Harvey). New York: Oxford University Press.

Palmer, M. (1997) *Freud and Jung on Religion*. London: Routledge.

Parkes, C. M. (1986) *Studies of Grief in Adult Life*. Madison: International Press.

Payne, M. (2000) *Narrative Therapy*. London: Sage.

Perls, F. S., Hefferline, R. F. and Goodman, P. (1972) *Gestalt Therapy*. London: Souvenir Press Ltd.

Perrin, N. (1963) *The Kingdom of God in the Teaching of Jesus*. London: SCM Press Ltd.

Pointon, C. (2005) 'Mind-body awareness', *Therapy Today* 16(9): 4–7.

Radiguet, R. (2005) *The Devil in the Flesh*. London: Marion Boyars Publishers.

Richards, P. S. and Bergin, A. E. (1997) *A Spiritual Strategy for Counseling and Psychotherapy*. Washington, DC: American Psychological Association.

Rogers, C. R. (1967) *On Becoming a Person* (1961). London: Constable and Co Ltd.

Rogers, C. R. (1975) *The Formative Tendency*. Paper presented at the Theory Conference of the Association for Humanistic Psychology, 5 April.

Rogers, C. R. (1980) *A Way of Being*. Boston: Houghton Mifflin.

Rowan, J. (1993) *The Transpersonal, Psychotherapy and Counselling*. London: Routledge.

Rowan, J. (2005) *The Transpersonal*. London: Routledge.

Rowling, L. (1996) 'Learning about life: teaching about loss', in R. Best (ed.), *Education, Spirituality and the Whole Child*. London: Cassell.

Russell, B. (1986 [1917]) *Mysticism and Logic and Other Essays*. London: Routledge.

Ryle, G. (1990) *The Concept of Mind*. London: Penguin Books.

Sacks, J. (2005) 'Why does God allow terrible things to happen to his people?', London: *The Times*, 1 January.

Sartre, J-P. (1973) *Existentialism and Humanism*. London: Methuen.

Schaeffer, F. A. (1972) *How Then Shall We Live?* Old Tappan, NJ: Fleming, H. Revell Co.

Schucman, H. and Thetford, W. (1996) *A Course in Miracles*, combined volume, 2nd edn. New York: Viking Penguin.

Scott Peck, M. (1978) *The Road Less Travelled*. New York: Simon and Schuster.

Self, W. (2004) *How the Dead Live*. London: Penguin Books.

Soskin, J. (1997) *Insight and Intuition: A Guide to Psychic Unfoldment*. London: Thoth Publications.

Steering Committee (2002) 'Empirically supported therapy relationships: conclusions and recommendations on the Division 29 task force', in J. C. Norcross (ed.), *Psychotherapy Relationships That Work: Therapist Contributions and Responsiveness to Patients*. Oxford: Oxford University Press. pp. 441–3.

Stern, D. N. (1985) *The Interpersonal World of the Infant*. New York: Basic Books.

Strupp, H. H. (1972) 'On the technology of psychotherapy', *Archives of General Psychiatry*, 26: 270–8.

Sutich, A. J. (1996) 'Transpersonal psychotherapy: history and definition', in S. Boorstein (ed.), *Transpersonal Psychotherapy*, 2nd edn. Albany, NY: State University of New York Press.

Swinton, J. (2001) *Spirituality and Mental Health: Rediscovering a 'Forgotten' Dimension*. London: Jessica Kingsley Publishers.

Tacey, D. (2004) *The Spirituality Revolution: the Emergence of Contemporary Spirituality*. Hove, East Sussex: Brunner-Routledge.

Tart, C. T. (1975) *Transpersonal Psychologies*. London: Routledge and Kegan Paul.

Tart, C. T. (1996) 'Helping the dying: science, compassion, and the possible survival of death', in S. Boorstein (ed.), *Transpersonal Psychotherapy*, 2nd edn. Albany, NY: State University of New York Press.

Thomas, R. M. (1990) *Life-Span Stages and Development*. London: Sage.

Thompson, K. (1982) *Emile Durkheim*. London: Tavistock Publications.

Thorne, B. (1998) *Person-centred Counselling and Christian Spirituality: the Secular and the Holy*. London: Whurr Publishers Ltd.

Thorne, B. (2002) *The Mystical Power of Person-Centred Therapy*. London: Whurr Publishers Ltd.

Tillich, P. (1976) *Perspectives on 19th and 20th Century Protestant Theology*. London: SCM Press Ltd.

Tolle, E. (2001) *The Power of Now: a Guide to Spiritual Enlightenment*. London: Hodder and Stoughton.

Toolan, M. (1988) *Narrative: A Critical Linguistic Introduction*. London: Routledge.

Tudor, K. (2000) 'The case of the lost conditions', *BACP*, 11(1): 33–7.

van Deurzen-Smith, E. (1984) 'Existential Therapy', in W. Dryden (ed.), *Individual Therapy in Britain*. London: Harper and Rowe.

Walsh, R. and Vaughan, F. E. (1996) 'Comparative models of the person and psychotherapy', in S. Boorstein (ed.), *Transpersonal Psychotherapy*, 2nd edn. Albany, NY: State University of New York Press.

Waugh, E. (1951) *Brideshead Revisited*. London: Penguin Books (1981) Granada Television Ltd., London.

Weber, M. (2003 [1905]) *The Protestant Ethic and the Spirit of Capitalism*. London: Dover Publications.

West, W. (2000) *Psychotherapy and Spirituality*. London: Sage.

West, W. (2004) *Spiritual Issues in Therapy*. Hampshire: Palgrave MacMillan.

White, J. (1996) 'Education, spirituality and the whole child: a humanist perspective', in R. Best (ed.), *Education, Spirituality and the Whole Child*. London: Cassell.

White, M. and Epston, D. (1990) *Narrative Means to Therapeutic Ends*. New York: W. W. Norton.

Wilber, K. (1984) *Quantum Questions: Mystical Writings of the World's Great Physicists*. Boston: Shambhala Publications.

Wilber, K. (1998) *The Marriage of Sense and Soul: Integrating Science and Religion*. Dublin: Newleaf.

Wilber, K. (2000) *Integral Psychology: Consciousness, Spirit, Psychology, Therapy*. Boston: Shambhala Publications.

Wilber, K. (2001a) *A Brief History of Everything*. Dublin: Gateway.

Wilber, K. (2001b) *Grace and Grit*. Dublin: Gateway.

Wilkinson, M. (2006) *Coming into Mind: The Mind–Brain Relationship: A Jungian Clinical Perspective*. London: Routledge.

Wright, N. T. (2003) *For All the Saints?* London: SPCK.

Yalom, I. D. (1980) *Existential Psychotherapy*. New York: Basic Books.

Name Index

Subject Index

Lightning Source UK Ltd.
Milton Keynes UK
UKHW02f1547110618
323801UK00004B/108/P